"In this book, Lou Tice shares the keys to building winning teams—including the visualization and affirmation of common goals."

Pete Carroll, Defensive Coordinator,
San Francisco 49ers

"The concepts presented by Lou Tice are an integral part of my life. Whether I'm in my office at Nordstrom, at home with my family, or anywhere in the world, these principles help me build stronger relationships, set and achieve higher goals, and enjoy a more fulfilling life."

Jack McMillan, Co-chairman,
Nordstrom

"In my profession as a physician, coaching and mentoring are essential but almost lost parts of the doctor-patient relationship. The 'healing relationship' is the moment when the doctor holds the possibility of cure or improvement as real when the patient has lost hope. Thus, the patient begins to dwell in the doctor's belief system of hope, rather than in his or her own despair. This requires sensitivity, credibility, and inspiration, and then patients can build a new belief structure, mobilize their own bodily resources, and begin to ally with medicine to heal.

In this book, Lou Tice brilliantly shows the hold that habits of thinking have on our behavior, sharing his personal experiences of escaping from his own 'prisons of thought' and building new possibilities. He explores the relationship of one person, a mentor, to another, that allows the latter to grow. He brings his vast experience as a teacher and inventor to this most critical of relationships in a time that some have characterized as one of isolation and loneliness. This is an essential, even core competence for teachers, parents, clergymen—and even friends—to have."

Matthew A. Budd, M.D., Assistant Professor of Medicine,
Harvard Medical School

"Commitment and service to others is the best work for the growth of an individual, a corporation, a community, and the world. *Personal Coaching for Results* is a book that will maximize your potential to help others. It is also an excellent handbook for natural team building."

Yoshiki Paul Otake, Chairman,
AFLAC Japan

"The Tice development process has enabled us to nearly double sales in the last year. Beyond that, my personal and family life are better than ever."

Carel Stassen, President,
Ackermans Limited, South Africa

"Whether you're looking for immediate help or for lasting improvement in performance and relationships, this book is pure gold."

John MacLeod, Head Basketball Coach,
University of Notre Dame

"This is not just another self-help book. It is about mentoring people of all ages, especially children, and teaching them to develop inner strength for the difficult times ahead. I recommend this excellent book for parents, teachers, and anyone whose responsibilities include the mentoring of others."

Glenn Terell, former president,
Washington State University

"I first came in contact with Lou Tice as a football player at the University of Texas. I have since used his affirmation process to drive my business success."

Johnny Johnson, former All-American defensive back,
University of Texas, and
All-Pro defensive back,
Los Angeles Rams
now a real estate corporation owner
and executive

LOU TICE

WITH JOYCE QUICK

PERSONAL COACHING FOR

How to Mentor and Inspire Others to Amazing Growth

RESULTS

THOMAS NELSON PUBLISHERS

Nashville • Atlanta • London • Vancouver

Published in Nashville, Tennessee, by Thomas Nelson, Inc., and distributed in Canada by Word Communications, Ltd., Richmond, British Columbia, and in the United Kingdom by Word (UK), Ltd., Milton Keynes, England.

Printed in the United States of America

1 2 3 4 5 6 7 BVG 03 02 01 00 99 98 97

Dedication

To Father James McGoldrick,
for his patience, guidance and inspiration
in helping me develop, both intellectually
and spiritually, a model of what it means
to be an intelligent heart.

CONTENTS

PREFACE

I believe that the desire to live fully is an inherent part of every human being. Deeply rooted within our heart of hearts is the longing to grow and bloom, to express our creative, life-affirming innermost nature, just as we ourselves are expressions of a superbly creative spirit, which most of us, including me, believe to be eternal and divine. This desire or drive to embrace life and to realize our full potential is most evident, perhaps, in healthy young children, who are almost without exception venturesome, trusting, energetic explorers, unrestrained by doubt and fear, eager to learn and grow, to be and do more every day.

But all too often as we become adults and go about our daily routines, we become caught up in the business of living—earning and eating our daily bread, solving our problems and socializing with loved ones and friends, entertaining ourselves and acquiring possessions, coping with the ever-present stresses and pressures of lives that seem to be changing and passing too quickly to even comprehend, let alone control. In the process, we often lose touch with these deep desires or sense them only vaguely and occasionally. When we remember and reconnect with them, we may feel that they are somehow beyond us, impossible to realize, out of reach, like some poignantly beautiful scene glimpsed from the window of a moving train.

As a result, our aspirations become smaller, our visions of what is possible become dimmer and more limited. We begin, in effect, shrinking to fit the size of our container—a world that increasingly seems to want us to believe that ordinary is good enough, that greatness is only for others who are luckier or more gifted, that making a good living and escaping pain or tragedy is the best that we can hope for.

Perhaps there are moments when we sense that much more is possible for us. In those moments, we know beyond a doubt that we will bitterly regret it if we live out our lives without exploring the possibilities. Even then, we may feel at a loss for a place to start, a path to take that will lead us in the direction of true happiness and the fulfillment of our dreams. Or we may be fearful that we don't deserve to even set out on such a path, leaving such a magnificent undertaking to others whom we judge as being far more able or gifted or well-equipped.

But there *is* greatness in you. I am as certain of that as I am of anything in this world. I don't know specifically what kind of greatness—that's for you to discover and decide for yourself. But I know it's there. As my friend Pat Given, whom you'll meet in Chapter 13, is fond of saying, "God does not make mediocre people. God makes only geniuses." Or, as the great psychologist Abraham Maslow said, "Geniuses are ordinary people who have had nothing subtracted from them."

Maybe your genius is in music or mathematics, in parenting or teaching or painting or cooking or photography. Maybe it's in arranging flowers or building a business, in developing new computer technology or repairing old automobiles. Maybe it's in coaching or mentoring—helping others to feel inspired and motivated to grow themselves. Perhaps you already have an inkling of where you think your genius lies but have downplayed it to something unimportant or ordinary, or maybe you have suppressed it for so long that you doubt it's even there at all. In other words, maybe you have been subtracting something from your genius.

If that is the case, all you need to do right now is to allow yourself to acknowledge the possibility of its dormant presence. Because the very act of doing so is the first step in creating the environment within which that possibility, like a seed, will come to life and grow. As you read this book and think about what you are reading and as you begin to put the ideas it contains into action, you will be adding light and water to the already fertile ground. And the next thing you know, you will start to notice changes, and so will the people around you. You will begin to feel that you are beginning to live in harmony with your deepest desires and dreams, with your innermost self, and, believe me, there is no better feeling.

I understand what it's like to want to be more and do more but, at the same time, not having a clear sense of how to go about it. I have always known in my heart that I was supposed to help people to live better lives, to bring out the greatness that is inside them, but for a long time I just didn't have the skills I needed to do it. When I first started out as a teacher and football coach, I could see greatness in many of the young people I was working with, and even, sometimes, in myself, but I often did just exactly the wrong things to encourage it. I tried to force it out, to will it into being, to enter into combat with the ordinary and win from the sheer strength of my determination. Sometimes it worked but, more often than not, it didn't. I helped a few people in spite of my "whip 'em into shape" methods, but I realize now that I probably hurt more than I helped. I don't know how many people I've seen and still see—coaches, teachers, parents, grandparents, corporate executives, military leaders and government representatives—who are just like I was, having the best intentions in the world, having a strong desire to help others to develop, but also having very little real understanding of how to go about it.

I have made it my life's work to gain that understanding, and as a result, I have become exponentially more effective at facilitating the growth process for myself and for others. I have also made it my mission to share what I have learned with as many people as possible, so I am delighted that you have this book in hand and hope that you will find its contents as valuable as I did.

One more thing. Before you go any farther, I want you to know that you have everything inside you—right now, this minute!—that you will need to bring your innermost desires into reality and to help others do the same. It may not be fully developed yet, but it's there. All that's required for the moment is that you believe in your ability to change and to grow toward those desires and dreams. I have no doubt that you can do it, because even though you may not realize it, you have already begun. And I'm certain because I have seen literally millions of people transform their lives in wonderful ways, using the information I'm about to share with you, and they were no more intelligent or gifted or specially equipped than you are.

It doesn't have to be a struggle. It doesn't have to be a battle to overcome or suppress or kill off who you are now in order to be a better person. On the contrary, as you develop and grow in the direction of your dreams, those parts of yourself that you're not happy with or that are causing less than satisfactory results will fall by the wayside. As you focus more and more on thinking and behaving in ways that bring you what you want, what you don't want will simply be nudged off of your agenda. As you nourish the seeds of greatness in yourself and others, the weeds of self-doubt and ineffective behavior will wither and eventually disappear.

You're on your way to a great adventure, more exciting and fulfilling than any I know—the adventure of becoming who you truly want to be and of helping others to do the same thing. Did you ever read a book or watch a movie that was so good you didn't want it to end? Well, this is an adventure that goes on as long as you do, because there will always be more exciting things and ideas to explore, more growing to do, more of your vast potential to tap into.

Thank you for allowing me to serve as your guide for this part of your journey. I take the responsibility seriously—but not somberly, so I hope we'll have some fun along the way. And now, I'm ready if you are. Let's get started!

Personal Mastery

Introduction

W hether we want to get to the summit of a mountain or create a successful business career, raise a happy, confident child or lower the time it takes to run a mile, no one succeeds entirely on his or her own. On the other hand, no one can do it for us, either. Most people who have achieved a significant measure of success have had plenty of help along the way. Then, once they have a good idea of what the terrain looks like, where the hazards and handholds are, they reach out to give those coming after them the benefit of what they have learned. In other words, they become, teachers, coaches, guides—mentors—helping others as they were once helped.

For more than twenty-five years, I have been in the business of teaching people, individually and in groups, how to succeed—on their own terms. Even before that, when I was coaching high school football, I was vitally interested in why some people who weren't especially talented or gifted were able to achieve far more than others. The answer, I have come to believe, is rooted in two central principles. First: **What you can do depends as much on your beliefs as it does on your ability**. And, second: **The quality of the help you receive along the way can make all the difference**.

I deliberately wrote this book in a way that reflects these two principles and takes into account a third, which is also vital: **All meaningful, lasting growth and change starts first on the inside and then works its way out**. That's why Part One has a largely personal, internal point of view. It is concerned with the mastery of self from an inside-out perspective and focuses on concepts that will help you build the beliefs it takes to excel in any area of life, no matter what your present circumstances. Then, in Part Two, we'll step back, expanding that intense, internal focus and extend what we've learned about the mastery of self to coaching, mentoring, and inspiring others.

As I see it, coaching, mentoring, and inspiring are closely related, yet somewhat different. I think of these activities as a progression, each built upon the same basic set of skills, but each taking the helping relationship to a higher, more influential level. A coach's activities are often limited to helping us perfect a specific activity or set of skills. A mentor can do the same thing, but our mentors may also become involved with many aspects of our lives, helping us to grow as whole people. And when a mentor becomes an inspiration, he or she touches our heart and soul in a lasting way. That's what this book will help you to do for others.

In the six chapters that comprise Part One, we'll look closely at our beliefs—beliefs about ourselves, other people, and our environment, and we'll discuss not only how we got these beliefs in the first place, but also how we can change them if we choose to. We'll also talk about how to make the critically important shift from having them work *on* us to having them work *for* us.

Optimism and pessimism, two distinctly different styles of explaining and interpreting the events in our lives, are belief-based habits we acquire over time. These habits have a powerful effect on how we experience life. Optimists generally enjoy more success, better mental and physical health, and have more harmonious relationships than pessimists do, and you'll discover why I say this in Part One. While we're at it, we'll take a look at how accountability, control, and power are connected and why self-fulfilling prophecies work.

Have you ever heard of scotomas? These are mental blind spots that all of us develop, and in Part One, I'll tell you not only how scotomas sabotage you, but also how to compensate for them and even use them to your advantage. Then, I'll introduce you to your reticular activating system, the "security guard" of your brain, and you'll see how a clear vision and systematic goal-setting work to allow vitally important information to get through.

Before leaving Part One, you'll learn how healthy self-esteem inoculates you against many of life's ills and how high self-efficacy enables you to become a super achiever. I'll give you a proven-effective, seven-step system for setting goals that will dramatically increase the likelihood that you'll achieve yours. I'll also show you how to harness the incredible power of your imagination to reprogram your subconscious mind and achieve the results you most want in life.

Part Two is all about how to use what you know to help other people grow. It's designed to give you the insights and tools you need in order to coach, mentor, and inspire others to greatness. In Part Two, I'll tell you why some people are so much more effective as coaches and mentors than others. I'll explain the differences between mentors and role models, and you'll see why mentors have far more influence. Then, I'll give you the three key factors that make a coach or mentor credible—someone to whom others want to listen—and talk about the importance of character in the mentoring relationship.

Because these skills are absolutely essential to any good relationship and particularly important for coaches and mentors, I'll tell you what I've learned about how to listen well, give useful feedback, and help others solve problems in ways that keep trust alive and lines of communication open. I'll also let you in on why attempts to motivate other people so often fail, and you'll learn, instead, how to help others to motivate themselves.

In Part Two, I'll share some valuable tips on how to help those you care about overcome obstacles and make it through tough times. Then I devote an entire chapter to mentoring children, because nothing is more important. You'll find out how to build self-confidence and self-esteem in kids and how to handle problems in ways that encourage positive change instead of pushback and resistance.

It doesn't matter what your circumstances are when you read this book. If you're already doing well, it will allow you to do far better. If you're not doing so well, it will give you new hope, new energy, and a wealth of practical, immediately useful tools that will empower you to change what you want to change. It will help you to become highly effective at empowering others as well.

At this point, perhaps you're feeling a bit skeptical. Maybe you've read a number of so-called "self-help" books that promised far more than they ultimately delivered. Or maybe you're thinking something like, "That's all very well for him to say. But this guy doesn't understand my situation. He doesn't know about the problems in my past or what I'm up against now." That's true, I don't. And if you're skeptical, I'm glad. Don't ever simply accept what you hear without questioning its validity and relevance.

But do keep an open mind. Much of the information I'll be sharing comes directly from world-class experts. A great deal of what you'll read is the result of twenty-five years of personal experience. Some of that experience was definitely gained the hard way—from false starts, major mistakes, and making my way through some very tough times. I know what it's like to struggle to change, to overcome a difficult and painful past. So, as you read, make some room in your belief system for new ideas about how to interpret your past experiences and your present circumstances, as well as new information that may change what you want for yourself in the future.

By all means, hold on to your skeptical attitude. Use it to discover what's true for you and what's genuinely useful. But don't hold on too tightly to any preconceived notions that may prevent you from getting the maximum value possible from this book—and from your life. What you see always depends as much on what you're looking for as it does on what's actually there. Similarly, your open-mindedness—your willingness—to learn, change, grow, and develop is what makes it possible for learning, growth, and development to actually take place.

Remember, the contents of this book are arranged in a sequence that builds on itself. It moves from the essential elements of personal mastery to the process of coaching and mentoring others, so be sure to start reading at the beginning with Part One. Take your time, take notes if you like, and, most importantly, apply the concepts and tools you'll be learning about on a daily basis as you go forward. Simply reading about them won't change anything for you any more than reading a book about lifting weights will make you stronger.

By the time you reach the end of Part Two, I think you'll find yourself feeling better able to create the life you most want to live and to successfully coach and mentor others to do the same. I hope you'll also find yourself feeling challenged and changed, moved to live and relate to others in more thoughtful, grateful, helpful, happier ways. That's what it's all about, really—getting to the levels of happiness that my friend, Father Bob Spitzer of Seattle University, calls "H-3 and H-4."

At the happiness level called H-1 all we want is to feel good, avoid feeling bad, and that's it. We don't give a hoot how anyone else is feeling. At H-2 we do a lot of work on ourselves, because we want to be better than the next guy. We have plenty of self-discipline, but it's all ego-driven, and we're not *really* happy, except when someone's telling us how great we are. Our relationships are usually full of conflict, and we sometimes feel like something's missing, but we're not sure what it is.

If we get to H-3, we're starting to make the best kind of happiness happen. That's because what we want most is to help other people, and it feels great when we do. We forget about ourselves. More than anything else, we care about others—our family, team, community, the whole darn planet, and we want to be a contributing part of all of it.

At H-4 we can see beyond the good of the team or the group to the *ultimate* good. We start to understand what unconditional love is all about, and we're always thinking about what we can learn and how we can give. We can see the highest good in everything, and we just naturally respond to it with the best, most loving part of ourselves. I hope this book helps you see yourself as an H-3/H-4 person.

Especially during periods of important change, many people find it valuable to track progress and record thoughts and feelings in a diary or journal. I highly recommend it, and, in fact, I do it myself all the time.

If you'd like to share some of your experiences as a result of what you've read here or find out more about the personal and professional growth education that my company, The Pacific Institute, produces, I'd be glad to hear from you.

CHAPTER ONE

How Your Mind Works: The Keys to Character

Could This Be You?

P icture this: You're living with your spouse in a beautifully decorated, warm and comfortable home that many people would describe as a mansion. It's located on the shores of a large, sparkling lake in what is arguably one of the world's most beautiful cities. You also own a working ranch a few hundred miles away that you visit often. It's nestled in a valley where the air is unbelievably sweet and clean and the scenery is spectacular. You look forward to going there to ride your horse through the countryside, fish in the stream, practice skeet shooting, and make plans for the future.

Your marriage is fulfilling and long-lasting—a true partnership in every sense

> *"What lies behind us and what lies before us are tiny matters compared with what lies within us."*
>
> Ralph Waldo Emerson

of the word. You and your spouse have worked as a team to build a widely respected international company. Your business is tremendously successful and satisfying because it helps literally millions of other people to become successful, too. Now you are a grandparent, and it's a great feeling to realize that when you die, you'll be leaving behind not only substantial material wealth and an extensive body of useful, meaningful work, but also a wonderful living legacy. Some years ago, you bought yourself a black Rolls-Royce Corniche convertible—the car of your dreams—that you have a lot of fun driving. And you spend much of your time traveling all over the world, talking to folks from all walks of life about your favorite subject: how people can use more of their vast potential.

Before I tell you what all of this has to do with coaching or mentoring, let me ask you a very important question: Do you have any trouble putting yourself in this picture? Of course, maybe the things I've described here aren't really your style. Maybe you'd rather imagine yourself creating art in a light-filled studio, or setting up free medical clinics in an urban ghetto, or raising llamas on a farm. Maybe your ideal of personal bliss would be reporting news direct from the world's hot spots or helping Mother Teresa care for the sick in India or taking photographs of artifacts from ancient civilizations for *National Geographic*. Or maybe it's living with your family in a comfortable, attractive home out in the suburbs, writing a best-selling mystery novel, or growing your own business to the point where you no longer have to worry about feeling secure in your senior years.

The specific images don't matter. What I'm asking is whether you can see yourself actually living the life you would most want to live. Do you have difficulty imagining that life? Does thinking about it seem like wasting time on a fantasy that could never really happen? Well, that's the way it would have seemed to me, too, twenty-five years ago. In fact, if you had tried to get me to see myself living the life I've just described in the first two paragraphs of this chapter, I would have told you that you were nuts. Born crazy and had a relapse.

Nevertheless, this is a fairly accurate snapshot of my life as it is today. Twenty-five years ago, though, I was a high-school teacher and football coach, struggling to keep the bills paid and raise a rapidly growing family on $1,000 a month. Some days I thought ends would never meet, and some days I thought I was doing all right—compared to the situation I was raised in, anyway.

I grew up with three brothers and a sister in a run-down house (*shack* might be a more accurate word) in one of the worst parts of the city. I don't know if they were alcoholics or not, but both of my parents drank a lot more than just socially. As a result, in addition to being dirt poor, we lived with chaos and turmoil. Episodes of intense physical and emotional violence were routine. After my father died when I was thirteen, we had to go on welfare. My mother tried to keep our household going, but she was, even in the best of times, pretty unstable. I went to work after school and during the summers to help out, but even then we never seemed to do more than just barely get by.

Some people would say without any hesitation that these kinds of early-life circumstances add up to a sure fire formula for failure. As a matter of fact, many people who have had similarly difficult childhoods would be the first to agree. For me, though, it turned out to be the first chapter in a wonderful success story.

The "Secret" I Refuse to Keep

So what's my secret? How did I get from that painful place where I started out to the wonderful life I have today? Was it dumb luck? Driving ambition? Exceptional talent? Well-placed connections with the "right" people?

Well, I'll admit to having plenty of ambition (which, to me, is just another way of saying that I have goals I take seriously). But anyone who knows me can tell you that I possess no great genius or extraordinary talent. As for luck, on the whole I don't believe in it. And twenty-five years ago, the only people I knew were my family members, a bunch of high-school kids, other teachers and coaches, and a few priests. What I *did* have, though, and still do, is the willingness to work hard and the determination to persist.

But hard work alone doesn't necessarily get you anywhere. In fact, it's extremely common to find people who work incredibly hard all their lives but end up just as badly off as they were when they started. The same is true of persistence. If you hang in there doing the wrong thing over and over, when what you *really* need to do is let go and try something new, all you'll have to show for it is a matched set of white knuckles.

I've given a lot of thought to the question of why I've been so successful, and I think I've done a good job of answering it. I've identified a number of key principles in the growth process that I've used to take me from poverty to affluence, from doubt and confusion to confidence, from a struggle for survival to an exciting, fulfilling life. And I've discovered that these principles work as well for other people—people from every walk of life—as they have worked for me.

But the secret of my success isn't a secret. Quite the contrary. Once I discovered how well these principles worked, I immediately began to teach others. This book is one way I can share them with you. It's also a way I can help you to become very effective at doing something I really love to do—sharing the "secrets" of success with other people.

Part One contains information that I consider absolutely essential for personal mastery—valuable tools and techniques that will enable you to use more of your potential and help others to use more of theirs. It amounts to a short course in human effectiveness—the missing "instruction manual" I used to wish our brains had come with—and it's information that I use myself, every day of my life.

In fact, it's information I share all the time with *Fortune* 500 executives and government leaders, four-star generals and professional athletes, Nobel Prize winners and college presidents, so there's no question about its value or usefulness. In a slightly different form, I also share it with the chronically unemployed, at-risk kids, social service workers, and inmates as well as staff in state and federal prisons, because it can benefit anyone. Put as simply as possible, it's about a process that will help you, no matter who you are, to make your future a lot better than your past.

Part Two tells you how to use these same tools to help other people grow, but it goes one important step further. It adds new, specific, immediately useful information—information that will allow you to coach, mentor, and inspire others in ways that make a positive difference. It builds on the solid foundation laid in Part One to help you create a lasting legacy you can be proud of.

So, now, let's get started. Just like so many other things, Part One really begins with your imagination.

Inventing the Future

Do you believe in the power of imagination? I sure do. Just look at the empires that the power of imagination has built through the advertising media alone. Then take another look, and consider the fact that *everything* that has ever been invented, built, composed, painted, created, or otherwise brought into this world by a human being first started out as an idea in someone's mind—a product of their imagination. Then, after the *what* part of the idea was conceived, one way or another the *how* got invented, and the thing itself was born into what we think of as "reality."

As humans, we invented our future, day by day, century by century, because we were uniquely equipped to do it. We had unbelievably fertile, incredibly powerful imaginations—the greatest gift, next to life itself, that we could possibly possess. That hasn't changed. You and I still invent our futures in exactly the same way.

Nature, Nurture, and Human Agency

Scientists used to argue heatedly about the relative importance of heredity and environment in understanding human behavior. This question was dubbed the "nature versus nurture" debate. These days, another factor has entered the equation, and the debate has settled down somewhat as a more complex possibility continues to emerge and assert itself. This factor is called *human agency*, and it simply means our ability to choose and change, to want and desire, to intend and imagine.

Human agency must now be taken into consideration whenever we are attempting to predict or influence human actions. It appears that our *thoughts* about our environment are as important as the environment itself and that our *thoughts* about our genetically inherited characteristics are as important as those characteristics themselves.

Human agency helps explain why two kids raised in the same abusive, impoverished family can turn out so differently. It helps us understand why one woman who loses her sight in a freak accident becomes an alcoholic recluse, but another who goes through an almost identical trauma becomes a best-selling author and teacher. Human agency is the reason one man lives happily weighing an extra fifty pounds, while for another it's a constant struggle of deprivation and relapse. It's why bankruptcy means deep depression, shame, and suicide for one investor but is only a painful learning experience to be avoided in the future for another. It's probably also why some people's health quickly fails when they believe they're not likely to live much longer, yet others survive and even thrive in spite of so-called *terminal* illness.

When the distinguished psychiatrist, Viktor Frankl, described his time as a prisoner of the Nazis during the Holocaust, he stressed the power of thought—specifically the collection of beliefs we call *attitude*—in determining the impact of the prison camp experience. Here is a short passage from his extraordinary book, *Man's Search for Meaning*:

> We who lived in the concentration camps can remember the men who walked through the huts comforting others, giving away their last piece of bread. They may have been few in number, but they offer sufficient proof that everything can be taken from a man but one thing: the last of his freedoms—to choose one's attitude in any given set of circumstances, to choose one's own way.

One of the central principles of this book, and of the programs my company produces and implements all over the world, is that **we move toward and become like that which we think about. Our present thoughts determine our future.**

This is by no means a new idea. "The soul becomes dyed with the color of its thoughts," Marcus Aurelius maintained. "There exists nothing either good or bad, but thinking makes it so," wrote Shakespeare. In the late nineteenth century, William James (medical doctor, Harvard professor, respected psychologist, and philosopher) proclaimed, "The greatest discovery of my time was that human beings can alter their lives by altering their attitudes of minds."

Unfortunately, there wasn't much information available in James's day about *how* to deliberately change an attitude or even about how to test the theory, so this discovery wasn't as immediately exciting as it might have been. Most folks knew nothing about this discovery. They just went on about their business of living as best they could, and, if their attitudes changed, it wasn't really seen as something they caused themselves. It was more like something that *happened to* them.

Even though we know a lot more than we used to about the human mind, thanks to many years of diligent work by scientists and psychologists, it's still pretty much the same story. Every now and then, something occurs that turns a light on for you, that helps you see yourself and others more clearly, think differently, let go of unproductive behavior and attitudes that stand in your way. Sometimes it's an event of major importance—a marriage, the death of a loved one, the birth of a child, a serious illness, an unexpected divorce, or even participation in a military conflict. Sometimes it's something that no one notices but you. Nevertheless, you feel changed for the better by it. And that's exciting.

What's even more exciting, though, is when you learn how to deliberately generate these enlightening experiences yourself in ways that spare the pain and harness the power. The material in this and the other chapters in Part One is designed to help you do just that.

Now, if you *move toward* that which you think about, then your ability to control what you think about, who you listen to, and how you interpret and explain your experiences becomes crucial. Your ability to control these things will, in turn, control your direction in life. And if you *become like* that which you think about, your character and integrity are involved, aren't they? Repeated thoughts generate actions; actions repeated over time determine character; and character, as the great writers and thinkers of the world will tell you, is destiny. In other words, what happens to you in life is not accidental. It's a direct or indirect result of what you think and what you do.

The Search for the Truth

A quote attributed to Lao Tsu, an ancient Chinese philosopher, counsels, "Do not seek the truth; only cease to cherish opinions." With that in mind, here are some things that I maintain don't exist: a beautiful day, an exciting story, a delicious meal, a boring party, a soothing melody, a fascinating conversation, a stressful situation, and countless others that could be similarly described.

Why not? Well, we behave, not in accordance with "the truth," but with the truth as *we perceive and believe it to be*. A meal may taste delicious to me, but if you were raised in a very different culture or are feeling ill, you might not agree. If you are in the hospital getting ready to have a second cancer operation, my beautiful day might seem pretty gloomy to you. And the conversation I find fascinating you might describe as obscure and irritating.

See what I mean? All of us live on the leash of our senses and our beliefs. Because of our physiology, the information our senses perceive is extremely limited. When we assume that we know the truth from what is apparent to us, we may well be deceived. If we want to see the details of our solar system, we need a telescope. If we want to see the details of the human body, we need a microscope. Even then, there is much that escapes us. Physicists tell me that the chair I am sitting in is not the solid object that it appears to be; they say it is composed largely of space. So, you see the truth often depends on who's looking, how they're looking, and how they interpret what they see.

Getting to the truth takes determination, persistence, and willingness to set aside preconceived ideas. Our tendency is to lock on to conventional and conditioned ways of thinking, adopting them as "the truth" and locking out other possibilities. We tend to be uncomfortable with paradox or thinking that is very different from our own. We like to feel sure of what we know, so we will argue for our version of the truth and try our darndest to make someone else's version wrong. We may even see ourselves as having won the argument, but in the process we have lost the opportunity of seeing and possibly understanding someone else's truth. Locking on to "the truth" can be a mistake that alienates others, limits our options, and locks out a world of possibilities.

Instead, you want to become a possibility thinker, someone who looks beyond convention, beyond conditioning. When you're a possibility thinker, you stop focusing on what you *don't* want—the problems, obstacles, and difficulties in your life. Instead, you look for options, solutions, and new ways of doing things that will give you the results you *do* want. You recognize your own biases, strengths, and weaknesses, and you can put them aside when they prevent you from seeing other possibilities. It's critical that you be able to do this, not only for your own success and well-being, but for the success of those you will be coaching and mentoring, too.

Now You See It, Now You Don't: Scotomas

Sometimes you can look right at something and not see it. How can that be? If you drive a car, you know about the dangerous blind spot that exists between the time something passes from the rearview mirror to the sideview mirror. Similarly, *scotoma* is the term that describes a blind spot within the eye's visual field caused by a physical defect or disease.

As I use the term, though, a scotoma is anything that keeps us from perceiving or understanding the truth. Most often, we inadvertently create these "blind spots" ourselves so that we can hold on to our version of reality, our beliefs about ourselves and the world in which we live. Scotomas cause us to see what we expect to see, hear what we expect to hear, and experience what we expect to experience.

If you're having a terrible time with your fifteen-year-old, whom you see as uncooperative, surly, and argumentative, you may have built a scotoma to the things he does that don't fit your picture. You won't notice when he cleans up after himself without being asked, but the mess he leaves in the living room will scream out at you. You won't hear him when he thanks you for the ride you gave him to the movies, but the silence will scream at you when he forgets. It's what you expect, and it confirms your belief, so, without fail, you notice.

If you believe that your company can't sell its services or products in a retail market, you won't see retail opportunities. You'll swear they're not out there. Your belief will create a scotoma. If you believe that women are poor drivers, you'll be on the alert for mistakes and dumb moves made by women behind the wheel. In fact, you'll notice nothing else, including the hundreds of expert female drivers with whom you share the road every day, and you'll find a way to rationalize any information to the contrary, such as your wife's flawless driving record or the insurance industry's statistics.

Now, scotomas can work for or against us, depending on our awareness and intention, and I'll tell you more about that in a moment. Unfortunately, more often than not, scotomas block our positive change efforts, flexibility, and creativity, because they make us selective information-gatherers. They keep us prisoners to our preconceived ways of seeing things and our habitual ways of doing things. Scotomas cause friendships to erode, marriages to fail, nations to go to war. Each side thinks, "What's the matter with you? Why can't you see the truth? Are you blind?" And the answer is, "Yes!"

Remember, when we lock on to "the truth," we also lock out other possibilities. What have you locked on to about your life? About other people? About the world you live in? What are you absolutely sure of? "She's just lazy, that's all." "I can't talk in front of a big group." "That won't work. It's never worked before." "You can't trust politicians." "He's a slow learner." "Getting old is the pits." "I'm no good at getting my boss to listen to me." "No way could I afford to go back to school." "I can't run an international business—I can't even do my taxes!"

It's important to realize that you manipulate your senses when you come to these conclusions, which are really opinions that may or may not have anything to do with the truth. You literally blind yourself to a multitude of opportunities, even when you're surrounded by them. That's because they might prove you wrong, so you just don't see them. You don't do it consciously, but it happens just the same.

Scotomas can also work to your advantage, if you realize you have them and use them with full awareness. For one thing, they are great concentration enhancers and energy focusers. In fact, the locking-on process is one of the things that gives commitment its incredible power. When you feel and declare a strong commitment to an idea, you blind yourself to distractions and irrelevant sensory input, which allows you to focus intently on your goal or challenge. When a professional basketball player is about to make a crucial free throw, he doesn't see or hear the crowd in the stands or feel the ache in his injured knee. Similarly, when you are totally committed to your marriage, the idea of a casual affair with your flirtatious neighbor just won't occur to you. In fact, you may not notice the flirtatious behavior that seems painfully obvious to your spouse. You don't see it because you have built a scotoma to it.

How to Get Lucky: Lock On and Open Up

So scotomas can help you achieve your goals, but they can also blind you to important information. The ideal way to manage this dilemma is to both lock on and open up. That is, focus intensely on your goals, but remind yourself to stay receptive to new information. Accept that what you "know" is only part of the truth, and be on the lookout for more of it. Go ahead and lock on to an imagined ideal or a desired end result, but remain open to unconventional options when it comes to figuring out how you're going to get there.

Don't think you know all there is to know about anything, no matter how long you've been learning, no matter how much authority you have, no matter how many people consider you an expert on the subject. In fact, the longer you've been doing something—running a company, raising kids, coming home to your spouse, being part of a friendship, mountain climbing, you name it—the more alert you need to be in order to avoid the blindness that is so often caused by complacency, tradition, and routine.

Diversity is a wonderful scotoma-buster. Even the benefit of one additional point of view gives you more information to work with and lets you see more of the truth. Many perspectives are available if you listen to the people around you, whether that's a widely varied work force or an extended family, a support group or a task-oriented team. Asking for input and listening carefully without preconceived judgments not only helps to eliminate blind spots and gives you an expanded view, it also says to the people you ask, "I value your opinion. I respect your ability to contribute." When you can base your decisions and actions on thoughtful consideration of this expanded view, a funny thing happens. You start to get "luckier."

As the quantity of truth that you see increases, so do the "lucky breaks" in your life. Only it isn't really about luck. It has nothing to do with coincidence or intelligence, either. It has to do with the way that you think, which causes a dramatic increase in the options available to you. Problems get solved because you *lock on* to solving them and then *open up* your mind to information about how. Relationships become more harmonious because you *lock on* to the positive, loving way you'd like them to be and *open up* your mind to finding the means to that end. Finances improve because you *lock on* to living a more abundant life and *open up* your mind to activities and behaviors that will earn it for you.

How the Mind Works

Psychology and psychiatry departments at large universities have entire libraries devoted to the workings of the human mind. So, although it's accurate, what I'm going to tell you about here amounts to skimming the surface—but that's OK, because you're not reading this book in order to become a psychologist. Also, the surface I've skimmed off to give you is, in my opinion, the cream—the essential things you need to know in order to be more and do more than you ever have before and to be the finest coach and mentor anybody ever had.

For some time now, a widely accepted way to look at the process of thought has been in terms of the conscious and subconscious. Occasionally, a third is added—the creative subconscious. These are purely theoretical terms, useful in helping us understand and explain human behavior. They aren't actually separated from each other by any physical boundary. Instead, these words represent different functions of what we commonly call the mind. Exploring a few basic principles of how these three functions work will help you understand why you sometimes behave as you do. It will also help you see why the affirmation and visualization process you'll learn about in Chapter 6 works as well as it does and why it is so critical to helping yourself and others grow.

The conscious mind deals with external and internal reality. It perceives, investigates, and interprets information that comes in through the senses. Once you perceive (see, hear, smell, touch, sense) something, you associate it with anything similar you have experienced before. Then, you decide whether any action is needed based on what happened in the past. That's why Jennifer, who was severely bitten by a neighbor's dog when she was coming home from second grade one day, is still afraid of dogs—*all* dogs—at age fifty. It's why the slightest whiff of barbecue sauce has made thirty-five-year-old Frank sick to his stomach ever since he became violently ill after eating a charbroiled hot dog when he was six. It's also why many people who have just had a painful divorce or relationship breakup are often reluctant to date or begin a new relationship. "I'm not about to open myself up to that kind of hurt again," they think, because they now associate intimacy with pain.

Your subconscious handles everything that goes on outside of your consciousness. It's a kind of autopilot that takes care of everything you don't think about—habits, attitudes, and beliefs; many body functions; memories; learned behaviors that have become automatic; feelings that have not been acknowledged or expressed, etc. The creative subconscious maintains order and sanity by making sure that you behave in ways that reflect your inner version of reality. In other words, it causes you to act like the person you know yourself to be. It operates very creatively to see that reality and your beliefs about reality match.

This is vitally important to remember as you attempt to change and grow, because your creative subconscious maintains your *presently dominant* self-image. If you see yourself as painfully shy and inept at making small talk, you don't have to remind yourself to be anxious about meeting new people or socializing at a party. If you believe that you are clumsy and uncoordinated, you won't have to remember to say, "No, thanks!" when you're invited to join the softball game at your company picnic. If you can't get out of playing, you won't have to remember to strike out or miss catches and feel uncomfortable the whole time, either. Your creative subconscious will take care of all of that for you.

By the way, it's not called the "creative" subconscious for nothing. It can create the body language that says "Leave me alone!" at the party, or it can give you the killer headache that keeps you from attending at all even though on a conscious level you've accepted the invitation and had your suit pressed. It can come up with something more important for you to do while the softball game is going on, or it can help you to accidentally twist your ankle during your first time at bat so you have to sit out the rest of the game. It can put you in the hospital, create pain where no injury or illness exists, generate such bizarre phenomena as false pregnancy and hysterical paralysis, or even cause death. Many people are convinced that it can also stop pain and heal injury or illness, and a great deal of research is being done to study the relationship between beliefs and expectations, the immune system and body chemistry.

Your creative subconscious is responsible for the stress and tension you experience whenever you feel out of place or try to act in ways that are out of sync with your self-image or beliefs. Just as the body warns you that something's wrong by sending you pain, your subconscious warns you that something's wrong by sending you tension and anxiety. Now, it's important to realize that your subconscious functions aren't even slightly concerned with your happiness or well-being, growth or development, success, wealth, or even health. All the creative subconscious has to do is make sure that the external reality you perceive matches your beliefs about reality.

If you're a woman who believes that men can't be trusted, and you find yourself in an intimate relationship, before long you'll begin to perceive only those behaviors that support your "untrustworthy" belief. You'll interpret those behaviors as deceitful, and you'll build scotomas to the rest. You just won't see the signs of love and loyalty. If you do, you'll discount or deny them. You'll feel hurt, angry, betrayed—but you'll also feel *right*: Once again, your belief about reality has been borne out by your experience in the world. Remember, this belief doesn't have to be conscious. You may never have articulated, even to yourself, the belief that "men can't be trusted." Yet if that's how you have interpreted your experiences on a subconscious level, it will be played out in reality.

My wife, Diane, and I have adopted or been foster parents to eleven children, many of whom were physically or psychologically abused before they came to us. I mean *badly* abused. Shot. Run over. Horribly beaten. Sexually violated. Things like that. Of course, we were determined to offer a better way of life to these kids who had gotten off to such a tragic start. We wanted to treat them as we believed they deserved to be treated—like the uniquely valuable, special, lovable human beings they were and still are.

But it didn't seem to matter how well we treated these kids. Time and time again, we were faced with major behavioral problems. Why? Because from the time they were born, they had gone through a long series of experiences that had utterly convinced them of three things: they were deeply flawed and somehow unworthy, the world was a painful place, and adults were the source of that pain and not to be trusted. We'd be putting our arms around them, patting them on the back, telling them that they were smart, great, super kids and that we were really proud of them, while everything they had assimilated from their past was screaming that they were no good.

So they'd steal the neighbors' mail or get into terrible fights at school or trample someone's prize-winning roses or something equally destructive. Because we didn't know as much then as we do now about the psychology of human behavior, Diane and I couldn't figure out what we were doing wrong. I still remember the time one of our boys started a fire behind the couch in the living room. Not half an hour before, I had been telling him how proud I was of him. After we put the fire out, I asked him, "How come you did that—how come you started that fire?" His answer was, "I don't know." When I told him to go to his room to think about it, he simply said, "Good."

You see, at that point Diane and I hadn't learned about how the self-image is formed and that it governs almost everything we think and do. We didn't understand that **human beings act, not in accordance with the truth, but with the truth as they believe and perceive it to be.** These kids believed that the truth about them was that they were bad, worthless, hopeless. Trouble with a capital T had been carved into their self-image, so they were acting like it. Even though their surroundings and the way they were being treated had changed, their subconscious picture of who they were hadn't yet altered at all. So their subconscious had to keep correcting for the "mistake."

It's no different for adults. If my deepest belief is that I'm a dismal failure in relationships with the opposite sex, when I start dating someone, and we're getting along well, chances are good that my subconscious is going to get very creative about correcting the mistake and setting things "right." One way or another, I'll find a way to sabotage the relationship. After the breakup, I'll be nursing my broken heart and saying, "Gosh, everything was going just great for a while, but then all of a sudden I couldn't stand her." It doesn't matter that my belief about how badly I do in relationships is based on old information—on what I saw of my parents' turbulent marriage, a girlfriend who cheated on me, my "best buddy" in high school who advised me to play the field because women were nothing but trouble, or all of this information together. All that matters to my subconscious is that my experiences match up with my beliefs about reality.

Because we base so many of our present and future decisions on past experiences, wouldn't it be great if we could go into our subconscious storage center and update "the truth" that is recorded there? Wouldn't it be useful to be able to deliberately adjust the negative self-image that was handed to us as kids so that it better reflects our true potential and leads us to health, prosperity, and love rather than to stress, failure, and conflict? Well, that's exactly what this book will show you how to do, and it's easier than you may think. First, though, let's look at the concept of accountability and the tremendous personal power it can generate.

Accountability, Control, and Power

Powerless people tend to blame others for their disappointments and failures. They blame their families: *"No one could succeed with the parents I had!"* They blame their friends: *"If my so-called friends would just come through for me once in a while."* They blame the system, society, their employers, the political party in power, and their individual circumstances.

Powerless people often feel that the deck has been stacked against them, and they have endless excuses for their lack of achievement and power over their own lives: *"All I need is some real money for a change." "It's because I didn't pay enough attention in school." "If only I was better looking (taller, shorter, a different race, a different age),"* and so on. They stumble through life feeling anxious, depressed, resentful, and bitter, dreaming of unlikely events that will magically transform them through little or no effort of their own. Because they're filled with envy, it's hard for them to feel real pleasure in other people's successes.

The cure is simple but not often taken: They just need to accept accountability for their own lives. They need to give up blame and learn to hope. Give up faultfinding and learn to set goals. Give up thinking about what they'd do if they won the lottery and figure out what to do with the money they have right now.

When we accept full accountability and responsibility for the results we get in life, we empower ourselves to change. When we believe that forces outside ourselves control us, we remain victims, feel powerless, and behave accordingly. It doesn't matter whether the outside force is the system, a disease or addiction, an employer, less than adequate parenting received as a child, the government, society, what others will think, the approval of a mate or spouse, peer pressure, and so on. Of course, these things do affect us to varying degrees. But when we make them *responsible* for what we do and say, for our failures and lack of effort, for our attitude that says "Why bother?", and for the pain we inflict on ourselves and others, we are, in effect, saying, "Until this outside force changes, I'm stuck." And so we are.

Accountability or responsibility (response-ability) suggests that we are able to thoughtfully choose the way we respond to life's events, rather than simply reacting by reflex. Feeling responsible is a good thing. As a matter of fact, it's essential if we are going to live up to our potential, enjoy fulfilling relationships with others, and live happy, fulfilling lives. John Kennedy became a true leader when he stood before the American people and said that the Bay of Pigs was an atrocity that should never have happened—and then took full responsibility for it.

It was then, that Kennedy was transformed from a promising young politician to a great leader. The same is true for you and me. When we take responsibility for our lives, we give ourselves power.

Accountability goes hand in hand with confidence and the feeling of controlling one's own life. When we're accountable, it means that we're capable of making rational or moral decisions on our own and that we are answerable to others for our behavior. It means that we can be trusted—that our word to others *and to ourselves* can be depended on.

The good news is that you can change the way you think. You can become accountable for your attitudes, expectations, and beliefs. You can deliberately change your self-image, your ideas about your attributes and capabilities, your convictions about what is possible for you and the world in which you live, your beliefs about who is responsible for your happiness and success.

This book will help you make these changes. Why would you want to? Just one reason I can think of. When you change the way you think, the way you behave changes. And when you behave differently, you get different results.

What's Good Enough for You

If you're already feeling on top of these things and in charge of your life, let me ask you some questions. Because you are accountable for your thoughts, they are focused, creative, and positive virtually all the time, right? Since you are accountable for your body, you must be trim and toned, healthy, fit, flexible, and active, correct? Because you are accountable for your emotions, you are filled with joy, enthusiasm, and a sense of inner peace on a daily basis, right? And since you are accountable for your time, your life is prioritized and balanced among many important interests and activities, isn't that so?

Do you see what I'm leading you toward? Even if you feel that you're already accountable and in control of your life, is there more you could be doing? Is there any less-than-ideal behavior or results that you're settling for, day after day, year after year? Is there more growing you could do in some areas? Could you be happier, healthier, more productive?

Did you find yourself feeling at all defensive when you read the last paragraph? I often notice that when I'm giving a presentation or a seminar and I start talking about accountability, some people begin to look uncomfortable. Maybe they're trying to cope with illness or injury, and they're feeling like victims. Their thinking probably goes something like this: "Are you trying to tell me that *I* am to blame for this? Do you expect me to believe that this is *my* fault?"

The answer is no. But neither do I want them to believe that it's someone else's fault. The accountability I'm talking about has nothing whatever to do with blame, guilt, or finding fault, and I get concerned when I hear so many people these days describing themselves as victims. So-and-so is the victim of an illness. Someone is a crime victim. Someone else is a victim of poverty or racism or sexism. Of course, I realize that these things exist and that no one deserves to have tragedy strike. But there's something in the label "victim" that tends to create a powerless attitude. Victims are helpless. If you think of yourself as a victim, you may begin to believe that you have no control over your life, that you probably aren't going to be able to have what you want, and that there's nothing you can do to change that.

Adopting a victim mentality can also be a way of avoiding accountability, like the man who filled out an accident report by saying, "The telephone pole was approaching. I was attempting to swerve out of its way when it struck my car." See what I mean? When you accept accountability for your role in creating a problem, you empower yourself to change the situation or to handle it differently next time.

By the way, the word *accountability* comes from an ancient Roman term that meant "to stand forth and be counted." That's the kind of accountability I mean—standing up more in your life and making it count. In the future, instead of playing the blame game ("Whose fault is this? Who's to blame here?"), examine as objectively as you can what your role may have been in creating the things that "happen to" you. Then, ask yourself how you would like to change your experience, what it would take to change it, and do what you need to do to make it happen. That's accountability in action.

How Personal Accountability Creates a Better World

Before we move on, I want to say one more thing about accountability on a personal level and how it connects to the social problems that plague us today. Some people think that we could solve a lot of society's problems with more laws, but the more laws we have, the more our prisons fill up. Others think that what we need is more money, but as a nation we are among the wealthiest.

I think the state of California was on the right track when it established a task force to promote self-esteem and personal and social responsibility. The report of that task force makes it clear that society's problems dwindle when its citizens feel accountable for their own actions, for the consequences of those actions, and for their own mental and physical health. People who feel this way don't expect others to make them happy and don't blame others for their sorrows. When a feeling of accountability arises from an inner choice rather than being imposed upon us by others, we operate with minimal confusion and self-deception and, therefore, we have better end results.

Accountability is definitely related to our feelings of self-esteem and self-efficacy. The more we appreciate our own worth and importance (self-esteem), and the more we feel able to cause the things we most want to happen (self-efficacy), the more we are able to act responsibly toward others. And the more responsibly we act toward others, the better our society as a whole will work.

All my experience, everything I know, tells me this is true. Winston Churchill once said, "The price of greatness is responsibility." I would add that when you take full responsibility for your life, you enable yourself to cause great things to happen. You help create not only a better life for yourself, but also a better world.

In the next chapter, we'll talk about the enormous power of the ideas that you accept as true—your beliefs and expectations—and we'll tie them to what you've just learned about how your mind works. I'll tell you some true stories about how my own beliefs have both held me back and helped me go forward. Then, we'll see how you can learn to create a belief system that will allow you to feel more optimistic, enjoy more success in every area of life, and become a first-rate coach or mentor.

CHAPTER TWO

Beliefs and Expectations: How Big Is Your Container?

The Pumpkin Jug

Your beliefs define the limits of what you will do and become as surely as the walls of your house or apartment define your personal living space. Have you ever heard the story of the farmer who brought a very unusual pumpkin to the county fair? This pumpkin appeared to be normal in every way, but it was shaped exactly like a two-gallon jug. Everybody at the fair thought it was really spectacular, and the farmer won a blue ribbon for it. When a reporter for the local paper asked, "How in the world did you ever get a pumpkin to look like that?" the farmer chuckled. "Nothin' to it," he said. "Soon as the blossom fell off and the fruit started to grow, I just stuck it inside a two-gallon cider jug. When it was ripe, I just broke the jug. The pumpkin and the sunshine did all the hard work!"

> "You're always believing ahead of your evidence. What was the evidence I could write a poem? I just believed it. The most creative thing in us is to believe a thing in."
>
> Robert Frost

In the same way, our reality is determined by the size and shape of our beliefs, our thoughts about who we are, and how we live. All too often, it is a painful or troublesome reality, due to beliefs we have accepted as true, even though they may not be. As children, how many of us were taught to think less than well of ourselves by adults who were replaying their own childhood experiences, or who just didn't know any better? How many of us, black or Hispanic, female or male, poor or illiterate, Muslim or Jew, disabled or disfigured, young or aged, markedly different or simply slow—routinely receive "not good enough" messages from the world? Sometimes these are blatantly cruel or violent messages. Sometimes they are much more subtle and insidious, but equally devaluing and destructive.

Fortunately, once we accept ourselves as accountable adults, we have the power to dispute, reject, and discard beliefs that no longer serve our best interests or express who we are or want to be. In their place, we can deliberately create new beliefs that will help us grow and realize our unique talents, skills, and abilities.

I know that this isn't always easy to do, especially if you haven't the slightest idea how to go about it. That's one of the reasons why, twenty-five years ago, my wife, Diane, and I decided to create our company. We wanted to give people a set of tools they could easily apply to change their beliefs and their lives for the better. To change not *what* they think but *how* they think.

We wanted to give these tools to people everywhere—in research laboratories, in corporate board rooms and assembly lines, in government and the military, in schools and correctional institutions and welfare offices. We wanted to give them to men and women in social service agencies and to people on both sides of the playing field, the battlefield, and the negotiating table. We wanted to give them to children and teenagers, parents and grandparents, the sick, the downhearted, and the elderly. And we wanted to give them to you. Because we were then, and still are, absolutely convinced that virtually everyone can benefit from them.

We feel this way because we know that, when it comes to human behavior, nothing is more important than beliefs. Absolutely nothing. The people who have changed the course of human history are those who were able to change our beliefs—about ourselves, our world, and what's possible. Think back on your own life for a moment. Haven't the people who have had a major influence on your personal history done the same thing? Whether their influence on you was positive or negative, didn't they somehow cause you to see things differently? To see yourself and your world differently?

Why are beliefs so important? What is a belief, exactly? How do beliefs "get in there"? How do they work? What makes them so powerful? In this chapter I'll answer these key questions for you. I'll show you how the answers fit into what we learned in Chapter 1 about how your mind works, and I'll tell you some true stories about the power of beliefs. Then, we'll talk about what all of this means to you, right now, wherever you are, whoever you are.

Beliefs and Behavior:
Your Own Virtual Reality

Remember the creative subconscious we talked about in the last chapter? We said that one of its jobs is to make your interior and exterior versions of reality match. Well, your beliefs are your *interior* version of reality. Beliefs can be thought of as clusters of repeated thoughts about certain things. Some of them you're aware of, some you're not. The important thing is that you believe in the truth of certain ideas. A vast number of them, actually.

For example, maybe you believe that foreign films are the only ones worth seeing, that your mother doesn't like the smell of chrysanthemums, that you look great in blue, that homelessness is a national disgrace, and that eating a lot of garlic every day is good for you. Whether your beliefs are true doesn't matter. All that matters is that you *believe* them to be true.

Once you believe them, you behave in ways that reflect your beliefs. You miss a lot of wonderful movies. You didn't see *Apollo 13*, *Forrest Gump*, or *Schindler's List*. You don't bring your mother bouquets that have chrysanthemums in them, even though it's really daisies she doesn't like. You own a closet full of blue shirts and sweaters and drive a blue car. You give money and time to a local shelter. And people occasionally leave the seat next to you empty at movies because you enjoyed a roasted garlic appetizer with dinner.

Besides affecting your behavior and influencing the responses you get back, your beliefs also regulate how you experience the world. They can change what you see or don't see, hear or don't hear, what you sense and feel. Because it's so vital to your efficient functioning and mental health, your powers of perception and interpretation work to confirm your beliefs out in the world. In other words, you see mostly what you look for, what you expect to see. You hear mostly what you expect to hear. We all do.

What You Get Is What You See: "Believing a Thing In"

Here's an example. Studies conducted by Dr. Andrew Weil, a Harvard-educated physician and author of many fine books, showed that the actual experience of drug users corresponds to their beliefs and expectations about that experience. In Weil's controlled experiments, people given sedatives *that they believed were stimulants* behaved as if they had taken stimulants. People given stimulants *that they believed were sedatives* behaved as if they had been sedated. So powerful was their belief in "the truth" of what they were told by the medical authorities who gave them the medication, their bodies somehow bypassed the physiological effects of the drugs. Instead, they created, without ever intending to do it, a physical reality inside their bodies that confirmed their belief.

Many fascinating studies now document the power of belief to create self-fulfilling prophecies—events that, because they are predicted and expected, are therefore more likely to happen, even caused to happen. Here's another example of how beliefs work to influence perceptions and behavior. According to *Success* magazine, two similar groups of psychologists were asked to observe the same child playing. One group was told beforehand that the child was emotionally disturbed. The other group was told that the child was a genius. When the psychologists reported their observations, each group had found evidence to support its preconceived belief, and all the psychologists were comfortably certain that their observations were accurate.

Just as with the drug users in Weil's studies, these psychologists unconsciously bypassed information that didn't support their beliefs or they interpreted it in ways that did. They were certainly trying to be objective. In terms of their behavior, the truth—that the child they observed was a garden-variety, developmentally unremarkable kid—didn't matter. All that mattered was what they *believed* to be true.

These two examples are just a tiny part of a large body of evidence that emphasizes the importance of our beliefs in determining what we see, feel, and experience as well as how we behave. If you're interested in self-mastery and in helping others to achieve more of their vast potential—and you must be, or you wouldn't be reading this book—it's essential for you to understand that **we behave not in accordance with *the truth,* but with the truth as we *perceive* and *believe* it to be.**

You must also realize that *self-fulfilling prophecies are everyday experiences,* not just laboratory experiments or studies that professionals read about in scientific journals. And there's nothing magical or mysterious about how self-fulfilling prophecies work either. How we *think* about a situation affects what we *perceive (see, hear, feel).* What we perceive directly influences how we *behave.* And how we behave, more than anything else, determines the *results* we get. Not mysterious at all. In fact, it's really nothing but common sense.

"Is-ness" and Resistance to Change

If you have believed something for a long time, can you deliberately change that belief to one that is better for you? Can you do it without betraying your values and without feeling foolish or phony? Sure you can—and you do, all the time. In fact, most of your beliefs about yourself and your environment are flexible, subject to change based on new, relevant information, new "truths." They *have* to be if you're going to survive in an everchanging world.

Right now, for instance, there are a lot of folks using laptop computers who once believed they'd never be comfortable with anything but those yellow legal tablets. Many of us are cutting fat and adding fiber to our diets because of new information and changing beliefs about nutrition and health. Many others are scrupulously recycling what they used to throw away. And every day, thanks to the work I do, I help literally millions of men, women, and young people to change some of their beliefs because they can now see the benefits of doing so and understand the process involved.

Think of it like this: Many of your beliefs are no more fixed, no more permanent than the length of your hair. I remember growing up during a time when no man, and I mean not one, would think of growing his hair long. Then, when the '60s and '70s hit, beliefs changed and so did hairstyles. Now we seem to have cycled around to short hair again, but it's not at all unusual to see a male wearing a ponytail, even with a suit.

Sure, you probably have a few core beliefs that are so rock-solid and fundamental you might even die for them. But the fact is that much of who you are is the result of beliefs that you picked up as you grew up, without thinking about them. When you were young, many of those beliefs were more or less handed to you by adults or older kids. Sometimes they were well-meaning but mistaken. Sometimes they weren't so well-meaning. But because they were authorities to you, you took in what they said, gave sanction to it, and accepted it as the truth. Then, you behaved accordingly.

What "truths" did you learn about yourself while you were growing up? Did you learn that you were strong and graceful or weak and clumsy? Interesting and funny or irritating and troublesome? Bright and quick or dull-witted and slow? Important and valuable, no matter what you did, or important and valuable depending on whether you lived up to certain adult standards?

What "truths" did you learn about the world? Is it a basically friendly place where your needs are likely to be met or a dog-eat-dog struggle for survival? Can people generally be trusted, or do you need to watch your back at all times? Do you treat the air, water, and land of your environment with respect and care, or do you think that it's already so polluted that nothing you do matters? Do you see issues and people in either-or terms of right and wrong, good and bad, or do you see a continuum of possibilities? Is there a loving, responsive creator watching over you? Or is your God a vengeful, controlling deity that you must constantly struggle to please? Maybe yours is a random universe without any guiding spirit at all. How locked on are you to the "truth" of your beliefs about yourself and the world?

What Do You See When You Look at Your Life?

It's not always easy to express or even recognize what your beliefs are. If you'd like to get a look at your deepest beliefs in action, take a look at your life. What you see will be everything you believe played out right there in front of you.

If you believe you can't handle wealth or that making a comfortable living is somehow evil, corrupt or a mystery you can't solve, then you are poor. If you believe that life is a combat exercise in which you constantly have to prove yourself capable or right, then your time will be filled with endless struggles and issues of control. If you believe that people are not to be trusted or relied upon, then you feel deeply alone. If you believe that people, including yourself, are basically good and that everyone deserves respect, then you enjoy many rewarding relationships. And if you believe that no matter what life sends, you can make something worthwhile from it, then evidence of that worth and value will be all around you.

If some of the things you see when you look at your life don't jibe with what you think you believe, remember this: Whenever there is a difference between a belief you hold consciously about yourself and one you hold subconsciously, sooner or later your subconscious belief will find a way to prevail. That's how persuasive and persistent your subconscious is.

So if you consciously want to be financially successful, but your subconscious picture of yourself doesn't support affluence, you'll sabotage yourself. You'll spend every penny you earn and then some, lose money in get-rich-quick schemes, invest impetuously, lend it to people who will never repay you. Maybe you talk a lot about wanting a more exciting career, but if your most deeply held belief is that you don't have anything of value to contribute or can't handle much more responsibility, you probably won't aim very high. Perhaps you envy people who travel extensively and live in foreign countries, but if your dominant subconscious image is that the world away from home is unsafe and that you don't do well in unfamiliar situations, how far do you think you'll get?

It's not that you don't have the *potential* to travel, achieve material wealth, have an exciting career, or do just about anything that you want to do. You have *tremendous* potential—probably far more than you realize. But your creative subconscious is guarding your sanity by making sure that your beliefs about reality are validated by your experiences.

As you honestly look at the life you're living right now, you'll probably see things you're not happy with. You'll see things that don't seem to fit with what you consciously want, things you do that are causing yourself or other people pain, things you do that are not in your best interests. When that happens, don't start looking for ways that you can change your environment or, even worse, for someone to blame. Instead, look at your deepest beliefs. Are there any sacred cows, things that you believe "just because"? How about beliefs that might have had a reasonable purpose once but are now in your way, holding you back, holding you down? Do you see any beliefs that serve only to keep you safe from imagined dangers or to preserve the status quo of your life so you won't have to change? What about beliefs that are downright self-destructive?

Becoming Your Own Authority

If you choose to change these irrational, exaggerated, or mistaken beliefs, your behavior is going to change as a consequence. And when your behavior changes, so do the events that you set into motion and the results that you get. **We change ourselves and the world from the inside out, not from the outside in.** I'm convinced that this is how the world works. I know that's a pretty strong statement, but if you're willing to question some of your assumptions as you read, and if you're willing to keep your mind open, I think you'll see what I mean.

It's especially important to question judgments that others have made about you and you've accepted as the truth. No matter what your individual circumstances, chances are that while you were growing up you took in some negative feedback about yourself. Most of us did. In his early years, Albert Einstein was a poor student who was called mentally slow and unsociable by his teachers. Abraham Lincoln's teachers described him as a daydreamer who asked foolish questions. And Thomas Edison was written off as a hopeless case when he was seven years old. His teacher said he was addled and predicted that it would be useless for him to continue in school.

Each of these extraordinary people might easily have believed the "you're not good enough" messages. If they had, I wouldn't be writing about them here, because no one would have heard of them. But instead of simply accepting what they were told about themselves, these people decided on some level that so-called authority figures couldn't determine their destiny without their tacit permission. And they refused to give it. Instead, they chose to generate their own life stories, to become their own "authorities." That's what I decided to do, too, before I was out of my teens, and that's what I am still choosing, day after day, year after year. That's what we all must choose if we want to live authentically and continue to grow, both as a species and as individuals.

Coaching at Kennedy

How many people do you know who shrug off their own undesirable behaviors and characteristics? They refuse accountability by saying something like, "That's just how I am," as if they emerged from the womb that way. How about people who respond that way to the world around them, the office they work in, the market they sell in, the family they live in, the political system that governs them? "That's just how it is," they say. "There's nothing I can do about it." Their minds are closed to other possibilities, and they resist, deny, or simply don't see anything that might shake up their belief system. "Is-ness" is fixed for them. Change is threatening, paradox is intolerable, and relationships tend to remain static and superficial.

Here's a true story about my own experience with "is-ness" and resistance to change. This happened years ago, when I was teaching and coaching football at Kennedy High School in Seattle, Washington. Kennedy was a brand new school, so I had my first team of players for four full years. As time went by, I became convinced that I knew these kids better than anyone, maybe even better than their parents. They were hardworking boys, but they weren't playing great football. They weren't even playing good football.

By the end of the third year, I had locked on to the "truth" about why we couldn't win. I believed that David, my quarterback, couldn't pass the ball ten yards. I had seen him play for three years, I was his coach, and I thought I ought to know. I had also locked on to the ideas that my ends couldn't catch and our team had no speed. So we moved the ball by slamming our fullback into the line for a couple of yards whenever we could. Our games were so boring, parents used to doze off in the stands while watching us play. We would win 7-6 or, more often, lose 6-7.

One day, we were playing a high school from a nearby town. I still remember this game vividly, because it was such an "Aha!" experience for me. It was third down with eight yards to go—a long yardage situation for us because we only averaged about three yards a carry. David called time-out and came over to me, asking what play we were going to call. We only had two plays, so I didn't know what was the matter with him, wasting a time-out like that. But when I told him to do what we always did, only harder, he really surprised me. He said, "Coach, couldn't we pass the ball to Marty?"

Marty was an end we used as a decoy, and everybody knew we didn't throw the ball to him. Besides, I didn't like the fact that David was trying to tell me what to do. After all, I was the coach. But David wasn't intimidated by the angry glare I gave him as a response. He looked me right in the eye and said, "Well, Marty's been open for the whole game. Just like he's been open for the whole *year!*" I paid no attention to him, and we ran our fullback into the line again. But David sent Marty down the field anyway, and he made faces at me the whole way. I can still see him standing wide open under the goal post, grimacing at me, making David's point more eloquently than any words could have done. "I'll be darned!" I thought. "Would you just look at that!" On the next play, we sent Marty downfield again, this time for real. David faked a handoff to the fullback and threw a touchdown pass to Marty. In fact, we scored three touchdowns in that game on the same play. And there I was, thinking, "Not all year! It couldn't have been that easy—not as hard as we've been working!" The next day, I reviewed our game films for that season, and there it was, right there on the screen, just as David had said. And now that I was really looking, I could see that it wasn't just Marty who had been in the clear. Other kids had been open, too, but we never called their plays. Suddenly, all at once, I could see it. Lights were going on for me so fast I felt like a Christmas tree.

At that point, I didn't know squat about scotomas, selective perception, or self-fulfilling prophecies. I didn't have a clue about the power of beliefs and expectations and how they influence behavior and results, but I sure was beginning to learn—the hard way.

There's more to the Kennedy High School story. A lot more. Because the incident with David had shown me that my players could see things I couldn't, I began to ask them for input. I'd ask them to tell me how we could score and which was their favorite play. I started listening to my players instead of just demanding that they listen to me. I started to let them run their plays and—what do you know—we started to win games! Before that, I'd been too worried about how it would look if I, the coach, the "authority," asked the players what they thought. My own self-esteem was so low that I couldn't ask for help. I didn't want anyone to show me—I wanted to show them.

After I began to change my style, the most amazing things started to happen. Not only did we win games, we started to see how much we could win by. Could we win by thirty points? By forty? Yes, indeed, we could. As a team, we would goal-set to do it, and we made it happen. You can imagine how good we felt. And the better we felt, the better we played. These kids always had the potential to be winners, but I had been holding them back because I couldn't see it. When my perception of them and what they could do changed, so did their performance. This is often called the Pygmalion effect, and we'll take a closer look at how it can help you coach and mentor others when we get to Part Two.

By the way, Marty went on to become a high school All-American. We had the state's leading scorer, and several others on that team became outstanding players, too. I still hear from some of them, only they're grown-ups with kids of their own now. From time to time, I ask one of them to spend a little time with me at The Pacific Institute. I do it for them, so they'll know that I'm still proud of them and to remind them of their ability to do anything they set their minds to. I do it for our staff, because they've heard a lot about these guys, and I want them to know I haven't made it up. And I do it for myself, to remember how far I've come and to remind myself of the dangers of "is-ness."

The *Wizard of Oz* as Parable

The Pacific Institute has a branch in Australia, so Diane and I go there often. On a flight home from Perth a few years ago, we stopped off in Hawaii to visit a client organization, a social service agency. They were working with the Alu Like people, a group of native Hawaiians who have been plagued with chronic problems similar to Dorothy and Toto's remarkable companions: a scarecrow who thinks he has no brains, a tin man who believes himself to be heartless, and a lion who is ashamed because he thinks he is a coward.

Their journey to Oz is long and often dangerous, but they persist, and by helping each other along the way, they finally get in to see the Wizard. Of course, it turns out that the Wizard is a blustering fake who is hiding behind the trappings of power. But he's also a nice guy with good intentions, and he doesn't want Dorothy and her pals to be sad. So he gives them more than they had ever hoped for—he gives them the reliable magic of high self-esteem.

"You don't need brains," he tells the scarecrow. "All you need is a diploma. You're already as smart as they come. Now, go act like it!" To the tin man, he says, "You don't need a heart. You're already both loving and loved. You just need a watch so you can hear it beating." "You don't need courage," he tells the lion. "You're the bravest of the brave. Here's a medal so you'll believe it. Now go behave like it, and hold your head high!"

Shortly afterward, Dorothy finds out that she never really needed the Wizard's magic to go home. All she had to do was really want it, visualize it, and believe in her own ability to make it happen: "You've always had the power to leave," Glinda tells her. But Dorothy couldn't make the power work until she believed in herself.

In my speech, I suggested to these young native Hawaiian graduates that they had spent too much time listening to people who were negative wizards. Negative wizards can seem very knowledgeable. Because we're taught as children to respect and listen to authority figures, and because we're too young or naive or scared to do otherwise, we give them bits of our power while they chip away at our self-esteem. They tell us we're not good enough, not smart enough, the wrong color, the wrong sex, that we worship the wrong way, and speak the wrong language. They tell us we don't measure up, that we'll never amount to anything. And we believe them.

I reminded these young people that negative wizards could take away their hearts, courage, and brains—but only if they were willing to let them get away with it. I told them that the graduation certificates I was presenting meant that they were setting out, not to *see* the wizard, but to *be* the wizard. And I told them that, as a result of their education and determination, they had everything they needed to become positive wizards for themselves and for the many others they were going to meet on the road.

Learned Helplessness, Learned Optimism

Was I selling those young people a bill of goods based on wishful thinking? Can we really learn to change our attitudes about ourselves and our beliefs about reality? Can we choose to be different and then actually do it, even though we may have been conditioned by many years of negative feedback from others? Even though we have internalized these negative messages so effectively that *we* are now the ones delivering them to *ourselves*? Can we change habitual but unproductive ways of thinking and make those changes last? Can people with low self-esteem turn that opinion around? Can pessimists learn to be optimists? And, if they can, does it really make any difference to what happens to them in life?

Yes, yes, yes! There is no longer any doubt about the answer to *all* of these questions. My twenty-five years of experience working with all kinds of people say, without the slightest hesitation, "Yes!" A large and growing body of reliable, valid research by the world's leading human behavior scientists says, "Yes," too.

Of special interest to me has been the work done by two widely respected scholars, Dr. Albert Bandura of Stanford University and Dr. Martin Seligman of the University of Pennsylvania. I'll introduce you to Dr. Bandura's work on self-efficacy in Chapter 3. First, though, I want to tell you a little about what Dr. Seligman has learned during the course of his groundbreaking work on learned helplessness and learned optimism, and what he and I learned from each other.

The *cognitive revolution* in the field of psychology and Martin Seligman's intense interest in why some people give up when others persist happened at about the same time, during the mid- to late '60s. Until then, theories of human behavior put forth by people called behaviorists were widely accepted as the truth. Behaviorists insisted that all animal and human behavior could be explained by a simple reward/punishment theory: They said that behavior that is reinforced or rewarded increases, and behavior that is ignored or that meets with unpleasant consequences diminishes or disappears. Period.

Then, during the '60s, a theory based on the process of thought, or cognition, emerged. Cognitive psychologists argued convincingly that the way we *think* about ourselves and the things that happen to us is what determines, in large part, how we feel and behave.

This interested Martin Seligman a great deal. First as a graduate student working with animals and later as a research psychologist supported by the National Institute of Mental Health, the National Science Foundation, the Guggenheim Foundation, and others, Seligman began to look at *how* thoughts, expectations, and beliefs influenced behavior. He was especially curious about how our habitual ways of explaining things that happen to us—our explanatory "style"—affected our mental and physical health and our success at work, school, home, etc. During the course of his research, Seligman designed some groundbreaking studies that proved two important things. First, pessimistic or helpless attitudes are not inherited, inborn traits. They are learned and gradually acquired. Second, because they are learned, they can also be *un*learned.

Here are Seligman's own words, from his 1991 book, *Learned Optimism*:

> Until now, if you were a pessimist you had no choice but to live in pessimism. You would endure frequent depressions. Your work and health would suffer. It would always be wet weather in the soul. In exchange for this, you might have gained a keener sense of reality and a stronger sense of responsibility. You now have a choice. . . . Learning how to think more optimistically when we fail gives us a permanent skill for warding off depression. It also can help us achieve more and have better health.

Seligman found that optimists tend to live more successful lives and sometimes longer lives, too. They enjoy higher levels of achievement, better health, and have less trouble with depression. Most exciting to me was the confirmation by Seligman's twenty years of work of something I deeply believed as a result of my own experience: Optimism can be learned and taught.

After I read his book, I invited Seligman to come to Seattle to share some of his ideas with our staff. He also spent a couple of days with Diane and me at our ranch, talking about the many ways in which his work and ours fit together. I was especially interested in how the results of his research can be applied in real life. During the twenty-five years that I've been studying the work of world-class researchers and struggling with the dense, highly technical language they often use, I've been asking the kinds of down-to-earth questions I think you'd ask: So what? Who cares? What difference does it make? I want to know how to *apply* what researchers like Seligman tell us so that our lives will change for the better. Otherwise, what's the point of all that work?

When he addressed The Pacific Institute's Global Leadership Conference in August 1994, Dr. Seligman told the crowd how he tested his theories in the real world with athletes, salespeople, students, even politicians. He found it invariably true that people with optimistic thought patterns could cope better with setbacks, obstacles, and failure. How come? Well, they didn't waste time blaming themselves and beating themselves up when things went wrong. Instead, they tried again, even harder, and were determined to succeed. And, in fact, they did succeed, far more often than pessimists did.

It's important to realize, though, that optimists don't wear glasses so deeply rose-colored that a clear picture of what's really out there can't get through. Optimism isn't about taking foolish risks or adopting a Pollyanna attitude that denies the existence of pain, difficulty, and struggle. It's a hopeful, encouraging, useful way of explaining your experiences in life. Marty Seligman talks about "the word in your heart." If it's yes, he says, you're an optimist. If it's no, you're a pessimist. And he and I both agree that you have the power to change it from no to yes, if you choose to.

Seligman teaches people one way to make that change. I come at the change process from a somewhat different angle, but we are both saying "Yes!" to your ability to take charge of your thoughts. And we are both working with scientifically sound principles of cognitive psychology. The important thing to realize is that these techniques for change really do work. They've been tested over and over again, and they're highly effective, if they're used consistently over time.

Winning by a Day and a Half

Here are two more stories about the power of beliefs. I have literally hundreds of these stories—I guess you could say I collect them, or they collect me—but I tell this first one because it's so graphic and really almost unbelievable. It's true, though. Check the newspaper and magazine archives at the library. It happened when Diane and I were on one of our trips to Australia. They were having a big footrace from Sydney to Melbourne—544 miles, one of the world's most grueling endurance tests.

Everyone was talking about a sixty-one-year-old potato farmer from the outback named Cliff Young who had entered this big-time race. The press interviewed him as if he were comic relief. When they asked how he trained, he explained that, because there were no horses on his ranch, he had to herd the cows on foot. He had never run a marathon race before, and he knew nothing about the "right" way to train or commonly accepted marathon strategy. He had no trainer or coach, and he showed up on race day wearing long overalls and old, beat-up shoes!

I was in Melbourne when the race ended, and by that time Cliff Young was a national hero. Not only had he surprised everyone by actually finishing, he had beaten the entire field and, in the process, he cut a day and a half off the previous record!

The accepted strategy for running a race like this had been to run eighteen hours out of every twenty-four and sleep six. But Cliff didn't know this. He didn't know "the truth" that everyone else knew about how to run this race. He had no idea that he needed about thirty hours of sleep over the five-plus days he was going to be running, so he slept a total of fifteen! Instead of lifting up his feet when he ran, he shuffled them along close to the ground. He didn't know that it was impossible for anyone to finish a day and a half ahead of the field. So Cliff Young ran outside of conventional wisdom and discovered his own truth. Since his sensational victory, several others have broken his record, and his strange, shuffling gait is now considered the "right" way to do it!

The same thing happened when Roger Bannister broke the four-minute-mile barrier in 1954. Until he did it, everyone "knew" it wasn't possible. That was the size of their container, their two-gallon cider jug. During the four years after Bannister blew it away, that barrier was broken more than forty times! Those forty runners weren't training differently and they weren't running under unusual conditions. But they were *thinking* differently. First it became *possible,* then it became possible *for them,* and finally it became routine, *a new standard* rather than something exceptional.

That's also how it works for you and me—in business, in fitness and health, in family life, and in personal and professional relationships. So, I'll say it again: When you change a belief, changed behavior follows. And changed behavior changes results. As you move ahead in this book, you're going to hear about some powerful techniques for changing beliefs that will make it easy for you. But first, I have another story to tell you about how beliefs can shut down or expand reality.

Building a Better Violin

Not long ago, I heard a fascinating report on National Public Radio about a new invention. Now, you probably know that any professional violinist is thrilled to have an opportunity to play a Stradivarius. The richness of sound produced by his painstakingly handcrafted violins made Stradivari legendary. Of course, only a limited number of these fine instruments are still around, and they cost a small fortune, assuming you can find one for sale.

But a British music lover, an engineer by profession, has redefined the possibilities. After a great deal of patient experimentation, he has been able to match the depth of tone and overall sound quality of a Stradivarius with his own, handmade violins. In blindfold tests, concert violinists couldn't tell the difference between the sound produced by his brand-new instruments and the ones made long ago by Stradivari himself.

What is truly remarkable, though, is that these new violins aren't made of wood at all. They're made of a new, high-tech polymer something like plastic. What's more, they cost only a tiny fraction of what a Stradivarius costs. Concert violinists are lining up to buy them. Of course, there's a long waiting list, so now this highly creative inventor is working on ways to build them faster. I have a feeling he'll succeed, don't you?

I think of this guy as the Cliff Young of violin makers. He just didn't accept the "truth" that would have limited his experiments to wood, and he didn't accept the "fact" that no one could ever duplicate the sound of the wonderful instruments made by Stradivari. Because he hadn't locked on to those ideas, he could see possibilities no one else could see. As a result, he has given a great gift to the world of music, and his fortune, if he chooses to make one, is assured.

I'm telling you these stories because I want you to think about your own life and ask yourself some important questions. What truths have you locked on to about yourself, about your career or business, about the people you live and work with? What "expert" advice have you accepted as the truth, without question, that may be keeping you from spreading your wings, from taking off and attempting to live your dreams?

What do you believe is possible for you, your children, your family, your community, your planet? How have your beliefs about what is possible shaped your reality and your behavior? How did you acquire these beliefs? Do they serve you well and help you to become the person you most want to be? Or do they keep you inside an invisible boundary, like the two-gallon jug, that limits your growth and stops you from taking the risks you need to take if you're going to continue to grow?

Think about these important questions before moving on to Chapter 3, where we'll talk about some beliefs that build personal effectiveness. Better yet, set aside some time to record your thoughts in a journal or notebook. Write about what you were taught about yourself and your capabilities as a child. Try to remember the messages you received about your intelligence, lovability, sexuality, creativity, health, agility, strength, and so on. What were you taught about money, work, marriage, responsibility, and individuality? Who were the positive wizards in your life, and what did they do for you? Who were the negative wizards, and what did they do to you? Write these things down to read later, and consider the implications.

You may want to share your answers and experiences with a close friend or family member. Even if you do your reflective thinking alone, remember that beliefs are just beliefs. Even the ones that seem to be in your way now served a purpose once upon a time. Classifying them as bad or good, positive or negative, weak or strong, isn't helpful. Instead, look at them as data—information about yourself to review in light of its current usefulness, then choose to retain, modify, or discard.

CHAPTER THREE

The Roots of Human Effectiveness: Self-Esteem, Self-Efficacy, and Self-Talk

Self-Esteem: What Are You Worth?

S trong self-esteem is as important to your psychological development as a good root system is to the growth of a tree. But what do we mean when we talk about self-esteem? Dr. Nathaniel Branden, often called the father of the concept of self-esteem, defines it this way: "The disposition to experience oneself as competent to cope with the basic challenges of life and as worthy of happiness."[1] I like this definition. Looked at in this light, it makes sense that the stronger your self-esteem, the better you're likely to perform and the happier you're likely to be.

Having high self-esteem doesn't mean you feel good about yourself every minute of every day. That's unrealistic. It's appropriate to feel guilty if you've behaved thoughtlessly or cruelly, or to feel deep regret if your self-interest has caused pain or difficulty for someone else. It's natural to feel sad if you've suffered a loss, or to be angry if you've been abused or betrayed. But if your self-esteem is generally solid, painful feelings pass more quickly. You tend to "pick yourself up, dust yourself off, and start all over again," trusting that you've learned something.

> "We must be arched and buttressed from within, else the temple will crumble to dust."
>
> Marcus Aurelius

Who Has Low Self-Esteem?

Unfortunately, the answer to this question is: Too many of us, for too much of our lives. If you were raised by people with poor self-esteem, you probably have to struggle with self-esteem problems yourself. If, under a confident or self-righteous veneer, your parents or caretakers felt inadequate, unworthy, and insecure, that's how they probably treated you. They sent you verbal and nonverbal messages about yourself that said you weren't good enough, and, after a while, you internalized those messages.

Soon, you didn't need them to tell you how inadequate you were. You started telling yourself with your own thoughts—your self-talk—routinely, day in and day out. You built a belief system that had as its foundation the shifting sands of self-doubt. As a result, self-destructive behaviors, such as substance abuse and other addictions, apathy, isolation, depression, hostility, or personal neglect may well have become part of your life.

I understand what it's like to be raised in such an environment. My early and middle childhood years were spent in poverty, chaos, and confusion. Alcohol abuse, violent anger, instability, and neglect were routine. When my father died, things got even worse for me and my brothers and sister. I was thirteen, and if it hadn't been for the influence of some wonderful people—mentors, role models, friends, and relatives—who took an active interest and showed me better ways, I don't know what would have happened. I can easily imagine how feelings of hopelessness and worthlessness might have overwhelmed me. My memories of those people and my ever-growing appreciation of what they did for me is one of the reasons why I wanted to write this book. Good coaches and mentors make a huge difference. So does your willingness to look unflinchingly at the forces that shaped your development, and then exercise your right to do things differently from now on.

Who Has High Self-Esteem, and Why?

It's easy to recognize someone with high self-esteem. They enjoy their lives and have plenty of enthusiasm. They also have a strong sense of purpose. They seem able to be what they want to be and do what they want to do. They make clear choices about how they want to live, and they use their talents, skills, and abilities in a balanced, harmonious way. No, they don't think they are perfect, but they accept the reality of their imperfections without denial or avoidance, even as they determine to improve.

Self-acceptance is an essential component of high self-esteem. Accepting yourself doesn't mean that you like or feel proud of your faults. But it does mean that you can experience the truth of who you are at this particular point in your life without feeling shame or guilt. You can't grow out of unwanted thoughts and feelings if you're not aware of them. If you judge yourself as bad or weak for having them, you'll be inclined to avoid that awareness. So give yourself a break. Self-acceptance means that you refuse to be in an adversarial relationship with yourself, and it is one of the basic building blocks of self-esteem.

And, no, high-self-esteem people are not arrogant. On the contrary. They feel closely connected to the rest of world and grateful for their blessings. They value themselves *and others* for who they are, not just what they do. They like themselves, on the whole, and they like other people, too. Their sense of worth doesn't depend on having a high-profile job or earning lots of money or looking like a movie star. As a result, they can recover from just about any loss or blow chance hands them, because they're determined to find their lives good, no matter what.

Sweet Fallibility

People with high self-esteem don't feel ashamed, embarrassed, or worthless if they make a mistake or a poor decision. Nobody enjoys being wrong or messing up, but we all do it. In fact, the higher your self-esteem, the more venturesome you probably are, and the more likely you are to be wrong from time to time. So what? Being wrong isn't as hard as some people think. If you catch yourself with your foot in it, just acknowledge it. "I made a mistake. Thanks for catching it." Or "Looks like I was wrong about that. Next time, I'll do better." Or "I shouldn't have blown up at you like that. I'm really sorry." Admitting it matter-of-factly when you're wrong is an important skill to perfect. Fortunately, I get plenty of opportunity to practice.

So, go ahead. Say "I screwed up." By proudly proclaiming yourself to be a normal, imperfect, fallible human being, you give others permission to do the same. Believe it or not, you also make yourself more lovable. While we respect each other for our strengths, it's often our human weaknesses that are most endearing. When you are able to openly confess a mistake or weakness without making a big deal about it, you are showing true humility, and your self-esteem and dignity are enhanced by your honesty. Besides, trial and error is one of the most effective ways to learn. It's only those whose self-esteem is like rust under chrome who have trouble admitting they were wrong. *Doing the right thing is always more important than being right,* and when you've made a mistake, the right thing to do is admit it.

While we're talking about making mistakes, maybe you've noticed that people with low self-esteem have a terrible time with anything they perceive as an insult. That's because, beneath their facade of self-confidence, they're really not convinced of their own value or competence. So whenever they think that someone has insulted or rejected them, they come unglued. They fret and fume, fly into a rage, spend a lot of time brooding about it, and sometimes they even seek retaliation or revenge.

People with high self-esteem just brush off insults. I once heard a story about Abraham Lincoln that illustrates what I mean. At the height of the Civil War, Lincoln and his secretary of war paid a visit to General McClellan to hear firsthand about how it was going.

When the general arrived, covered with mud, he brushed by them, trudged upstairs, and sent his maid to tell them he was tired and had gone to bed. The secretary of war was offended. "Surely you won't allow him that sort of rudeness," he said. "Surely you will relieve him of his command." Lincoln thought for a moment, then said, "No, I will not relieve him. That man wins battles, and I would hold his horse and clean his boots if it would hasten the end of this bloodshed by one hour." Lincoln was so secure in his power and purpose that very little could unsettle his sense of self-worth. The same is true for anyone with high self-esteem.

Once you realize that making mistakes is no big deal, you free yourself to look at the criticism you're getting from others and ask yourself if it's justified. If it isn't, you can just shrug it off. If it is, you can learn and grow from it. You can apologize if you've behaved badly or hurt someone, try to make amends, and affirm your intention to do better next time, without groveling or feeling humiliated. When you take responsibility for both your strengths and weaknesses, you also take charge of them.

Self-Esteem and Risk Tolerance

A positive sense of self-worth encourages an expansive, adventurous worldview. This view of the world allows for the creative experience of choice. It enables you to take risks without becoming a nervous wreck and to encourage others as they take calculated risks, as well. Risking isn't easy, because there's the possibility of loss involved, but it isn't a white-knuckle experience when you have high self-esteem and self-efficacy. Then you know that risk-taking is involved in everything worthwhile, and you realize that without taking risks you'll never feel truly confident, create a lasting love relationship, be respected by others, or raise happy kids, for that matter.

Because they aren't worriers, people with high self-esteem don't spend a lot of time fretting about the possible losses involved in the risks they take. They stay focused on what they have to gain (the only reason we take risks in the first place), what they have chosen to do, and they keep moving forward.

So much of your experience is determined by where you focus your attention. If you think loss, talk loss, see loss, day after day, don't be surprised when you end up losing. But if your purpose is worthy, your commitment strong, and your thoughts focused on a positive end result, you'll behave like a winner. And, regardless of whether any particular risk pays off, in the long run, if you behave like a winner you'll be one.

Freedom to Change

When you have high self-esteem, you are free to change yourself and develop an action-based lifestyle. You can express your needs and desires clearly, say no when you mean no, and behave in ways that respect the needs of others without sacrificing your own needs or betraying your principles.

On the other hand, people with low self-esteem protect the status quo and have to be right all the time. They are usually masters of the put-down and like to point out the faults, flaws, and incompetence of everyone around them. Of course, they are good at these things because they have had so many lessons, and they are simply reflecting out into the world what they have learned about themselves. Psychologists sometimes call this kind of behavior "projecting," because we project onto other people those things about ourselves that we secretly fear, dislike, or condemn. If those things are outside us, then we don't have to deal with them. We can continue to deny our own blindness if we can see the blindness in others.

People who continually put others down are really trying to put themselves up so they can feel powerful and in charge. They can't recognize and validate the good in other people because they can't do it for themselves. They have been invalidated so often, they have become emotionally disabled.

If you suffer from low self-esteem, you probably don't believe you deserve anything better than what you already have. This belief is a bottom-line barrier to change. No matter what you say you want to achieve or become, you aren't going to do it unless you first *believe* you deserve it and can cause it to happen.

If you think you can't change, you won't try. If you believe you don't deserve the best life has to offer, you won't be able to summon up the drive and energy to create and sustain it. Needless to say, if you don't try, you can count on failure. Of course, you *will* have the cold comfort of knowing that you were right. Your inner and outer reality will be a comfortable match.

Self-Efficacy: What Can You Make Happen?

Like strong self-esteem, high self-efficacy is a crucial factor in determining what you can be and achieve. Self-efficacy is simply your own estimation of your ability to cause, bring about, or make happen those things that are important to you. It's your confidence in your ability to learn, make good decisions, and think effectively.

Self-efficacy is not just a matter of knowing what to do or possessing a collection of specific skills. It also involves your *belief* in your ability to persist in the face of setbacks and obstacles, to learn new skills and problem-solve, to enlist support and outside resources. In other words, to do whatever it takes to get the job done, whether the job is mastering a new computer program or getting a shaky relationship back on track, completing an advanced degree program or finding a new job, getting a real estate license or learning how to service and repair your bicycle.

Dr. Albert Bandura of Stanford University is considered the world's foremost authority on efficacy. He has visited us several times at The Pacific Institute and has been keynote speaker for several of our Global Leadership Conferences. Dr. Bandura tells us that people with strong self-efficacy share several characteristics that make it far more likely that they'll succeed in their endeavors. Here they are:

People with Strong Self-Efficacy

- Approach difficult tasks as challenges rather than as threats
- Set challenging goals and sustain strong commitment to their goals
- Direct their analytical thinking at the task in order to perform most effectively
- Attribute failures to insufficient effort or unfavorable conditions
- Heighten effort in the face of difficulties and setbacks
- Quickly recover their sense of efficacy after failures or setbacks
- Are fairly resistant to stress and depression

On the other hand, Dr. Bandura confirms that people with a weak belief in their own efficacy, as we might expect, display an opposite set of characteristics that make achieving success much harder:

People with Weak Self-Efficacy

- Shy away from difficult tasks and see them as threats
- Have low aspirations and weak commitment to the goals they choose
- Direct their analytical thinking at themselves, thereby disrupting performance
- Dwell on personal deficiencies, obstacles, and adverse outcomes
- Attribute failures to their own deficiencies
- Slacken their efforts or give up quickly in the face of difficulties
- Are slow to recover their sense of efficacy after failures or setbacks
- Are susceptible to excessive stress and depression

Dr. Bandura and his colleagues have also done a great deal of research to find out how people develop a strong sense of self-efficacy. They have found four factors that influence our perceptions of personal efficacy. The first is *mastery experiences*, which simply means you know what it's like to put forth sustained effort and succeed. You've encountered similar situations and similar obstacles in the past, and you've conquered them, so you know you have what it takes. It's another way of saying that success breeds more success.

Vicarious experience means that although you may not have succeeded at doing something yourself, you've seen others who are like you persist in their efforts and succeed. You've learned, not necessarily from your own experience, but by watching someone else. And you say to yourself, "Hey—if they can do it, so can I."

Social persuasion can help boost your own appraisal of your efficacy, too. If I have credibility in your eyes and I tell you that I believe you can be or do something, that's social persuasion. It's what good coaches and mentors do. It's also what good parents do. Picture a mother who is helping her child learn to walk. She places low tables close at hand for him to reach out to, making success more likely. She praises his efforts, causing him to feel a sense of accomplishment and pride. And she encourages him to keep trying when he wobbles and falls, so he learns that persistence pays off.

Physical and emotional states influence your perceived efficacy, but you already knew that. When you're in poor health, fatigued, under exceptional stress, or in a dark mood, you don't feel as competent and capable as you do normally. Even routine tasks may seem like too much to handle during these times, but when your health is restored and your mood improves, you feel ready and able to take on much bigger challenges.

Sources of Self-Efficacy

- **Mastery Experiences**

  Successes build a robust belief in your personal efficacy. Failures undermine it.

  A resilient sense of efficacy requires experience in overcoming obstacles through persistent effort.

- **Vicarious Experiences**

  Competent models transmit knowledge, skills, and strategies for managing the demands made on you by your environment.

  Seeing people similar to yourself succeed by sustained effort raises your belief in your own capabilities to do the same.

- **Social Persuasion**

  Social persuasion raises your belief that you have what it takes to succeed.

  Your activities are structured in ways that promote success.

- **Physical and Emotional States**

  Efficacy is raised by improving your physical state, reducing stress, or changing how you interpret your bodily sensations. A positive mood strengthens your perceived efficacy, while a despondent mood weakens it.

I hope this helps you see the importance of your sense of self-efficacy when it comes to influencing the results you get. The higher your own estimation of your efficacy, the more energy and effort you'll probably put forth, especially when facing difficulties and obstacles. The more you doubt your capabilities, the more likely you'll be to slack off or give up entirely when the going gets tough. Very little can be achieved without sustained effort and perseverance.

We see the difference that high self-efficacy makes all the time in school settings. Teachers who understand the importance of self-esteem and self-efficacy, and who know how to build these qualities in their students, are incredibly valuable resources. They make a great difference in our lives and in the lives of our children. Many experiments in the classroom and in the laboratory have confirmed it.

In one now classic study, teachers were told that certain children in their classrooms were gifted and that certain others were "slow learners." In reality, all of the kids had roughly similar abilities; and the classifications given to the teachers were chosen at random. By the end of the school year, not only did the children's performance directly reflect the teachers' preconceived notions, but IQ scores went up or down according to the teachers' beliefs, as well.

How can this happen? Because the teachers, who are tremendous authority figures to little kids, influenced the children's perceptions of themselves through social persuasion. They built up the self-efficacy and self-esteem of the kids they saw as bright, and they diminished the self-efficacy and self-esteem of the kids they saw as slow. They didn't *consciously* intend to do this, but it happened, nevertheless. Time after time, day after day, some kids were getting the message, "This is hard, but you can do it. You're smart, and if you hang in there, you'll get it." Others were receiving messages that said, "This will be hard for you. You may not do very well, so try not to feel too badly." And what do you know! The children started to act like they were being treated.

I hope you'll think of this story the next time you're coaching or mentoring someone and trying to raise their sense of self-efficacy. I hope you'll remember it, too, when you listen in on the conversations you have with yourself every day. The principle works in exactly the same way for adults as it does for kids, and it works the same way for you as it does for others.

Self-Talk: What Do You Tell Yourself?

Self-talk is what we call the continual, ongoing dialogue we all have with ourselves. It's the way you explain your past and also what's happening right now. It's the raw material from which you manufacture your self-image, self-esteem, and self-efficacy.

Whatever you repeatedly tell yourself with your self-talk determines your beliefs, your behaviors, and your emotional responses to events and experiences. When you record an event or experience in your memory, you don't simply record the facts and sensory details. You record your *interpretation* of all these things. That's why self-talk, self-esteem, and self-efficacy are so completely intertwined and interdependent.

For example, suppose your boss comes in one day and tells you that your services are no longer required. That's it, you're out on your ear, fired. If your self-esteem and self-efficacy are in the basement, you may become despondent, even depressed. You may feel like a failure, believe that no one will ever hire you again, start drinking heavily to dull your emotional pain, lose your house and car because you can't make the payments, and maybe even choose, consciously or unconsciously, not to live any longer. Would those things be results of getting fired? Nope. They are results of your *response* to getting fired.

Take the same scenario, but imagine now that you have high self-esteem and a strong sense of personal efficacy. You've been fired, and you're naturally upset for a little while. But you're not seriously worried. Within a day or two, you're telling yourself that you've actually been given an opportunity. You think, "I probably wasn't going anywhere at that company anyway. They didn't appreciate me, and they treated all their employees badly. Now I'm free to find a better job, one I enjoy more." You expect the future to be successful because you see yourself as valuable and resourceful. Same event, different response.

What Goes On When You Worry

Worry is negative self-talk about things that haven't happened. It's interest paid on trouble before it comes due. You'd never do anything like that with your money, would you? But I'll bet you do it with your thoughts. Most of us do, from time to time. Some poor folks seem to do it almost constantly. Our awareness of the future is an important part of our search for meaning and purpose. But when that awareness becomes dominated by uneasiness, restlessness, and fear, then worry takes over. Worry is really negative goal-setting. We've already said that we move toward and become like that which we think about. So if we're always thinking about what could go wrong, we're just naturally going to move in that direction.

Worry is what some people do to feel like they're in control: Nothing bad can sneak up and surprise them if they've already imagined the worst that could happen. Worry is also how some people show they care. Although their expressions of doom and gloom aren't really welcome or appreciated, they continue them because they just haven't learned a better way.

Even if many of the things you worry about never actually happen, worry and negative self-talk put a tremendous strain on your mental and physical resources. Prolonged, heavy doses of stress and tension can cause some illnesses and contribute to the severity of others. How much back trouble and high blood pressure, how many ulcers, headaches, heart attacks, and digestive problems are caused directly or indirectly by worry and negative self-talk? How do fearful or pessimistic thoughts affect our immune systems? How do calm, positive thoughts affect them?

The answers to these important questions are still unclear, but one thing is certain. Mind and body are not separate entities. They are different aspects of the unified, unique being that is you, that is each of us.

Brain and body chemistry depend on many factors, including the kinds of thoughts we run through our minds, and it is not at all uncommon to find a serious illness developing after a serious emotional trauma. Dr. Andrew Weil's bestseller, *Spontaneous Healing*, all of Dr. Bernie Siegel's books, and many others published during the last ten years or so are beginning to help us see that our thoughts and beliefs have just as much effect on the health of our bodies as they do on the success rate of our accomplishments and relationships.

Choosing to Change

When you were growing up, your self-talk was a reflection of the messages you received from your parents, teachers, and other authority figures in your life. If you were treated with respect and affection and saw those around you dealing optimistically and positively with life's challenges, your self-talk was probably positive. If you were constantly criticized, put down, and saw others blaming, worrying, and expecting the worst, your self-talk more than likely mirrored those negative attitudes.

Once you become accountable, though, you have a choice. You can choose to reject the thought patterns and internal dialogue your grew up with in favor of more useful, productive habits. You can learn to dispute irrational, rigid, illogical thoughts and substitute life-affirming, self-affirming, positive self-talk instead.

Every time you deliberately affirm a positive belief about yourself, you shift your attitude slightly. You add weight and power to the part of you that wants to live a positive, productive, happy life. This doesn't mean you ignore problems or difficulties. It's important to stay grounded in reality and to anticipate and face trouble. But if your focus is strictly on what's wrong, if all you can see and think about and talk about is what's *wrong,* you'll just continue to live out the problem. When you shift your focus to the *solution*—to what it will look like when the problem no longer exists—to what you *want* instead of what you *don't* want, you begin to move toward those things.

Rumination and Imagination: I x V = R

One very effective way people learn is by repetition. But you don't have to actually repeat an experience over and over again to build a belief. You can relive a positive or negative event hundreds of times in your imagination, and every time you mentally "see" and emotionally "feel" it, it affects your body and your mind as if it were happening again.

Some victims of post-traumatic stress syndrome suffer terribly because they keep reliving the traumatic events. Even though the experience is purely imaginary, their suffering is very real—they may have heart palpitations, cold sweats, shortness of breath, severe muscle spasms or tension, blinding headaches, sexual impotency, and so on. That's because **our subconscious minds can't tell the difference between something that is** *actually* **happening and something that we vividly** *imagine* **to be happening.**

This is an important principle that you'll soon be able to use to great advantage. For now, though, remember this formula: I x V = R. I (Imagination) times V (Vividness) equals R (Reality, to the subconscious mind). Any time you imagine something vividly and feel the related emotions, it makes an impression in the neuron system of your brain. If you mentally replay the imagined experience over and over, the impression becomes more deeply etched, more permanent each time. Eventually, it becomes a belief that your subconscious accepts as true (even if it didn't really happen), and you begin to behave accordingly.

Here's one rather dramatic example of how it works, taken from Charles Garfield's wonderful book, *Peak Performers.* Jiu Chi Kung was a virtuoso pianist who was jailed for seven years during the Chinese cultural revolution. During this time, he had no access to any musical instruments whatsoever. Upon his release, he was back playing on the international concert circuit within three months, a feat that was considered impossible. When asked how he had done it, he explained that during his incarceration he had practiced his repertoire every day in his mind. His fingers "remembered" those mental practices.[2]

Kung was able to do what he did because of the I x V = R principle. Here's another example you may be able to personally relate to. Suppose you're a little kid who is just learning how to draw.

You're not thinking about whether you're any good at it or not, you're just having a good time. You make a picture of your house, color it in, and when you're done you feel happy and proud.

You take your drawing to your older sister, whose artwork hangs on the refrigerator door, which, in your eyes, makes her an expert. "See what I made? I made our house!" you tell her, expecting approval and praise. She takes one look and decides to play art critic. "This isn't our house," she tells you. "Look, you didn't even put in a door, and our house isn't blue, and it doesn't have a chimney like that, and what are those blobs in the middle? Are those supposed to be people?" Because you look up to your sister, her judgments make an "impact" in your subconscious: "I'm no good at this. In fact, I'm lousy at it! I can't draw."

Her sarcastic, belittling statements aren't meant to cause you pain, but they do. And every time you remember them, it's as if it were happening again. You reinforce them with your own self-talk ("I can't draw") and begin to build a belief. But you like to draw, so you keep at it anyway.

The next time you make a picture, you decide to avoid the house and try animals instead. When it's finished, you avoid your sister and take it to your older brother, who knows even more than she does. After all, he's in sixth grade and can ride a two-wheeler anywhere he wants. So you say, "See what I made?" hoping again for approval and praise. But he's busy and can't be bothered. "Go away," he tells you. "I'm busy." "Look at my drawing," you persist. He glances at it and says, "What's that supposed to be? I can't tell if that's a fat horse or a weird looking dog. Is that a tail or another head? That's dumb."

This makes an impact, too, as soon as you give it sanction with your self-talk. "He's right. I should have listened to my sister. I can't draw. I'm no good at this art stuff." Do you see how you're beginning to build a belief? When you get to school, you find out that drawing and painting are apparently important, at least to your teacher, because she sets aside time every day for the class to color and paint. But the very idea makes you nervous, because your self-efficacy in this area is so shaky. You give it a try, anyway, because you don't have a choice, and you keep stealing glances at what the other kids are doing to see if you can copy it. When the teacher collects the pictures the class has made, she selects some to pin up around the room. Yours isn't one of the chosen few, and you're deeply disappointed, but not surprised.

Now, every time the paints and crayons come out, you turn off inside. You can't wait for art to be over with, and what do you think happened to the effort you used to put forth and the enthusiasm you once felt for these activities? Gone, right? Later on, in junior high and high school, you won't even consider taking art as an elective, and you sure as heck aren't going to volunteer to make any posters or drawings for the class play or create any artwork to go along with your science project.

You may wonder what's wrong with you that you can't draw like so many of your classmates can. You may figure it's something they were born with, an ability they inherited from their parents, and you just don't have it. Or you may adopt a "who cares" attitude: Art is a waste of time, an activity for people with nothing better to do. When you become an adult, are you going to be interested in looking at great art or visiting art galleries and art museums? Not a chance! Will you remember your early, efficacy-destroying artistic experiences and understand why you feel the way you do? Probably not. Will you understand that your beliefs about your talents as an artist and your opinion of art in general were shaped by authority figures who didn't know any better? Will you realize that they have nothing to do with your true abilities or the value of artistic endeavor? Not likely.

Every single belief you have about what you can and can't do, every internal "truth" you "know" about yourself was built in much the same way. Your estimation of your attractiveness, lovability, intelligence, friendliness, strength, courage, ability to learn, and a host of other characteristics were originally shaped by the perceptions of authority figures, or "who-saids," as I sometimes call them ("Who said? Someone who knows more than you do!"). They encouraged you to grow and express yourself, or they shut you down through intentional or thoughtless negative feedback. Sometimes they did both.

From the overly critical "who-saids" in your life, you learned how to put yourself down. By now you may even have surpassed them at making critical, belittling judgments about who and what you are. Where these early-life negative wizards—whether parents, teachers, preachers, or peers—left off, you took up the task. Harsh, sometimes irrational criticism has now become routine for you in those areas where you took their words and actions to heart.

Listen for the Voice That Says, "Yes!"

No one can build a belief inside your mind but you. That's the bad news, but it's also the good news. Most of your beliefs about yourself were formed before you had any idea of what was happening. When you were young, you couldn't think to yourself, "Gee, when Daddy says I never do anything right, he's just talking out of his own low self-esteem. I'm really very competent." You couldn't say, "They only picked me last for the softball team because I haven't yet had as much experience as the other kids—it doesn't have anything to do with how good I am at sports or how much they like me. I know I'm strong and fun and smart!"

Nowadays, though, you can deliberately question criticism, even when it's coming from your own mind, and decide whether to accept or reject it. If you're aware of how beliefs are built and how self-talk works, it's much easier to build or restore your self-efficacy and self-esteem. And, as we discussed in Chapter 2, you can choose to change, to become your own authority about who you are, what you're like, and what is right for you.

I'm not saying it's going to be easy. Even though many of the beliefs you hold about yourself are unproductive and limiting, you may find yourself feeling tense or defensive just thinking about changing. If you believe you aren't good enough, you probably also believe you don't have much chance of altering that. If you think you're already doing the best you can, you may not be open to the idea that you can do much better.

These are the core beliefs that you want to reconstruct, and it will take time and effort. The years of experience that built those beliefs aren't likely to be counteracted overnight. There is one thing that *can* happen quickly, though, and that is your commitment to doing the work of change.

I can't give you any magic formulas that will instantly transform your life for you. I can, however, give you a scientifically sound set of tools that will enable you to increase your self-efficacy, improve your self-esteem, and enhance your ability to set and accomplish bigger and better goals. I won't tell you *what* to think, but I will help you to change the *way* that you think. Taking charge of your thoughts is how you take charge of your life.

As we progress, I ask you to listen for the affirming voice inside you—the word in your heart—that says, "Yes, I *want* to do this. Yes, I *can* do this. Yes, I *will* do this."

At the same time, I'm also asking you to be aware of the other, perhaps louder, voices that may be saying, "No way. Not me. Maybe other people can do things like this, but I can't." Acknowledge them and recognize them for what they are—voices from your past that want to keep you "safe" by avoiding risks, keep you small by avoiding growth. Then tell them to shut up. Put them in an imaginary box, put a lid on the box, and get it out of your way. Put it in cold storage. Then, see yourself moving forward into the success and happiness you truly deserve, no matter what your past has been like, no matter what your circumstances are right now.

In Chapter 4, we'll talk about your comfort zones. Knowing you have them and how they can work both for and against you makes it a lot easier to move out of them. And moving out of them is essential, if you truly want to grow.

CHAPTER FOUR

Comfort Zones: The Tyranny of the Familiar

Stability, Change, and Your Comfort Zone

ll of us live within an imaginary area I call a comfort zone. If the term "comfort zone" sounds like something you'd read in the directions for how to adjust your home's heating system, it's no accident. Your heating system's thermostat operates on electrical feedback based on temperature. If you feel comfortable with your room at 68 degrees, you set the indicator at 68. When the temperature rises above 68, an electrical current shuts off the heat. If the temperature drops below 68, another impulse tells the system to turn the heat on again.

> "The desire for safety stands against every great and noble enterprise."
>
> Tacitus

Now, if your furnace was turning off and on the moment the temperature rose or fell even a fraction of a degree beyond 68, it would be very inefficient. It would be turning off or on virtually every moment, and the motor would quickly burn out. So your thermostat has a tolerance of plus or minus a couple of degrees on either side. It lets the temperature drop to 66 or rise to 70 degrees before sending the change signal to your furnace. This four-degree tolerance is often called a comfort zone.

Your own comfort zone works in much the same way. It's the physical or psychological area of tolerance within which you feel comfortable and at ease. Inside it is everything you've done often enough to feel confident about. It encompasses all your ideas and images of who you are and what you're like, where you belong, how you live, with whom you associate, etc.

You don't have to think too much about what you're doing

when you're operating within your comfort zone, because it's all very familiar. As a result, life within this zone has the benefit of being fairly stable. We all need a certain amount of this familiarity and stability. If we couldn't run on autopilot at least some of the time, we'd be like the thermostat that was turning the furnace on and off every single second—we'd burn out in a blaze of confusion. But if the familiar stabilizes our lives, change is the vehicle of our progress.

We absolutely must change if we are to grow. We must do things we've never done before, sometimes things we never dreamed we could. This means venturing into the unfamiliar territory outside our comfort zones. And when we're attempting to operate in unfamiliar territory, the signal we receive is not electrical current, but rather discomfort—tension, anxiety, stress, and sometimes full-blown fear. These feelings of discomfort are felt in the body and in the mind. You know what I'm talking about. You've been there.

Some of the typical physical signs of being outside your comfort zone are obvious. You trip over your own feet. Your speech becomes disjointed and halting. You bump into things, spill your drink, drop the folder that contains your notes, dump the contents of your purse into someone's lap.

How many situation comedies have been written around the slapstick scenes that result when people are out of their comfort zones? How about the guy on a date with a girl he desperately wants to impress, unable to form coherent speech and behaving like a bumbling idiot? Or the eager new hire, trying way too hard to be noticed by the big boss and making a horrendous mistake? What about the penny-ante gambler who blunders into a high-stakes game and loses his shirt? Or the family trying to pretend they're wealthier than they are to impress snooty guests? The individual circumstances differ, but the results are almost always the same: When you try to act like someone you really believe you aren't, you're probably going to fall all over yourself.

Some of the physical consequences of moving outside your

comfort zone may be less obvious than tripping over your own feet, but if you're paying attention you can feel them. As your body moves into the fight-or-flight mode that it adopts when it feels threatened, your breathing becomes more shallow and rapid. Your vocal chords tighten, so your voice may quaver and break, making you sound anything but confident. Your stomach secretes more digestive acids than it normally needs, which is why you may feel queasy or nauseated or even actually throw up. The muscles in your upper body tighten; your knees get weak and wobbly and your balance is impaired (definitely the raw material for slapstick comedy, as long as the joke isn't on you!). Your blood pressure rises and your pulse rate accelerates. In fact, your entire cardiovascular system has to work harder. It's no wonder we say things such as, "I've been under a lot of pressure lately." That's exactly what's happening. You're so tense, you literally feel squeezed.

In athletics, it's called "choking" or "freezing." Imagine a rookie basketball player stepping up to the free throw line with the outcome of the game at stake. He's trying to look cool, but he's so tense he can hardly catch his breath. His hands are sweating, and his shoulders, arms, and neck are tied up in knots. So is his stomach. Performing under intense pressure is not something he's used to. He's way out of his comfort zone, and he doesn't know how to handle it, so his body and his self-talk go berserk. His performance usually follows. The throw he's been able to make easily in practice sessions becomes an "air-ball" or a "brick," meaning it falls five feet short of the basket, or it bashes off the backboard, because he just can't relax.

Some years ago, an index was developed by medical researchers that listed a number of significant life changes, such as marriage, divorce, job loss, death of a spouse, promotion, career change, child leaving home, etc. It gave each change a numerical rating depending on the average degree of emotional impact. You could go down the list of life changes, see how many you had experienced within the last year, and, on the basis of your score, you could predict with reasonable accuracy whether you were likely to suffer a serious illness within the next twelve months. It didn't matter whether the changes you had gone through were positive or negative. Change itself was the determining factor.

You see, your subconscious doesn't care whether the move outside your comfort zone is good for you or not, whether it's going to result in a net benefit or loss. Your subconscious is only concerned with making sure that your inner and outer pictures of reality match. So when you venture outside your normal area of familiarity and tolerance, it sends you some of the powerful discomfort signals we've just discussed to tell you something is wrong—signals that say, in effect, get back where you belong!

No wonder change can be so difficult. No wonder we often feel tense when meeting new people, moving to a new city or neighborhood, starting a new job, course of study, or career. Even though the new job may have more to offer and actually represents a promotion, even though the move may be to more attractive or roomier surroundings, even though the new people may be nicer and more interesting than our present set of friends, it doesn't matter. It's new, it's different, and that's what produces stress.

Comfort Zones, Self-Image, and Self-Esteem

Our comfort zones directly depend on and accurately reflect our beliefs. They are a natural outgrowth of the self-image we've developed over time—our composite mental picture of who we are and what we're like, where we belong and where we don't fit in, what we can and can't do or learn to do, and what is good enough for us.

In general, the higher your self-esteem and the more positive your self-image, the broader your comfort zone. And the broader your comfort zone, the less stress you'll experience and the bigger your life will be. With a broad comfort zone, you'll feel at ease even when you're in an environment that is very different from the one you're used to. You'll be poised and confident when meeting new people, visiting new places, taking on new roles and responsibilities, even when they are not at all like those you've encountered or experienced in the past.

Years ago, when I first started organizing what I had learned about personal and professional growth into seminars so I could share it with other people, I had a very narrow comfort zone. At first, I was only at ease when my audience was made up of people who were a lot like me—coaches, teachers, students, parents of students. And I was only at ease if the group wasn't too big.

When one of the parents suggested I come to his office at a local bank to present my information, I got very nervous. After all, I wasn't a businessman or a banker. I knew a lot about football and a great deal about goal achievement and motivation, but I hadn't even thought about teaching in the world of business. What would I have to say that the president of a bank or the owner of a major department store chain would want to hear? These people were wealthy, cosmopolitan, world travelers. I had never been around wealthy people in my life, and I had barely been out of Seattle, except on trips with my football team. I was pretty sure they'd eat me alive, so I resisted the idea. I came up with all kinds of reasons why I couldn't possibly do such a thing. (Does any of this sound familiar? Do you ever catch yourself resisting when it looks like you might have to leave your comfort zone?)

Fortunately, I was scared but not stupid. My wife, Diane, and my friends who believed in what I was doing helped me to reaffirm my conviction that the information in my seminars should be common knowledge. They helped me to imagine the benefits that could accrue if people in business had access to these concepts. They helped me to see that I was having a comfort zone problem. Then, because I believed one hundred percent in the effectiveness of the principles I was teaching, I used them to help myself.

Today, I do things I never dreamed I could or would do. I give seminars to hundreds, even thousands of people at a time without a problem. In fact, I have found that I really enjoy working with very large groups. It's not unusual for me to have breakfast with a congressional leader, lunch with a Nobel Prize winner, or dinner with a four-star general. Some of the most respected people in government, education, business, and industry have been my house guests, and many have become personal friends. In addition to our home base in Seattle, our company has offices in England, Japan, Spain, and Australia. We have representatives throughout Europe, Latin America, Africa, and Asia. And Diane and I spend a great deal of time traveling to places that once seemed very exotic; now they feel just as comfortable as home.

Do I still have comfort zone problems? Sure, every once in a while. But I have stretched and grown so much over the years that it doesn't rattle me anymore. I know how to handle it when I notice that I'm feeling anxious about my ability to perform in a new setting or a bit intimidated by a new person or experience. And, after twenty-five years of working with them, I know without a shred of doubt that the concepts, principles, and techniques I teach really work, so I'd be crazy not to use them.

A newspaper reporter recently described me as my own greatest success story. I don't know about that, because when I think of the people in prison, the at-risk kids, and the chronic welfare recipients whom we've helped to turn their lives around, my own personal transformation seems much less dramatic. But if I didn't use the concepts I teach to create success and happiness in my own life, how could I ask you to do it in yours? I'd be a fraud, and you and I would both know it. If I didn't take these principles and techniques out as far as they could go for myself, how would I know where their limitations were? (By the way, I haven't found those limitations yet.)

Can a Narrow Comfort Zone Be Good?

I don't mean to imply that we *always* want to have a broad comfort zone. Sometimes it's a good thing to feel uncomfortable, particularly when it reminds us that we are in a place where we really don't choose to be, or when we're operating in a way that conflicts with our values.

For example, I have a very narrow comfort zone when it comes to being around cruelty or violence. I don't like to see a lot of blood and gore in movies or on TV, and I sure as heck don't like to see it in real life. I get very uncomfortable, very tense, and stressed out. As soon as I can, I remove myself from the situation and get back where I belong. So, if you feel anxious or tense when you're around people who are using drugs, drinking to excess, doing things that are illegal, or engaging in activities you consider immoral or hurtful—good! If you're uptight when people are abusing themselves or each other—good! It's because you're out of your comfort zone, and the signals you're receiving from your mind and body that say, "Get out of here!" need to be listened to.

It's not just other people's behavior that can set off your comfort zone alarm. If you're used to living up to a certain standard and your income drops for some reason, you'll probably feel anxious, too. Suppose you're a salesperson who is used to making $4,000 a month. Suddenly, you have a couple of months when you make only $2,000. You've moved out of your financial comfort zone and are operating in a way that doesn't match your internal picture of how things are supposed to be. As long as those pictures don't line up, you'll be very uncomfortable. You'll also be highly motivated to analyze the situation and generate the income it'll take to get you back where you belong.

Similarly, if you're used to cleaning up your house every day because you like things neat and tidy, it will put you out of your comfort zone to wake up in the morning to a sink full of dirty dishes and clutter all around. So you'll generally plan ahead to make sure that doesn't happen or, if it does, you'll clean it up as soon as you can.

It works the same way in every area of your life—family relationships, finances, physical and mental health, job or career, social and leisure time activities, community or political involvement, and so on. Whenever you aren't performing up to your own internal standards, whenever you sense a deterioration in your usual level of growth, whenever you don't behave in ways that match your self-image, you'll be uncomfortable. And you'll be motivated to take action until your inner and outer pictures once again match.

Getting Used to It

Sometimes, though, we get used to things being a certain way without really thinking much about it. We develop a comfort zone that has far more to do with familiarity and routine than conscious choice. It's been said that people can get used to almost anything—if it happens gradually and incrementally, if it goes on long enough, or if the pressure to adjust is great enough.

For example, did you ever move into a new house or apartment, and as you looked around the place you thought about all the changes you were going to make. "We're going to fix that cracked window, and those drapes will definitely go. We'll have to put up new shelves in the closet and get rid of that stained countertop. We'll replace those missing switchplates and repair the sagging front porch step." But weeks went by, and then months. Next thing you knew, you had been living there for five years, and you hadn't done any of those things. What's more, you didn't even notice them anymore. You had become so used to them, you've built scotomas to them.

Then, your in-laws call from out of state and say they want to come for a visit. Pow! Instant scotoma-buster. Suddenly, all those things you've gotten used to are jumping out at you. They were good enough for you, but they aren't good enough for the image you want to present to your in-laws. Within days, you have amazed yourself with what you've accomplished—practically a complete makeover on the house. You've cleaned it from top to bottom, painted, bought new drapes, fixed everything that was broken, and added new sheets and towels.

But what happens after your in-laws go back home? Do you

retain those high standards of cleanliness, order, and good repair? Or do you gradually, week by week, month by month, slip back into old ways, letting broken things stay broken, letting dirt and disarray take over again? In my experience, what you do will depend on whether the alterations you made were purely external, or whether, in the process, your internal comfort zone changed.

Because my company works in many state and federal prisons, I have had the opportunity to get to know administrators in various correctional systems. Kathy Hawk, director of the Federal Bureau of Prisons, is a special friend. She tells me that it only takes a couple of months for most convicts in federal prisons to adjust. When first arrested, people who are used to being free experience enormous tension and stress. Surrounded by armed guards, stripped of personal possessions, and dropped into a world with many new written (and unwritten) rules, they're so far out of their comfort zone, they might as well be on the moon.

If they resist the new environment and stubbornly refuse to conform, the pressure from the system becomes unbearable—far more painful than the pressure to remain autonomous that is coming from inside them. So their subconscious goes to work to change their internal pictures. Within six or eight weeks, they usually fall into line. Once that happens, they can do what corrections people call "easy time," but only because their comfort zones have altered. "This is the way it's supposed to be; this is now where I belong," the new pictures tell them. They have gotten used to it.

What happens when they're released back into society? Often, it's the same thing, only in reverse. They feel so far out of their comfort zone on the street that their subconscious starts working to get them back where they "belong," even when that means getting arrested again and returning to prison. The longer they've been inside, the harder it is to adjust once they're out, if they don't know how to change their internal picture and self-image. That's one of the reasons why our recidivism rate is so high. When people see themselves as "cons," when for years they have associated only with other prisoners, they feel uncomfortable around those who have never been locked up. When your self-image says "convict," your behavior is just naturally going to match.

Remember the example I gave you earlier of a salesperson who is used to earning $4,000 a month? Suddenly income drops to $2,000 so they get busy generating sales to correct for the mistake. Well, the same thing is likely to go on when a $6,000 month occurs, too. "That's not like me," their subconscious says. It doesn't match their internal self-image but, instead of not being enough, it's too much. So, on a subconscious level, they get very creative about correcting for the mistake. They buy things they don't need to eat up the extra money. They take an expensive vacation. Or they decide to kick back for a while and take it easy, thinking, "After all, I deserve a break." The next thing you know, their earnings are right back in the $4,000 groove where they feel most comfortable, and they write off the $6,000 month as a fluke.

Two Jonahs Who Refused to Grow

Whenever I see this sort of thing happen, it reminds me of Jonah, the goldfish. As I heard the story, there was a woman with a pet goldfish named Jonah. One fine spring morning, the woman decided it was time to clean his bowl. She couldn't find a temporary container large enough, so she filled the bathtub with a few inches of water and slipped Jonah into the tub. When she came back about an hour later, she found the fish engaged in some thought-provoking behavior. It was swimming around in one little corner of the tub, in a circle no bigger than the fishbowl.

Abraham Maslow, one of the twentieth century's most respected psychologists, coined the term "Jonah complex" to describe people who are afraid of success, because the Jonah in the Bible story chose to turn away from the greatness God had planned for him. The Bible tells us that Jonah eventually found himself consumed by a great fish, which may or may not be better than feeling consumed with regrets over things that might have been.

Both Jonah stories can be seen as parables that can help us to embrace our own greatness. Most of us develop fairly comfortable lifestyles. Then, when we get the chance to go beyond them, we often choose to remain in our tiny but comfortable corner of the world, even though it offers little challenge, growth, or opportunity for meaningful service.

We like to believe that our comfort zones keep us secure, safe, and protected, and sometimes that's true. As we've seen, though, they can also keep us from growing and getting what we want. Sometimes we get so nervous about moving out of our comfort zone that we just stop wanting anything more than we have, because it's easier and less stressful. We lose touch with our hopes and dreams, because we don't think we can bring them into reality. Soon we may forget we ever had them.

We may discount or discourage the dreams and goals of others, too, because people who choose to avoid risk and keep their lives small usually feel threatened (out of their comfort zone) by people who are actively growing. Sometimes we manage to stay in touch with our dreams, but we feel powerless to do anything more than talk about them. It's as if we kept them in an imaginary box, and every now and then we bring the box out from where we've hidden it, open the lid, and check to see that they're still there.

"Someday," we say, "I'm going to go back to school," or "open a little restaurant," or "start my own business," or "visit Ireland to see where my ancestors lived," or "learn to fly a plane." But it's always "someday." Eventually the people around us get tired of hearing us talk about what we're "going to" do, because they know it's just talk. One day we may no longer be able to avoid the realization that we blew it—that we grew old and "someday" never arrived. I've heard it said that the only people who are afraid to die are those who have never truly lived. What could be sadder than a life whose final days are spent regretting what might have been?

The more we give in to our fears and anxieties, the smaller our comfort zone becomes. For some poor folks—like Jonah the goldfish—their comfort zone is just about the same size as their apartment, and there they sit, making up reasons why it's better for them to stay put and trying hard to convince themselves that they really are better off where they are. People who suffer from agoraphobia actually suffer severe panic attacks when they try to move outside the narrow boundaries of the world in which they feel safe. Sometimes that's no farther than their front door. They know it's not rational, but the subconscious doesn't operate in a "rational" way.

Taking the Risk of Growth

If you want to live life masterfully and be able to inspire others to do the same thing, there's simply no way around it: You're going to have to take some risks. You'll need to risk rejection, disappointment, criticism, being ignored, looking foolish, trying new things, failure, and—yes—even success.

Does it surprise you to know that a great many people are afraid to succeed in a big way? It takes courage to rise above the crowd, guts to take on the responsibilities that come with success. Timid people have tiny goals, unremarkable ideals, and ordinary concerns, usually focused on themselves. They are terrified of doing anything that will make them stand out too much. They have ho-hum relationships, ho-hum lifestyles, and they tend to put down or ridicule anybody who is different. They don't ask too many questions, don't exert too much energy, and don't step too far out of line. They don't want to take the risk.

Do you have the courage to rise above the ordinary? Are you willing to stop trying so hard to please others and, instead, strive for excellence according to your own standards? Are you willing to say, "Ordinary is not good enough for me. I want a *great* life, a *great* career, *great* relationships, and I'm ready to do whatever it takes to get them!" A great life does take bravery, and if you want to build your courage, self-esteem, and self-efficacy, taking calculated risks is one sure way to do it. Start with small ones, and then, as you gain confidence and resiliency, risk a bit more.

The fact is that you have plenty of experience taking growth risks, but you may be discounting it. You stood on your own two feet and learned to walk. You faced the world without mom or dad by your side when you went to school. You mastered a two-wheeled bicycle, double Dutch jump rope, and algebra. You sold Girl Scout cookies door-to-door and went away to summer camp, where you learned to dive and helped write a skit. You called a girl (or boy) you liked and asked them out. Later you may have taken the plunge into marriage. You earned a diploma, maybe a college degree or two, and you got your first real job. You took up cross-country skiing. Perhaps you had children and learned how to care for them.

Now, I know that not every risk you've taken appears on the surface to have paid off. I know there were plenty of times that you put yourself on the line and the results were disappointing, maybe even disastrous. Maybe your marriage ended in divorce or you got fired from that job. Perhaps some of the girls you called for dates laughed at you, and perhaps you can still remember the burning shame you felt when you got stage fright and forgot all your lines.

If you choose to, you can use those disappointing results as reasons not to try anymore. The unaimed arrow never misses, and by not trying, you can attempt to control your environment so that you'll never again feel the pain of defeat. Or you can choose to see failures and disappointments as proof that you are a player, not just a spectator, in your own life. You can see them as testimony to your willingness to bite off a little more than you are absolutely certain you can chew every now and then, and give yourself a pat on the back.

Expanding Your Comfort Zone the Hard Way:
Toughing It Out

One way to expand your comfort zone and cause yourself to grow is to throw yourself into a new situation and just tough it out—hang on, take the stress and tension, hope it doesn't make you sick or crazy, and wait until you adjust. All of us have done that sort of thing from time to time. It's the kind of experience about which people sometimes say, "That which doesn't kill me makes me stronger." And sometimes it works.

I grew up thinking that toughing it out was the only way you could grow. One of the reasons I felt that way came from the summers I spent on a small ranch owned by my cousins. It was located in the eastern part of Washington, and life there was hard—no electricity, running water, or indoor toilets, none of the creature comforts most of us take for granted now. Nevertheless, being there felt good.

I could tell that my cousins cared about what happened to me. They gave me my first pair of cowboy boots and bought me my first pair of Levi's. They gave me a horse to take care of, one I had to break myself. Every morning meant a long day of hard work and more hard work, but everybody else was working just as hard, and there was an unspoken pleasure and pride in it. When I had something new or hard to do, they would help me a little at first. Then they left me on my own to figure it out. In some ways, I guess it was like teaching a little kid to swim by throwing him in the water. But I knew that they'd be there to pull me out if I ran into serious trouble, and the message I got was "we believe you're tough enough to do it."

At the ranch, you learned to ignore physical pain, and complaining or whining was simply unheard of. Even broken bones were considered relatively unimportant, unless they were actually poking through the skin. You just wrapped it up and went back to work. So I learned to swallow discomfort and to do all sorts of things that other kids my age couldn't, including driving a car when I was only eleven. I felt deeply proud of these skills and abilities, and found that I could take on and master very difficult challenges, if I just persisted. I could expand my comfort zone by sheer force of will, and it didn't matter that I often had to endure tremendous physical and mental pressure to do it. It was the only thing I knew that worked.

When I became a football coach, I brought that "tough it out" philosophy into the locker room and onto the playing field. I used to think that when a kid threw up before a game, it was a sign that he really wanted to win, and I believed that the best thing to do about it was ignore it. Later, I realized that it meant the kid was so far out of his comfort zone, he couldn't control his tension. He was thinking things like, "Oh, get me out of here! I don't want to go out there and get creamed!" But in the old days, I figured that the kids who were calm and relaxed didn't care enough, and I treated them like it.

A Safer, Easier Approach

If the "tough it out" approach to change and growth is all you know, it's not surprising that you'd want to avoid change as much as possible. But change doesn't have to be a sink or swim proposition, nor should it be. We now know so much more than we used to about the process of change and about how the mind works that it's no longer necessary to throw yourself into a new situation and hold on with your fingernails until you adjust—if you adjust. Now you can approach change in a much safer, easier, relaxed way, a way that will help you enjoy the process and seek out growth.

Imagine for a moment that you're the parent of a little girl who is almost old enough to begin kindergarten. Her world is a very safe one, about as big as your front yard when she's alone, and everywhere else she goes, mommy or daddy is there holding her hand. All that is about to change. She'll be on her own for a big part of the day, in a strange place called "school" that she's never seen before. A stranger will be telling her what to do and when to do it. She'll be surrounded by unfamiliar furnishings, unfamiliar equipment, kids she's never met, and a whole new set of rules.

What do you suppose would happen if you, as her parent, decided to make school a complete surprise? On the first day of school, you drive her up to this big building and say, "OK, now, honey. You're going to school in there from now on, and I know you're going to just love it." You take her inside and try to leave, but what do you think her reaction is? Does she love it? Does she feel excited and proud to be there? Judging from the hysterical, sobbing child clinging to your legs, it doesn't look like it. You'll probably have a devil of a time getting her out of bed in the mornings for quite a while. "Well, she'll get used to it eventually," you reason. But no loving parent would really do it that way, would they? It's just too painful.

Instead, you'd be painting word pictures for her of how great school was going to be from the time she was three years old. You'd describe the classroom and the equipment, tell her about all the fun things she was going to get to do, and you'd probably take her on at least one visit to see her room and meet her new teacher. She'd be looking forward to the change, and she'd probably be driving you nuts with her impatience as she eagerly awaited the day when she'd "get to" go to school just like the big kids do.

In the same way, I'm going to show you how to prepare yourself for change so that it becomes a "get to" instead of a "have to." And I'm going to give you tools that will allow you to transform your feelings of fear and anxiety into excitement and anticipation instead.

In the next two chapters, we'll look at a safe, comfortable approach to opening up your comfort zones and improving the quality of your life. You'll learn about a systematic method to reduce the stress associated with change and dramatically broaden your comfort zone. It will allow you to deliberately change on the inside first, so that the changes you want to make on the outside will feel natural and free-flowing. And so that, once made, those changes will last.

The approach I'm going to share with you is the same one I teach in my seminars all over the world, the same one I share with top corporate executives, professional athletes, and world leaders. When used correctly, there's no doubt about its effectiveness, and it's not difficult to learn. Like anything worthwhile, it requires some practice and willingness to persist. But if you're willing to make it part of your strategy for positive change, I know you'll be delighted with the results.

I don't want to mislead you, though. I'm not saying that change will be a snap. I'm not saying that once you've mastered these techniques, your life is forever after going to be smooth sailing. You're still going to encounter obstacles and setbacks, I guarantee it. But you'll be better equipped to deal calmly and effectively with them. You'll still have to make tough decisions, too, but you'll make them with a new clarity and faith in the future.

Current Reality: A Good Place to Start

The fact that you're reading this book tells me that you are interested in being and doing more than you are right now. That interest is the critical first step. Before you begin reading the next chapter, I recommend that you spend some time doing two very important things: looking at exactly where you are right now in your life and deliberately fanning the flame of your desire to grow.

So get out a notebook or open a computer file and start talking to yourself. Take a personal inventory. Make lists, if you like, or simply write a narrative, as if you were writing in a journal. Use drawings or visual images, anything that helps you express your thoughts and feelings. Ask yourself questions that will help you discover your own personal truths, and take as long to answer them as you need.

For example: What things about yourself and your life are you currently dissatisfied with and what would you like to change? What are you pleased with? What do you want to maintain or have more of? Look at every aspect of your life—your relationships with family and friends, job or career, physical and mental health, finances, spirituality, intellectual growth, creativity, community involvement, etc.

What do you really enjoy doing? What do you despise? Why do you get up in the morning? Do you feel that you *have* to get out of bed, or do you really *want* to do it? How do you feel, as a rule, when it's time to go to bed at night? What would your life look like if you could have it any way you wanted it? What would you try if you were certain you wouldn't fail? What would you like to accomplish or experience before you die? In the next ten years? Five years? One year? How would you like your epitaph to read?

List the qualities you possess that you see as strengths. Then list those you see as shortcomings or weaknesses. While you're at it, list the changes you've already been through, including those you sought out and those that just seemed to happen to you. What was hard about them? What was easy? How did you feel after the transitional period was over?

Maybe you'd prefer to skip the introspection and just get on with it. Perhaps you have a strong but vague sense of simply wanting to improve your life, have better relationships, make more money, have a more satisfying job, and that's OK, as far as it goes. But it doesn't go far enough. If you really want to make the most of what you read in this book, you're going to need to move from those generalities into images and goals that are much more specific. Taking time for a clear, unflinching look at your current reality as well as a glimpse of some of your dreams, hopes, and desires will be extremely useful.

One important word of caution: As you explore and question, resist all urges to judge or blame yourself or anyone else. Right now, all you want to do is compose a fairly accurate picture of your current whereabouts in life and begin to get a specific sense of how you want to change that picture. Even if you've made some major mistakes (and who hasn't?), even if you're very unhappy with your current state, even if your problems seem overwhelming, resist the temptation to beat yourself or anyone else up about it.

You may find yourself feeling some tension as you review your life. If this happens, simply acknowledge it, and give yourself permission to let it go. Don't dwell on it or keep replaying it in your mind. Believe it or not, the tension you may experience as discomfort right now is going to be useful to you later on as you move along in the growth process. You will learn how to use that tension creatively to resolve conflicts, accomplish new goals, expand your comfort zones, solve problems, and grow.

If it helps, go for a brisk walk or run, engage in some high-energy dancing or housecleaning. Take out those aluminum cans you've been saving and stomp on them, play a set of tennis, or simply try some deep breathing. Then get back to your personal inventory, and remember to take it easy on yourself. There are no good or bad questions, no right or wrong answers, no single best way to go about it. Keep the goal in mind—a sketch of your current reality and a glimpse of where it is you'd like to go with your life. Then, when you're ready, begin Chapter 5.

CHAPTER FIVE

High-Performance Goal-Setting

Do You Really Need Goals?

I worry about people who have no goals, and it isn't just because they're probably not going to enjoy much success in their lives. It's because they may not have much of a life, period! You see, human beings are teleological creatures. In other words, we think in terms of purpose and we're naturally goal-oriented. Having a teleological nature means that in order for us to change and grow, we need something tugging at us from the future, something to—quite literally—look forward to.

When you give up on your important goals, or when you have no goals at all, your whole system slows down and eventually shuts down. You become depressed and sluggish, maybe even seriously ill. Prisoners of war have been known to simply curl up in a corner and die when their hopes for the future were extinguished. They didn't succumb to mistreatment or to malnourishment or disease. They just didn't see any point in going on. We'll never know how many suicides or terminal illnesses have been caused by lack of meaningful goals or sense of purpose.

> *"If a man proceeds confidently in the direction of his dreams and endeavors to live the life he has imagined, he will meet with success unexpected in common hours."*
>
> Henry David Thoreau

Having specific goals is like having a rudder on a ship. The cruise companies wouldn't be in business long if they said to people, "Oh, we're not really sure where this cruise is headed because we don't have any steering devices, but it *might* be someplace you'd really like, so buy your ticket, take your chances, and welcome aboard!" Of course, it's theoretically possible that you'd wind up in a lovely place such as Hawaii or the Bahamas, but the odds against it are astronomical. It's far more likely that you'd find yourself going around in circles, grounded, or smashed against some rocks.

It's no different with your life. If you feel as if you're on auto-pilot much of the time, you're right. But it's important to realize that your "autopilot" is really a part of you. It's your subconscious self-image that we talked about earlier—the mental pictures that tell you what you're like, what's good enough for you, what you deserve, and where you feel comfortable. Remember, these internal images control what you do, where you go, and what you can achieve. Remember, too, that they're largely composed of informa-tion you've taken in from other people—*their* ideas about what's good enough for you and what you deserve—and *their* ideas may very well be keeping *you* in dry dock.

When you have goals—specific goals—and accurate feedback about how you're doing, you appoint yourself captain of your own life. You're then able to set a course to take you where you really want to go, while avoiding many of the dangers along the way. You're the one who's in charge, not only of your destination, but also of the route you take to get there.

Goals, especially when they're broken down into smaller sub-goals, also provide you with the feedback you need to stay on course. They give you a map to follow and, ultimately, a sense of accomplishment and reason to celebrate when you get there.

Goal-Setting: The Practical Habit That Makes Dreams Come True

Putting aside for a moment the way achieving a goal makes us feel, let's ask a very important question. Does goal-setting really make a difference when it comes to what we actually accomplish? The answer, in a word, is absolutely! For years I've been helping people to see why the right kind of goal-setting is a practical habit that makes just about everything else possible. Here's just one example. Back in 1953, a study was done on Yale University's graduating class. It asked seniors a long list of questions about themselves, and three questions had to do with goals. They were, "Do you set goals?" "Do you write them down?" and "Do you have a plan to accomplish them?" Only three percent of the class answered yes to those questions.

Twenty years later, a follow-up study was done. It turned out that the three percent who had said yes to goals reported that they were more happily married, were more successful in the careers they had chosen, had a more satisfactory family life, and had better health. And listen to this. Ninety-seven percent of the net worth of the class of '53 was in the hands of that three percent! You see, once you have clear goals, you open yourself up to a pattern of opportunity that remains closed to you otherwise, and you begin a process—much like the one we'll talk about here—that will serve you well all of your life.

Of course, everyone in that class of '53 had hopes and wishes for themselves. Practically all of us do. Hopes and wishes are important, and they're similar to goals in that they concern something we'd like to see happen in the future. So how is a goal different from a wish or a hope? Well, a wish or hope is something we long for, but it's probably not something we think about very much. If it should happen to come true, we may consider it a miracle, something a fairy godmother or guardian angel might grant, but not something we caused ourselves.

Goals are much different. They cause us to focus our energies, something like a goal in football or hockey, and they're very specific, achievable, and measurable. A clearly stated goal tunes us in to our environment. We become very sensitive to things we may not have noticed before—things that can help us do what we want to do, and we'll talk more about this special sensitivity in a moment. But here's the most important difference. *Goals are much more likely to happen than wishes or hopes.* Why? Because we write them down, spend time thinking about them, develop strategies to make them happen, and, in general, take them very seriously. So, if you have any wishes or hopes that you'd love to see come true, why not use what you're learning in this book to turn them into goals? That's the way to lift your dreams out of fantasyland and into the middle of your very real life!

If your dreams don't have anything to do with daily life, what in the world are they for? Jenny Craig, founder of the highly successful national weight-loss clinics, says, "It's not what you do once in a while—it's what you do day in and day out that makes the difference." It's just as true for your dreams as it is for health and fitness. If you have a dream packed away in a box somewhere, take it out again, dust it off, and see if it still stirs your heart. If it does, bring it out into the light again. Set goals that move you toward it. Affirm it in words and mental images every day. Do research on it, write about it, share your ideas with those who can help you, and don't let a day go by without making some progress toward it. In short, breathe life into your dream. One day, you'll have to retire it and get a new one, because you—not your fairy godmother!—will have created a dream come true!

Commitment and Consciousness: Your Reticular Activating System

Your nervous system contains a built-in screening device that blocks out or admits information, depending on whether that information is important to you. It's a network of cells called the reticular activating system, or R.A.S., and its job is to determine which of the thousands of sensory messages bombarding you every second are going to get through to your awareness.

Without your R.A.S. you'd be overwhelmed by an incredible barrage of perceptions. Can you imagine what it would be like if you were simultaneously aware of every single sight, sound, smell, taste, and touch in your internal and external environments? You certainly couldn't focus long enough to read this book or to read anything, for that matter. You couldn't carry on a conversation or watch a movie or balance your checkbook. It would be impossible for you to live like you do now.

Thanks to your R.A.S., which operates without your being aware of it, this is not a problem. Like a good executive secretary, it serves as a screen to protect you, the "executive," from unwanted and unnecessary distractions. It functions in a way that is very sensitive to the choices you make about what matters and what doesn't. For example, imagine a young couple with a new baby. The mom has taken some time off from her job to care for the child, and the dad is working late to make up some of their lost income. It's the middle of the night, and everyone is sound asleep. They sleep through jet planes roaring by outside and the racket of a party in the adjoining apartment. But what happens if that baby wakes up and begins to fuss? Mom wakes out of a sound sleep instantly. Dad, however, continues to sleep like a log.

Mom wakes, not because the baby is louder than the jet plane or the party, but because these sounds are important to her. Dad sleeps on because it's been agreed that Mom will respond if the baby wakes. He's not even conscious of hearing the baby cry. If their accountabilities were to change, though, what they hear would probably change, too. For the time being, Dad's R.A.S. is working for him, allowing him to screen out certain sounds, while Mom's is also working, letting small but critical noises in.

It works the same way for you. Whenever you declare something to be important, either because it possesses value or poses a threat, you put your R.A.S. on alert to let that information through. Did you ever decide to buy something—maybe a new television set—and as soon as you decide, all you see are advertisements for special offers that feature TVs? You see television sets for sale on billboards, in store windows, in the newspapers, on garage sale signs. Of course, these sales are always going on, and the TVs are always out there. You just didn't notice them before, because they weren't important to you. You built scotomas to them. My daughter tells me that she never realized how many pregnant women there were walking around until she became pregnant, and suddenly they were everywhere!

The same thing will happen to you, once you declare yourself committed to a specific goal. Suddenly, you'll see things you couldn't see before, hear things that would previously have gone by you, get hunches you can't explain. Your R.A.S. goes to work, expanding your awareness in amazing ways. That's why you don't need to know *how* you're going to achieve something at the time you set the goal. You're going to discover all sorts of things that will help, but you just don't know what they are yet.

Before we move on, I want to say one more thing about the power of commitment. Commitment is the key to success in achieving any goal, whether it concerns a relationship, a business, health and fitness, education, personal and professional growth, or sports. Larry Bird was one of the best basketball players ever, yet he wasn't physically outstanding. Even he had to admit that he was relatively slow, and he couldn't really jump. But he succeeded because he was totally committed to success. He practiced more and played more intensely than almost anyone, and he used his talents for all they were worth. The same is true of Tom Watson, the great golfer. Tom was nothing special when he played in college, but his coach still talks about him, saying "I never saw anyone practice more." The difference in physical skills between athletes can't tell you that much. It's the quality of their commitment that really separates the good players from the great.

If you're fully committed to a goal, it means that you're willing to do whatever it takes to achieve it, and everything you do is going to reflect that commitment. Being committed means that you've made a choice and that you take time to fully involve yourself with what you've chosen. That's real time, by the way, as measured on the clock, not just a few hours here or there that you justify by calling "quality" time. If you're deeply committed to an activity, person, goal, or project, the time you spend on it will reflect that commitment, in *both* quantity and quality.

Being committed also means that you're willing to give the best you have without reservation and that you pay close attention to the results you're getting. It means accepting the limitations of your choice as well as the benefits (when you choose one thing, it also means you *don't* choose many others). And it means entering into a *relationship* with whatever you are committed to, be it a person, a career, creating a work of art, or remodeling the basement. So you need to understand that you can't gain any greater satisfaction from that relationship than you're willing to put into it. Ultimately, I hope you'll also come to understand that it is only through deep commitments that you can discover who you really are, grow to your fullest capacity, maintain meaningful connections to the rest of the world, and give freely to others.

Commitment requires a significant investment. I'm using the word *investment* here deliberately, because there are tremendous potential dividends down the road for you as a result. That's why I entitled the centerpiece of my company's educational programs *Investment in Excellence.* Putting your money into investments can be risky, but investing your time, energy, and resources in a goal you care deeply about is guaranteed to return benefits that you can't put a price on.

See the End Before the Means

Now that you know how your R.A.S. works, you can see why you begin to see all sorts of things that will help you—things you never noticed before—whenever you commit yourself to achieving a goal. That's why it's a mistake if you think you have to know exactly *how* you're going to achieve a goal *before* you commit to it. When you operate that way, you cripple yourself unnecessarily and limit your scope severely. You're goal-setting inside a box that is only as big as your present knowledge.

That's also why it's important to be careful about who you listen to and share your goals with. If you want to do something—say, start your own business—and you share your idea with people who don't understand how goal-setting and the R.A.S. work, they may say, "How do you think you're going to do that? Where will you get the money? Where will you get help? You don't know anything about how to run that kind of business." "Well, I'm not exactly sure . . ." you reply, and your confidence will falter and your enthusiasm will take a dip. Next thing you know, you're backing up your goal and lowering your aspirations to fit what you *do* know right now.

When I decided to put my educational curriculum on video tape and set up my own distribution system, I knew absolutely nothing about video production. Almost everyone I talked to about the idea told me to be realistic, be sensible. "Just keep on doing what you do best," they said. "Keep on teaching live seminars." But I wanted to reach many more people than I could doing live teaching. I wanted to get this information out to *millions* of people, all over the world, and there was no way I could do that in person, even if I spent every minute of my life traveling.

So I didn't listen to the naysayers. And—what do you know!— as soon as I positively committed myself to the goal of going to video, I began to hear about people from California to Canada who could help. It didn't matter that I knew nothing about video education. I could learn, and I could find others who knew the rest. I could find all the people and resources I needed, and, together, we could invent the "how-to" as we went along.

That's exactly what will happen to you. When you set a goal, you declare a new significance. You say, "*This* is important to me. This *matters*." And when you do that, all sorts of information and resources become available to you that weren't available before because they were getting screened out by your very efficient R.A.S. You weren't even aware of their existence before you set the goal, but afterwards you can't miss them. That's how your mind works and that's how goal-setting works: First you set the goal, *then* you see how to do it.

This is "end-result thinking." It's the way you want to train yourself to operate for high-performance goal achievement. Sure, the "how-to"—the processes you use and the actions you take toward achieving your goals—are important. But without a clear picture of the end results in mind, you hobble yourself unnecessarily, and you increase the likelihood of veering off course due to setbacks and obstacles.

For example, imagine that you're heading for an afternoon of doing something you really enjoy. Let's say it's reading a fascinating new book in the park under a magnificent maple tree. With your book, a snack, and a thermos of coffee in your backpack, you start walking toward the park. Halfway there, you meet friends who are on their way to the latest hit movie, and they invite you to join them. What will determine whether you continue on your original course to the park or accompany your pals to the movie?

The quick answer would probably be something like, "I'll do whichever I want to do more." But, in fact, you will decide which you most "want" to do based on the clarity, staying power, and emotional appeal of the pictures in your mind. If the picture of reading in the park is more compelling, detailed, and dominant than the one with your friends at the movie, you'll choose the park. Even though this is an example of a pleasant "obstacle," it works the same way for those that are not so pleasant. You move toward the picture that you are able to hold uppermost in your mind.

When you're an end-result thinker, you create a clear, vivid mental picture of your goal, and you strengthen it by thinking about it regularly, in a very deliberate, systematic way that we'll talk more about in the next chapter. You use the power of your conscious and subconscious mind to create a picture that is so emotionally forceful, so vivid, that you are driven to bring it into reality. Nothing, whether pleasant or unpleasant, can dissuade you.

Out of Order, on Purpose

This bring us to the critical principle of *cognitive dissonance*, which means just what it sounds like—a state of disharmony or disorder (dissonance) having to do with thoughts (cognition).

Cognitive dissonance occurs whenever we try to hold in our minds two conflicting ideas about reality at the same time, and it inevitably creates a strong desire and drive to resolve the conflict.

For example, you have a picture in your mind of what the inside of your house should look like. Maybe it's a neat and tidy place—beds made, dishes washed and put away, no clutter, very little disarray. Then a friend comes to stay with you for a while, and your friend is much more casual about his surroundings. You don't realize this, until you come home from work and find newspapers and magazines left open everywhere, clothes thrown over the backs of chairs and on the floor, evidence of a shopping expedition on the dining room table, candy wrappers crumpled up and left on the couch. The place, to your eyes, is completely out of order.

How do you resolve the cognitive dissonance you're experiencing—the difference between your mental picture of how things should look and the picture of how they actually do look right now in reality? Well, you could attempt to adjust the environment. You might return the house to order without saying anything. You might have a discussion with your friend about housekeeping standards in your home. If you're upset enough or if the dissonance continues long enough, you might even ask your friend to leave.

Or you could decide to adjust your belief. Maybe you've been running yourself ragged trying to keep your house neat as a pin because that's the way your mother, who never worked at a job outside the home, always said it should be. But maybe that belief is hurting you more than it's helping. You have a fulfilling, full-time career, children to raise, an active social life, a husband who seldom has your undivided attention, unopened books you've been dying to read, virtually no time to exercise or even relax and just do nothing. Maybe you'll choose to take some of the pressure off yourself by deliberately relaxing your housekeeping standards. Or maybe you'll decide it's time to get some household help.

So there are options when you're dealing with cognitive dissonance, but one thing is certain. When you're experiencing it, you'll feel powerfully motivated to resolve the dissonance and restore harmony and order. Even if you're not consciously aware of it, you'll be driven to adjust your outer and inner pictures of reality so that they once again match. This is simply how human beings are built in order to maintain sanity. We need to see our beliefs about reality confirmed by what we see and experience. When this happens, we feel that we have a handle on things, that we're in our comfort zone, and, as we've already seen, that is where we like to operate. When this doesn't happen, we feel compelled to correct the mistake.

Now, here's something else about cognitive dissonance you really need to know. Whenever your system is thrown out of order in this way, a tremendous amount of drive and energy is generated to restore order. Then, as you might expect, after order is restored, the extra drive and energy turn off, because they're no longer needed.

That's why so many people experience a dramatic letdown after they've achieved an important goal. There's no longer any cognitive dissonance. The picture in their minds (the desired goal) and the world they live in (current reality) used to be different, so they generated drive and energy to achieve the goal and make those pictures match. After the goal has been brought into reality, there is no dissonance. So they flatten out emotionally, and their energy shifts into neutral. They feel deflated, restless, maybe even depressed.

To avoid this trap, all you need to do is set your goals to take you *through*, not just *up to*, your end-result objective. In other words, don't wait until after you've achieved a goal before setting a new one. Goal-setting is a powerful force, but it needs to be continuous and ongoing if it's really going to get you anywhere. Of course, you can kick back and rest whenever you want to, but if it's a choice instead of something that feels as if it's happening to you, it will be a refreshing time-out instead of a draining experience.

Are you beginning to see how high-performance goal-setting works? When you set a goal and hold in your mind a vivid, emotionally charged picture of the end result you want, and you affirm that end result as the truth, you're deliberately throwing your system out of order. The reality you experience in your mind and the reality you experience in your environment don't match! You imagine yourself doing challenging, satisfying work that you really enjoy, but every day you go to your dreary, dead-end job. The handsome new car you visualize yourself owning with pride turns into your old rattletrap jalopy when you walk out the front door. The loving, mutually supportive marriage you can picture so clearly clashes with the conflict-filled relationship you presently have.

And, in the past, that's probably where you stopped. You opened your eyes, the bubble popped, and you abandoned your vision. You were choosing—without being conscious of making a choice—to resolve your cognitive dissonance by eliminating your hopeful but rather weak mental picture. By doing so, you were missing a tremendous opportunity.

What do you think might happen if you held on to that mental vision of your imagined ideal? What if you deliberately strengthened that vision day after day, week after week, by replaying it over and over again in your mind and adding to its detail? What if, at the same time, you affirmed your vision with powerful, emotionally charged words, so that, over time, it grew to be even clearer and more compelling than current reality?

Well, I'll tell you. Something really exciting would begin to happen, and it's not in the least mysterious. It has nothing to do with magic and everything to do with the predictable, psychological principle of cognitive dissonance. You would experience a tremendous increase in drive and energy, motivating you to resolve the cognitive dissonance by closing the gap between your mental image and reality. As you visualize the new, you would become increasingly dissatisfied with the old. You would be energized and motivated to phase out the old and phase in the new, to transform your reality.

Closing the Gap: Energy and Enthusiasm

I'm not exaggerating when I say you would be energized. Have you ever noticed how much energy some people have? They're always working on some project, working toward some goal they care about, and they appear to be blessed with unusual stamina and enthusiasm. These people are somehow magnetic—they enjoy what they're doing, draw others to them easily, and have a real passion for living. They always seem to know what they want and where they're going. Maybe you've just assumed that their metabolisms naturally run faster than yours or that they were born that way. Perhaps you wonder whether nutritional supplements or ginseng tea might give you some of the get-up-and-go that they have.

But I believe the energy and vitality you observe in these people come from cognitive dissonance. They have an intense desire that is focused on a clear vision, a specific end result they want to achieve. And then they have another and another and another. They are constantly throwing their systems out of order as they create new and challenging goals, new mental images of the way they want things to be. They experience the self-generated drive and energy it takes to close the gap between their images and external reality. Then they do it over again, with new images, new goals, new results.

In addition to illustrating how the principle of cognitive dissonance keeps us moving, high-energy people are also good examples of something called *reciprocal causation*. Reciprocal causation just means a cycle or spiral of cause and effect that builds on itself. For example, the more you exercise, the stronger you get, and the stronger you get, the more you are able to exercise. The more you play the piano, the better you get at it, and the better you get, the more you play. The same is true for successful goal achievement: The more you set and achieve meaningful goals, the more energy you generate, and the more energy you have, the more you will be able to achieve.

Seven Steps to Achievement: A Goal-Setting System That Works

The reason many people fail to achieve their goals is that they never really set them in the first place. Oh, if you asked them whether they have goals for the future, they'd probably say they do. But they don't understand that wanting or hoping for things isn't the same as having specific, clearly defined goals. And though they may be reluctant to admit it, the truth is that they spend more time planning a wedding or a vacation than they do their lives. By failing to plan they are planning to fail, by default.

Goal-setting works. That is, it does if you do it systematically. Literally hundreds of studies have proved that setting specific, moderately challenging goals results in improved performance when compared to not setting goals at all and just doing whatever comes naturally.

I don't want to suggest that people who don't set goals can never be successful. Once in a while they do succeed, because they have somehow developed the desire and determination to do well. But often they allow circumstances or other people to determine the direction they take, and then they literally make the best of it. They frequently describe themselves as having been very lucky. Would they have been even more successful if they had systematically set goals? There's no way to tell, although I admit I believe so.

With that in mind, I want to give you a seven-step system that will enable you to approach goal-setting with confidence. It's easy to use, and it has been proven effective. I guarantee you that if you employ this system, it will dramatically improve the likelihood of your success.

Step 1: Put your goals in writing.

There's something about writing things down that makes us take them more seriously, isn't there? "Will you put that in writing?" we ask when something is really important to us. Major life changes such as births, weddings, graduations, and deaths are always documented. Writing your goals is a way of declaring to yourself, "This matters. I am taking this very seriously!"

Writing also has permanence. Thoughts and speech, unless they are recorded, do not. When you write your goals, you're much less likely to forget them or inadvertently alter them over time. Writing them also forces you to really think them through, to imagine them specifically and clearly. Which brings us to step two.

Step 2: Define your goals clearly and specifically.

If you try to achieve nonspecific goals, vague desires, or fuzzy ideas, the feedback you get will be vague, as well, and feedback is critical. For example, if you goal-set for a better standard of living or losing weight, how will you know when you've achieved it? Any improvement at all will qualify as something "better," right? If you have a highly specific goal, such as doubling your income or losing twenty-five pounds, you'll always know when you're on track and how far you have to go at any given time. You'll be able to reward yourself at predetermined milestones, and you'll know the moment you've achieved your desired end result.

Most goals should be expressed in terms of behavior or action, for the simple reason that these things can easily be tracked. Even if the end result you ultimately want is to change the way you feel (from depressed to content, for example, or from self-doubting to self-confident), the only way to achieve it is to change what you are *doing*. As a general rule, each of your short-term goals should be specific enough to answer the following questions: **Who** will be doing the behavior? (The answer to this first question will most often be you.) **What** will that behavior be? **When** will the behavior happen? **Where** will it happen? **How often** will it happen?

For example, if your end-result goal is to make a healthful and enjoyable exercise regime part of your life from now on, how are you going to do it? **What** sort of exercises will you do? How will you make sure you are building cardiovascular health as well as toning muscles and maintaining flexibility? Spell it out: Brisk walking? Weight training? Swimming? Jogging? Bicycling? Yoga?

When and **how** often will you exercise? A graduated program of brisk walking: week one, ten minutes a day, five days out of seven, rain or shine; increase to fifteen minutes the second week, twenty minutes the third, and so on up to forty minutes a day, five days out of seven. **Where** will you exercise? Outdoors, around the neighborhood, on a moderately hilly, up and down route. In extremely bad weather, on a treadmill indoors.

If you're going to adjust your diet at the same time, you'll need to spell out those behaviors, as well. What foods will you eat every day, what will you avoid altogether, and what will you limit to occasional consumption? How do you define "occasional"? Will you take vitamins and/or nutritional supplements? Which ones and how often?

Step 3: Turn your end-result goals into short-term subgoals.

Some people say that long-term goals are the only kind you need if you really want to get anywhere. Others maintain that long-term goals are too distant to get their arms around. The latest research indicates that the best way to approach goal-setting is with a combination of both short- and long-term objectives.

If you have only long-term goals, you may indeed find it rough going. The realities of life are that you probably have many pressing demands on you in the present—things you must get done on a daily and weekly basis. These things often cause you to put off your long-term goals . . . and put them off . . . and then put them off some more. In addition, you may begin to feel discouraged or demoralized if your target is way off in the distance, because you can't see that any significant progress is being made.

On the other hand, if you have only short-term goals, you may feel fragmented, without an overall direction and purpose. Or you may not experience the powerful motivational pull that a meaningful, long-term goal can generate. When you combine short- and long-term goals, you have the best of both worlds. So, by all means set long-term goals, but break them down into subgoals that you can accomplish in the near future.

Your eventual objective may be to become financially independent, but what can you do today, this week, this month, to move you closer to that desired end result? Your long-term goal may be to speak fluent Spanish and travel in South America, but this week your goal may be to learn the pronunciation and meaning of fifty new words. Your down-the-road goal may be to run in a marathon, but this week you're working on breaking the ten-mile barrier.

Step 4: Make sure your end-result goals are both challenging and attainable.

Your goals should be neither too easy nor too difficult for you to attain. If they're too easy, you won't feel the satisfaction and pride that comes from having pushed yourself a little and succeeded. You'll have a "so what, no big deal" response to achieving them. On the other hand, if they're too hard, you're likely to become frustrated or discouraged and give up. You do, though, want to challenge yourself. The higher the goals, the harder you'll work to attain them and the better your performance will be—assuming the goals are not unrealistic or beyond your reach.

My experience has shown that your long-range goal can be exceedingly difficult, as long as the short-range goals leading up to it are arranged in a gradual progression of difficulty. It's something like training to run the marathon I mentioned above. If I suggested to you that you could run twenty-six miles, you probably wouldn't believe it. But if you started with smaller goals—first mastering a quarter mile, then a half mile, then a mile, then up to three, five, ten, and so on, and you stuck with it over time, you'd probably be able to do it. And as you drew closer and closer to the twenty-six mile end-result goal, it would seem much less formidable than when you originally imagined it.

Step 5: Anticipate obstacles and setbacks.

So you've decided to change something about your life, and you're committed to doing it. Maybe you've decided to kick the smoking habit or develop a healthy lifestyle, including exercise and good nutrition. You've set specific long- and short-term goals that are both challenging and attainable, and you've begun your new behavior. You're using affirmations and visualizations (we'll discuss these powerful tools in Chapter 6) to support your goals and make the change easier. But, sooner or later, you're probably going to be tempted to slip back into old ways, especially when you're feeling tired, lonely, discouraged, or sad.

You may be further tempted as a result of spoken or unspoken messages from your spouse, friends, or family members that say, in essence, "change back to the way you used to be!" You see, your personal changes, even though they are intended to be positive, may seem threatening to others. They may prefer the certainty of the you they know to a new, improved you they don't. On a subconscious level, they may be wondering, "If you improve, will you still like me the way I am?" Or they may feel guilty watching you improve while they continue to postpone or ignore their own need to change. If their self-esteem is shaky, they may even disparage or put down your efforts.

If you understand that obstacles, setbacks, and slips back into old behavior are common, it'll be easier to deal with them if they happen. Anticipate some of the obstacles you may encounter, and develop strategies to overcome them. If it's a matter of hanging on until the temptation to revert to old behavior passes (as with smoking withdrawal, for example), prepare a list of possible alternative activities—a walk around the neighborhood, a trip to the movies, reading a good book, deep breathing, enjoying a low-cal snack, etc. Make the list as long as possible so you'll have plenty to choose from.

List situations that are likely to tempt you back to old behavior, too. In fact, list every potential obstacle you can think of, whether it's a friend or family member who indulges in the behavior you're trying to eliminate, situations you strongly associate with old behavior, or internal resistance that may be triggered by any number of things. After you've identified them, list several possible ways you could deal with each one.

If you do have a slip or relapse into old behaviors, don't for a moment think that it's a sign that change is impossible. Treat it as a temporary setback and an opportunity to learn something valuable. Maybe it means that one element of your goal-achievement strategy isn't working well, so review it with that in mind. Maybe you're asking too much of yourself too early in the goal-achievement process, and you need to adjust your expectations a bit. Or maybe a specific situation is causing you to slip, and you can plan to avoid or change it. Whatever you do, don't let a slip throw you, and don't expect yourself to be perfect. Getting back on track after a relapse can make you stronger. It can also help you to be more understanding of other people's occasional slips.

Step 6: Track your progress and reward achievement.

Keeping track of your progress, or self-monitoring as it's often called, is an essential part of successful goal achievement. It gives you accurate feedback that tells you how you're doing and helps you to better understand how your environment is helping or hindering your progress. Besides, have you ever heard the saying "that which gets measured gets done"? Goal-achievement improves when performance is monitored. So, if you want to be successful, develop a tracking system that works for you. Your system should be simple and easy to use and portable enough to carry with you, if that is appropriate. A sample self-monitoring chart is included at the end of this chapter. Feel free to use it as is or adapt it so that it makes sense for what you are doing.

Every day, at the end of the day (or every week, if your goal involves weekly activities or behaviors), identify whether you did or didn't achieve your goal(s) for that day. Make a few notes to indicate the things that helped or hindered your goal achievement. Note also what you did well and how you might have done better.

For a long time, it's been recognized that behaviors that are rewarded or are rewarding in themselves tend to increase in frequency. Behaviors that are punished or ignored tend to decrease in frequency or even disappear. So it's also important that you reward yourself at intervals as you work to accomplish your goals. For maximum impact, rewards should come immediately upon attainment of a goal or very soon after.

Rewards can be tangible or intangible. Tangible rewards are things you can touch or pleasurable activities that take place in your external environment, such as an article of clothing you've been wanting, dinner out at a special restaurant, a facial or massage, or a new putter. Intangible rewards involve things that take place in your internal environment, such as self-praise and congratulations.

I believe a combination of tangible and intangible rewards works best. Don't just give yourself a treat and skip the self-congratulation and praise. Do both. Whenever you achieve a significant subgoal or have successfully overcome an obstacle, treat yourself to something you really like and tell yourself, "I deserve this! I worked hard, and I came through for myself. I'm rewarding myself for a job well done and helping myself stay on track." Rewards are an important part of your goal achievement strategy, so don't disregard them.

Step 7: Support your goals with affirmations and visualization.

In Chapter 4, we looked at the close relationship between performance and self-talk (your ongoing silent or spoken evaluation of yourself and your environment). In Chapter 6, we'll focus on a specific kind of self-talk—affirmations—and we'll explain how you can use them to support change and increase the probability of success.

For the moment, all you need to know is that an affirmation is simply a statement that confirms the truth of something. The

Apostles' Creed that many people repeat in church every Sunday is an affirmation of religious belief. The American Pledge of Allegiance is an affirmation of patriotism and national loyalty. Traditional wedding vows are an affirmation of the marital relationship. But an affirmation doesn't have to be traditional or formal. Whenever you state (or think about) something as "the truth," you're making an affirmation.

Visualization is just what it sounds like: a mental image, picture, or vision. When you combine affirmation and visualization, you give yourself a powerful ability to "see" yourself behaving differently. Repeated often enough, this can change your self-image. And when you truly come to think of yourself differently, as we discussed in Chapter 3, you naturally begin to behave differently. We'll describe affirmations and visualizations more fully in the next chapter. For now, just be aware of them as powerful tools to your goal-achievement strategy.

Let's review the seven steps to goal-setting success.

1. Put your goals in writing.
2. Define your goals clearly and specifically.
3. Turn your end-result goals into short-term subgoals.
4. Make sure your end-result goals are both challenging and attainable.
5. Anticipate obstacles and setbacks.
6. Track your progress and reward achievement.
7. Support your goals with affirmations and visualization.

Enlist Support from Others, Too

Here's an eighth step that, while not essential, is a highly desirable option. Consider organizing a weekly support group of people who are also using this goal-achievement strategy. Having others to meet with on a regular basis will provide all of you with valuable support. It will also give you the benefit of each other's thinking when it comes to dealing with obstacles and problem solving.

As we discussed in Chapter 3, one of the best ways to increase self-efficacy (the belief that you can accomplish a specific task) is to actually succeed at the task or goal. Another way is to observe someone else (a model) who is successful at it. A weekly meeting of this kind will give group members the opportunity to participate in "modeling" observation and discussion of other people's successes. In addition, feeling accountable to others as well as to yourself can help intensify your commitment. It's no accident that Weight Watchers, which is just this sort of support group, has been so successful.

If you want to organize such a group, try to meet for at least eight to ten weeks. You may want to continue meeting for even longer, but if you decide to stop at that point, consider a reunion every three months for a year or so. This will help you make sure that the use of systematic goal-setting will become a regular, ongoing part of your life.

As each group member shares information, I suggest you focus on three agenda items: (1) Compare goals, action steps to accomplish them, and tracking procedures. Do some seem to be more effective than others? (2) Ask "What's working well?" Describe successes in detail. Ask "What's not working well?" Share problems, setbacks, and obstacles. (3) Compare strategies for overcoming obstacles. At the end of each meeting, adjust individual goal statements, rewards, and obstacle strategies as needed, incorporating what each has learned.

How Long Will It Take?

You have a goal. You're very clear about what you want. You're affirming and visualizing the end result. You have a plan of action, a system that includes short-term and long-term goals, monitoring, and rewards, and you're following it. Maybe you even have a strong support group. So how long is it going to take? How much work is enough? How much affirming, planning, and new behavior will it require in order to get what you want?

The answer is simple. When you have what you want, that's long enough. Now, I know this isn't the answer some of you want. We're so used to schedules and timetables that pinpoint exactly when something will happen that we expect our goal-achievement process to work the same way. But it doesn't.

In most cases, your estimate of the time it will take you to accomplish a goal is just that—your best guess. Some things you'll achieve sooner, some later. If your goal isn't reached in the time frame you've set, set a new one. Do whatever needs to be done. If you've done just about all you can, but it's not enough and the goal is still important to you, rest a bit; then do some more. Reevaluate your strategy. Enlist some fresh thinking to help you out. Consider not what you've been doing, but how you've been doing it. Don't accept the limited judgments of other people who say, "It's too late," or "I told you so—it can't be done." And stop negative self-talk before it starts.

When do you stop working on a goal? When you've stopped wanting it or when you've gotten what you want.

Weekly Self-Monitoring Chart

(Sample)

Name: Bob Smith

Goal: To achieve a positive state of physical strength and cardiovascular fitness appropriate for my age, sex, and body type, as determined by a YMCA fitness consultant.

Week of: November 20

Check each day you achieved your objective.

Goal	Sun	Mon	Tue	Wed	Thu	Fri	Sat
Walk briskly/jog at least 30 min. no fewer than 4 times a week							
Weight training at least 30 min. no fewer than 3 times a week							
Repeat affirmations & visualizations twice a day, 10 min. each session							

Affirmations to support my long- and short-term goals:

1. I take pride in my body, love feeling strong and healthy, and feel great when I exercise.
2. It's easy for me to keep my fitness commitments because the benefits are so pleasurable.
3. I have a positive expectancy of reaching my fitness goals, and I bounce back quickly from temporary setbacks.
4. My daily affirmations and visualizations make change a natural, free-flowing process.

CHAPTER SIX

The Adventure of Growth

What You See (and Say) Is What You Get:
Affirmations and Visualizations

A t the end of Chapter 5, I introduced you to the concept of using mental tools called affirmations and visualizations to support and maximize goal achievement. Now, we'll take a more detailed look at these two closely related, very powerful techniques. You'll see how and why they work and how you can incorporate them into your daily routine to decrease anxiety and make your life richer and more fulfilling.

Some communications systems, such as those used by our armed forces, use the word "affirmative" instead of "yes." That's as good a definition as I know of an affirmation—saying yes to something, clearly and with conviction. In a formal debate, the side that upholds the truth of the proposition is called the affirmative side. When you make an affirmation, you are saying, "Yes, I believe in the truth of this."

> "Our duty as men is to proceed as if limits to our ability did not exist. We are collaborators in creation."
>
> Pierre Teilhard de Chardin

To affirm something means to literally make it firm, solid, more real. On the surface, thoughts don't appear to be anything we could call solid. But when you repeat them over and over again, they become beliefs. Beliefs, as we've seen, become behaviors. Behaviors create experiences and results. That's how we move toward and become like that which we repeatedly think about.

In our discussion of self-talk in Chapter 3, we said that it isn't necessary to repeat an experience over and over to build a belief. You can do it just as effectively with your memory, revisiting and reliving it as if it were happening again. The effect on your body and mind is as if it *were* happening. We introduced you to the formula I x V = R (Imagination times Vividness equals Reality) as an easy way to remember this extremely important principle. As far as your subconscious is concerned, a vividly imagined experience really *is* happening to you—right now, not weeks or months or years ago.

Perfect Practice

Professional athletes were among the first to see the value of using these concepts in a practical way. It meant they could practice any time, any place, in their minds. They could practice on airplanes, in busses, even in a hospital bed. Not only that, they could practice performing *perfectly* whenever they wanted to—something that was in "real" life a highly desirable but unpredictable, even rare event. When they added these mental rehearsals to their training regime, they found their performances improved, sometimes dramatically.

I remember reading a story about a javelin thrower in *Esquire* magazine some years ago. He had been using visualization techniques in earnest to supplement his practice. Listen to how he described the throw that surpassed his own personal best record: "I thought, 'I know this throw, I've thrown it before,' because I've seen myself do this so many times before in my mind."[1] I knew exactly what he was talking about.

In his book, *Golf My Way*, Jack Nicklaus explains his use of visualization:

> First I "see" the ball where I want it to finish, nice and white and sitting up high on the bright green grass. Then the scene quickly changes, and I "see" the ball going there: its path, trajectory, and shape, even its behavior on landing. Then there's a sort of fade-out, and the next scene shows me making the kind of swing that will turn the previous images into reality.[2]

Notice how Nicklaus starts out with the end result—the ball at its destination point. And he doesn't stop there. He says he sees the entire process of getting the ball to the green, in a kind of reverse motion. We know he puts in countless hours of physical practice, too. But he's just as disciplined when it comes to what's going on in his mind. He leaves as little as possible to chance, because he wants to succeed so badly. The results are sports history.

Just about everyone knows who Jack Nicklaus is, and it's safe to say that few outside of Canada know the name Silken Laumann—yet. I know about her through a Canadian business associate. Nicklaus and Laumann, I believe, have a lot in common. In the summer of 1992, Laumann, a world-class rower, pulled off one of the most inspiring comebacks in Canadian sports history. She won an Olympic bronze medal in Barcelona, even though she had broken and badly mangled her right leg in an accident just ten weeks earlier. She was in considerable pain and wearing a brace. No one expected her to compete, let alone win a medal. These days, she takes time out of a rigorous training schedule to speak to audiences—especially groups of young people—who want to know more about how she managed to overcome truly incredible odds to do what she did.

I want to pass the gist of what she says along to you. First of all, Laumann tells people that success is not a destination, but a process—a journey that begins with a dream or vision and that is carried out in small steps. She reminds them that confidence is not something that some people just naturally have and others don't. Rather, she says it's something we build ourselves over time, with each attempt and each victory. She also talks a good deal about the power of positive affirmations to control performance: "It sounds really dumb," she says, "but it works."

Because of my coaching background, I have worked with many top professional sports figures over the years—individuals and entire teams. Although most of my activities these days take place far from the locker room, I still really enjoy working with athletes.

Not long ago, I spent some time in New York with the Jets, which I'll tell you a little about later. But when I think of all the people in sports our education has helped, I invariably recall the work we did almost ten years ago with Detroit Tigers superstar Kirk Gibson.

Perhaps because it was such a dramatic transformation, and those are always memorable. Or maybe it's because of the tremendous enthusiasm with which Kirk embraced these concepts. As you may remember, Kirk had a reputation for being baseball's "bad boy." He was a brilliant and powerful player, but, by his own admission, he was arrogant, egocentric, and erratic: "I was a self-centered, egotistical jerk who had no perception of who I was walking over and didn't care." In 1982, Kirk suffered some injuries and was forced to play a short season. In 1983, he had a disastrous year, with a batting average of .227. He was so unpopular because of his hostile behavior and deteriorating performance that he was mercilessly booed whenever he stuck his head out of the dugout. He felt lousy about himself, and his behavior showed it. "I would go to the park and suffer for eight hours," he said in an interview for the *Kansas City Times*. "I went up to that bat thinking, 'I'm going to show you!' and the next thing I knew, I was sitting down." He was convinced he couldn't hit against left-handed pitchers, and his previously optimistic nature seemed covered by a dark cloud of doom and gloom.

Then, his agent, Doug Baldwin, arranged for him to visit us at The Pacific Institute. Kirk spent a full day with us, a very intense day. We taught him about comfort zones, self-talk, affirmations, and visualizations—the same things you are reading about here, and he connected with the information like a Louisville Slugger with a fastball. His quick mind just soaked up the concepts we introduced him to, and his desire to improve was obvious. It was, said sportswriter Alan Steinberg, "like giving Icarus tools to make wings that would work."[3] When he left our offices, we were convinced that things were going to change for Kirk, and we waited confidently for the evidence. Sure enough, before long it began to come in.

From that point on, interviews with Kirk seemed to have a new flavor. The old anger and arrogance were gone. In their place was a new humility. His manager, Sparky Anderson, described what happened at Spring training in March of '84 by saying, "There wasn't a livin' soul around here that didn't see the difference in Kirk Gibson."[4]

But more than his attitude improved. In 1984 Kirk batted .265 against lefties compared to .150 in 1983. He was elected the American League Championship Series' Most Valuable Player, with a .417 average. He led the Tigers to a World Series victory in five games over the Padres with six hits, seven RBIs, and two home runs. In 1985, though the Tigers did poorly, Kirk hit several career highs with a .287 batting average, 96 runs scored, 30 stolen bases, 29 home runs, and 97 runs batted in. Talk about peak performance!

So What? Who Cares?
What Difference Does It Make?

I'm telling you these true stories not so you can admire other people's accomplishments, but to help you realize that change, even dramatic change, is possible for you, too. These people are not genetically superior to you. They were not born achievers. But they know some things about how to take charge of their thoughts that give them an edge, and they use those things routinely. They've learned how to build beliefs that help them grow. They've learned how to control their self-talk and mental images to create the best possible outcomes. And what they've done, you can do, too.

As you process this information, keep in mind that the notion of thoughts influencing the body is nothing new. "As a man thinketh in his heart, so is he," the Bible tells us in Proverbs 23:7. The ancient Greeks believed in a holistic approach to sports life. They saw the mind and body as two vital aspects of a single, unified, interdependent system. Physicians who practice holistic medicine today see it in the same way. So do many physicists and other professionals in the so-called "hard" sciences. They believe that the thoughts we think have a profound effect on our bodies, even though we may never fully understand the process that causes it.

The combined use of affirmations and visualizations gives us a way to take control of some of those thoughts—to deliberately construct "memories" for our minds that are positive, healthful, and conducive to peak performance of every sort, including the functioning of our bodies.

Rehearsing Your Optimal Future

Mentally rehearsing a "personal best" future isn't just for athletes. A growing number of health care professionals teach their patients how to use affirmation and visualization techniques to help them get through procedures with less stress and pain, less bleeding, and shorter recovery times. Sales professionals use affirmations and visualization to mentally role-play how they'll deal with difficult customers or rebound from a slew of "thanks, but no thanks" responses. Men and women in business use them to imagine specific situations that might crop up, including important presentations, and then picturing exactly what they'll do. Entrepreneurs use them to imagine the results of exciting new ventures. Event planners use them to "see" what a successful conference or meeting will look like long before the actual event takes place.

In his book, *Peak Performers*, Charles Garfield, who began his career as a mathematician, explains the power of visualization this way: "Most people use words to describe their plans and activities, even silently to themselves. . . . Language is arguably the most powerful of all human creations. But even more than words, *images* motivate people to perform at peak efficiency. . . . Mental rehearsal is far from casual daydreaming. Peak performers give it concentrated and repeated practice."[5]

That's how it works. You repeatedly affirm in language and clearly visualize what you want for yourself in the future, as if it were completely real. Then, thanks to your R.A.S., you experience new insights and perceptions. Cognitive dissonance generates an increase in goal-directed energy and drive. And then you take action, in a systematic way, doing what it takes to claim your vision as your own.

It's not magic or mumbo jumbo. In fact, it's a system based on some of the oldest, wisest teachings in the world and verified by the most current, valid, and reliable scientific research. It has been practiced by a great many people, including me, for decades. Sure, it takes work. It takes commitment, time, and energy to create reality from a vision, but it happens all the time. Whenever you look forward to something and create a picture in your mind of how you want that something to be, you're using visualization, even though you may not know it. When you plan your Christmas dinner, you're using it. When you think about how wonderful your summer vacation is going to be, you're using it. When you imagine a life together with someone you love, you're using it.

Think about this: Every single man-made creation in the world, past and present, first started out as mental energy—an idea inside someone's head. Where thought goes, energy flows. The more thought, the more energy, and the more energy, the more likely the reality becomes. If you can clearly see yourself being and achieving what you want, you're far more likely to be and do those things. If you can't *see* it, how in the world can you expect to *be* it?

You can only grow as far as you can imagine yourself growing. You can only be as successful as you can envision yourself being. You develop your vision over time, step by step. First you see it, then you become it, inventing the "how" as you go along. Then you see the next level of development and grow into it. And on and on you go. If it sounds like it could be fun, you're right. And it's more than fun—it's a wonderful, satisfying, inspiring way to live your life!

Writing and Visualizing Affirmations

You've seen the importance of beliefs, particularly self-image, in shaping reality. You've also seen how self-talk and comfort zones work, and you've learned why all of us need to set clear goals in order to achieve our full potential and take charge of our personal future. Now you're ready to learn exactly how effective affirmations are written and how to work with them until an imagined, ideal future becomes current reality.

Written affirmations provide a blueprint for growth and change and a consistent frame for visualizations. They are goal statements that help you to move forward with minimal stress and anxiety into the life you most want, the relationships you most desire. They aren't magical incantations or exotic mantras. They are powerful tools that can help you improve your internal picture of who you are and what you are able to do. With them, you equip yourself to anticipate and smoothly handle change in a natural, free-flowing way.

Here are my step-by-step guidelines for how to write effective affirmations:

1. *Affirmations celebrate achievement in the first person, present tense.* You can't affirm or visualize change in anyone or for anyone but yourself. My purpose in writing this book is to help others grow, but it wouldn't have done a bit of good had I affirmed and visualized something like the following: "Because of the logic, clarity, convincing examples, and spirit in which this information is offered, readers will easily understand and apply the concepts in this book to create happier lives for themselves." That affirmation is not about me. Its end result concerns someone else's behavior (yours, in this case), and it would be a waste of time for me to affirm it. What I did affirm is that "I have my purpose uppermost in mind as this book takes shape, and I consistently strive to write clearly, logically, convincingly, and from my heart." Whether you apply the concepts and grow from the experience is entirely up to you.

So you need to put yourself at the heart of every affirmation you make. You need to be able to see *yourself* doing or behaving whatever it is you affirm. If you have trouble seeing yourself as you want to ultimately be, the short-term subgoals you've developed can help. For instance, maybe your end-result goal is to be independently wealthy, but right now you just can't comfortably see yourself that way. There's nothing in your background to give you the pictures you need, although you have seen plenty of others who live this way, at least on TV and in the movies. Perhaps it's easier for you to see yourself making an additional $1,000 a month. If so, that's what you need to affirm and visualize right now. It's a step in the right direction, and if you take enough of them, you'll get there.

Perhaps you want to get a Ph.D. and teach English at a university, but you don't even have a high school diploma yet. You've never been inside a college classroom, so you're having trouble seeing yourself in that setting. Back up a little and visualize yourself getting your G.E.D. or collecting a two-year degree from junior college. Then continue to goal-set for bigger things as you get closer to your dream. It doesn't do you much good to see *others* doing what you want. You have to be able to see *yourself* doing it, convincingly and comfortably.

This first-person focus is in no way selfish or vain, but it does require a healthy self-interest. After all, you *are* interested in changing yourself, in growing to be more than you presently are, and there's nothing wrong with that. Of course, when you change yourself, you are also giving others, especially those who are closest to you, something different to respond to. So you may very well see changes in other people as an indirect result of the changes you are making in yourself. But you can't force them to change or control how they respond to you, and it's certainly never wise to make superficial changes in yourself in an attempt to manipulate others into changing.

There are several other reasons why you want to phrase your affirmation in the present tense—that is, as if it has already been accomplished. First, and probably most important, you want to imprint your affirmation into your subconscious as an accomplished fact, something you have already achieved, even though you really haven't—yet. So if you're presently unemployed or unhappy with your career, and your ultimate goal is to find satisfying, challenging work, you might write an affirmation such as "I love getting up in the morning because I can't wait to get back to work!"

Write a number of affirmations to support the subgoals that are going to get you to your end result and to handle any setbacks or slips that may occur. For example: "Every day, I do at least three things that move me closer to achieving my career goals." "I have a clear understanding of the value of my many skills and abilities, and it is easy for me to talk convincingly to others about myself." "I am relaxed, confident, and persuasive during job interviews." "I love networking, and am always alert for ways I can help others and ways they can help me." "I am so completely committed to my career goals that if I occasionally slip into inactivity, I correct it immediately."

Are you lying to yourself because these things haven't really happened yet? Not at all. Your intention is not to deceive yourself or to deny the truth of current reality. Rather, you are putting the principle of cognitive dissonance that we talked about in Chapter 5 to work for you. Remember, cognitive dissonance is what happens whenever we try to hold two conflicting ideas about reality in our minds at the same time. The result is a strong desire to resolve the conflict.

When you affirm a new truth, you are deliberately throwing your system out of order and triggering a conflict in order to stimulate the energy to resolve it and accomplish your goal. You are affirming and visualizing the "truth" of challenging, satisfying work, vividly and repeatedly. At the same time, you know that you don't actually have it, yet. So your subconscious gets the message, "Something's wrong here." There's a problem that needs correcting (cognitive dissonance). And it goes to work, generating drive and energy to correct for the mistake, to get you back where you "belong."

Another important reason for writing and visualizing your affirmations in the present tense is to prevent you from affirming potential or ability instead of actual achievement. For example, instead of affirming "I *am* patient and affectionate with my children," you might affirm "I *can be* patient and affectionate with my children." But no cognitive dissonance is created when you say it that way, because you already have the *ability* to be patient. It's *use* of that ability that you want to bring into reality, right? Keep in mind, too, that when you think in terms of "I *can be*" or "I *intend* to be" or "I *want* to be," there is a silent ". . . but right now I'm *not*" implied.

Finally, you affirm and visualize in the present tense so that you don't become caught in the trap of affirming the past. If your goal is to go back in time to "the way things used to be" while you're immersed in present reality, you'll be creating cognitive dissonance, all right. The pictures won't match, and you'll be creating lots of energy, but instead of improving the present and moving toward a growth-filled future, you'll be trying to relive a past that is permanently and forever out of reach, except in memory.

Don't misunderstand. The past is important. It teaches us a great deal about who we are and where we want and don't want to go. It contains our memories, pleasant and painful, and our personal and collective histories. But the past is fixed, beyond our power to reach or change. If we don't learn from it, it's been said, we're doomed to repeat it. No matter how pleasant our memories of the past may be, persistent repetition of them without forward motion and fresh, new, challenging goals will cause us to stagnate. People who hold too tightly to the past can't reach out to embrace the future. As George Eliot wrote, "It's no good you'll do watering last year's crops."

The present, on the other hand, is your doorway to the future. In today are the seeds of tomorrow, so affirm all your goals in the present tense, or your tomorrows will look like yesterday.

2. Affirmations are phrased positively. Your affirmations should describe what you want to be and do, not what you *don't* want or are trying to change. Instead of saying "I never miss an exercise class," say something such as, "I keep my exercise commitments." Instead of "I don't have the desire to smoke cigarettes" or "I no longer lose my temper when my children misbehave," try "I am proud of being fully committed to breathing only clean air," or "I remain calm and reasonable with my children, because I love them and want to set a good example."

Why is this so important? Remember that the language we use, to ourselves (self-talk) and to others, automatically triggers images or pictures in our minds. These pictures, in turn, cause emotions. It's hard to avoid creating a picture of yourself smoking when you use the words "desire to smoke cigarettes." You almost have to see yourself doing it when you say the words "lose my temper." The words themselves create the undesirable image. What you're doing, in effect, is affirming the problem, perpetuating current reality.

On the other hand, when you deliberately use positive language, you trigger positive images and positive emotions. You're affirming the solution rather than the problem, the end result rather than current reality. To make sure you're doing this, first imagine the problem or the behavior you want to change. Then ask yourself, "What will it look like when the problem is completely fixed? How will I behave when I no longer do this?" Describe *that* picture in your affirmation.

Here's a scenario: You have high standards, and that's fine. But you also have a tendency to routinely criticize other people's behavior, and it's causing some problems. Your kids say you're always picking on them, and they're starting to avoid you. Your spouse tells you she feels the same way. At first, you deny it. Now you realize, with some discomfort, that there's truth in what they say. As you think about it, you wonder how your critical behavior might be connected to the conditioning you received from your own overly critical parents. In any event, you decide you want to change. You consciously set an end-result goal of becoming a much less critical person. Your short-term, much more specific, and easily tracked goal is to genuinely praise each of your family members at least three times every day.

In this case, which would be the more effective affirmation?

"I no longer harshly criticize my family members," or "Because I love my family and want to build their self-esteem, I notice and appreciate their many talents, abilities, and positive personality traits on a daily basis." See what I mean? The second one contains the loving, appreciative, behavior-specific images you want. The picture called up by the first one just perpetuates the problem.

3. Affirmations are brief. Your affirmations are goal statements that declare a new truth about how things are going to be in the future. They help you say, very clearly, to yourself, "*This* is the way I want my life to be." "*This* is the way I want to look." "*This* is the way I want to relate to my spouse." "*This* is the way I want to feel when I wake up in the morning." "*This* is how I want to handle pressure at work." "*This* is how I want to treat my children." "*This* is how I want my home to look."

A one- or two-sentence statement, as opposed to a paragraph or page, provides a manageable definition that is easy to visualize and incorporate into your daily routine. Remember, it isn't the writing so much as the process of repeated visualization that will cause the changes you seek. So it's essential that each goal you affirm be described simply, clearly, and concisely.

You don't have to limit yourself to just one brief affirmation per goal. Some goals will naturally be more complex than others and may call for several affirmations, each addressing a particular aspect. For example, a long-term goal of optimal health and fitness may mean one affirmation for attending a weight-training class, one for regular cardiovascular or aerobic conditioning activities, one for maintaining a healthful diet and good nutrition, perhaps another for a daily meditation period, and one more for supporting the writing and use of your affirmations themselves.

If your overall goal is to improve the quantity and quality of your personal relationships, you could write one "umbrella" affirmation, such as "I am receptive and friendly toward everyone I meet. I treat everyone with consideration, attentiveness, and respect."

But you might want to add several others to address particular areas or subgoals. For example, "I am kind and patient with my mother, even when I disagree with her opinions." Or "I stop what I'm doing and listen carefully when my children talk to me." Or "I enjoy being the first person to offer a greeting and comfortably initiate conversation with people I'd like to get to know better."

4. Affirmations put you wholeheartedly into an experience. Remember the formula I x V = R (Imagination times Vividness equals Reality—to the subconscious)? We have now reached the point where use of that formula will be critical. At the end of this chapter, I'm going to suggest to you a daily routine that will help ensure the most effective use of your affirmations. As you go through that routine day after day, it's important to realize that simple repetition alone is not enough. If you just repeat your goals by rote, without real conviction and vivid sensory and emotional detail, you won't be doing yourself any good.

When you repeat your affirmations, you want to create a kind of "virtual reality" in your mind that is almost as vivid and lifelike as the real thing—a reality that has you at its center. Only then will your subconscious experience and record it as if it were actually happening. Only then will you create the cognitive dissonance, and therefore the energy and drive, you want. So check to make sure your affirmations are written in richly descriptive language.

See the colors, feel the textures, smell the aromas, hear the sounds. Make these imaginary experiences so vivid that you experience a positive emotional response to them. Practice writing and visualizing vivid, sensuous, richly detailed descriptions of the goals to which you are committed until you're satisfied with the results.

The importance of this positive emotional response can't be overemphasized. If your affirmation states that you feel happy and energized, *feel* those feelings as you repeat the words. If it says that you feel proud, *feel* proud. If it says that you really enjoy doing something, summon up a genuine feeling of enjoyment as you affirm it. If you have difficulty calling up the appropriate feelings on the spot, the "flick back, flick up" technique that follows these guidelines will make it easier for you.

5. *Affirmations are specific.* We've just talked about the importance of including sensory details. This need for detail is so important, it deserves to be set apart. If your subconscious is going to record the achieved goal as if it were reality, you need to provide it with the details of reality.

If you affirm "I am a strong leader," or "I am a friendly person," you are partway there. But you want to go farther. What are the characteristics of a strong leader? How should one behave when demonstrating strength? Is strength all that's needed in order to be an effective, strong leader? What behaviors could be considered friendly? Spell them out. How about smiling and maintaining good eye contact? Asking questions that demonstrate interest and listening attentively to the answers? Initiating conversations? What is the body language of a friendly person? Write affirmations that incorporate the behaviors you want to adopt.

Vague, nonspecific affirmations are like going into a restaurant and saying "Please bring me some food" or booking an airplane flight to "the West coast." What you get may not be acceptable because you weren't clear about what you wanted. Concrete, detailed affirmations, on the other hand, are like saying, "Bring me the roast chicken, rice pilaf instead of potatoes, small Caesar salad, no bread, and a glass of iced tea with a lemon wedge." Now the waiter knows exactly what you want, and you get it.

The same principle holds true when a group is setting goals together. It doesn't matter whether it's a corporation, a work group, a class of students, or a family. Imagine trying to work with other people to achieve an end result of "a clean house" or "a good sales year" or "better attendance in school." Each group member will have a different ideas of what "clean" or "good" or "better" means, and everyone will be working to bring their own, unique vision into reality. The result, as you can imagine, is a group working at cross-purposes—confusion, turf-building/protection, big wastes of time and energy, resentment, and, very often, chaos.

That's why, when my company goes into an organization to help them improve their quality and productivity, we begin by gathering information and building consensus about current reality. Later, there's a critical strategic vision-building process that creates a clear, specific common vision, including desired end results, short- and long-term goals, and accountabilities. Everyone involved has a voice in creating affirmations to support these agreed-upon goals. At that point, everyone has a crystal clear picture of exactly what they're aiming at as a group and what their individual roles are in making it happen.

6. *Affirmations are realistic.* Only you can decide what's realistic for you. If you can vividly see and feel yourself in a new reality, then it's realistic. If you can't, add a few subgoals. Can you imagine asking a kindergartner how it will feel when he's in college? You might as well ask how it will feel on the moon, because what you'll get will be pure fantasy. Similarly, if you're sixty pounds overweight at age forty-five, it may be difficult for you to visualize yourself as slim as you were at seventeen. You may have no trouble, though, seeing yourself one dress size smaller. That's what your affirmations and visualizations should focus on, for now. Once you're close to achieving that goal, you can begin to see and feel yourself moving ahead to the next step.

The trick is to visualize and affirm your goal close enough to current reality so that you can see yourself experiencing it, but not so close that you lose your motivation and drive. When I left high school teaching, I couldn't imagine myself living or thinking the way I do now. It would have been too far out of my comfort zone, much too unrealistic. Because I grew up in poverty, thinking of myself living a life of prosperity was, at first, a stretch and a half for me. When we took the plunge into our new business, Diane and I had $1,000 in the bank, and that seemed like a lot. We also had nine adopted and foster children, a stack of bills, and big butterflies flapping in our stomachs. I set a goal to double my teaching income. I could see myself doing that much, because I had unshakable faith in our ability to work hard, in the value of the information we were sharing, and, above all, in God, with whom we had and still have a strong working partnership.

As time passed and I became more and more successful at using the techniques I was teaching, my goals became larger and farther out. It felt less difficult for me to take some pretty big leaps in my personal development, as well as in our company's. These days, I have a hard time imagining limits to how far I can grow or to the size and scope of the projects I'm willing to take on. Sure, there are limits to my physical abilities, and, like you, some days I feel them tugging at me more than others. But I believe that full achievement of my intellectual, spiritual, emotional, human potential is always going to be just outside my grasp. Until the day I die, perhaps even afterward, there will always be room and reason for me to grow.

I want you to know my story, just as I want you to know the other true stories I've been telling, because what we have done, you can do, too. I want you to see where I came from, where I am today, and the process I used to get there, because that process is the key to what I've been able to achieve. I can go anywhere in the world, talk comfortably with anyone in the world. I enjoy a bountiful, satisfying lifestyle because I have used and still use the information I'm sharing with you. I expand my comfort zones, set and achieve goals that are in reach, bounce back from adversity and failure (I know plenty about what it's like to fail). I use the incredible power of my conscious and subconscious mind to make change feel like an adventure instead of a threat. I refuse to accept the circumstances of my early childhood as the defining boundaries of my existence. I choose to be my own authority when it comes to my life, my future, what I can or can't do, and my capacity to grow.

You are your own authority when it comes to what's realistic for you. That means that you don't simply accept the judgments of other people who want to define your capabilities and your reality. You don't look at yourself through other people's scotomas. You are your own judge, and you know that trial and error is a way to learn. You also know that there's something to be said for biting off a little more than you're absolutely certain you can chew.

7. Affirmations make no comparisons. There will always be people who are more advanced than you are in some areas of development, just as there will always be others who haven't come as far. There will always be people who have more and do more than you and those who have less and do less. Comparisons aren't useful in your strategy for personal growth, except as you compare yourself to yourself, to how you used to be or how you want to be in the future. The need to compete with others ("I want a bigger, prettier house than theirs!" "I want our kids to go to a better school than their kids." "I want to make twice as much money as he makes.") often points toward shaky self-esteem, the need to prove something, to be one up on someone. Competition with self, on the other hand, indicates an expanding spirit.

A fiercely competitive "us-against-you" spirit can mean the winning edge if you're on a team playing against another team or a soldier going into combat. In that kind of situation, an adversarial relationship encourages a confident "attack" mentality that says, "Our side is better than yours, and we're going to prove it!" Away from the playing field or the battlefield, though, this kind of thinking can do more harm than good. Competing against other family members can fuel resentment and conflict. Competing against friends and neighbors often creates friction and resentment. Employees competing against each other within a company breeds mistrust in an environment where cooperation and openness are essential.

Your achievements need to be uniquely yours, made for your own reasons, not anyone else's. Besides, you may have enough *internal* competition going on to make things interesting, even rough. You may be listening to self-talk that says, "I can't. I'm not good enough, not strong enough, not smart enough." You may have old habits and attitudes that have become deeply ingrained, scotomas to bust, comfort zones to expand. You may have doubts and fears and worries that are keeping you smaller than you want to be. Don't *drain* your power and energy by comparing yourself to others. *Gain* power by comparing where you are now with where you want to be.

That doesn't mean that you don't look at and learn from others. But when you notice other people who are farther along than you are in some way, don't compete. Study them. Identify what you admire, what you'd like to see more of in yourself. Then set a goal to incorporate it into your own style, your own agenda, your own life.

I believe that I'm a good teacher and public speaker, but I wasn't born that way and I'm continually working to improve. When I started out in my business, I wasn't competing with anyone, but I was wide open for input from people from whom I could learn. So I studied Jack Benny for his timing and Bill Cosby for the way he can be funny without making fun of anyone. I studied Sir Winston Churchill and Billy Graham for their ability to engage an audience. I watched flamenco dancers who could draw your eyes to their hands, and I studied Tai Chi to learn something of its language of grace and control. I even studied French cabaret singers, though the only French I know is *oui*, because I was fascinated by their impact and expressiveness.

I do this in other areas of life, too. When I see someone who strikes me as special—especially admirable or highly effective—I pay attention. "I like that," I think. "Do I want to be more like that?" If the answer is yes, I create goals and affirmations that will help me do it. But I don't compare myself to these people, and I don't put myself down because I'm not as accomplished or skillful or talented as they are.

The only person in the world I want to be better than is me. I want to be a better husband, father, grandfather, friend, teacher, leader, citizen, servant of God. I want to be more creative, more interested and more interesting, more loving, more effective as a peacemaker and educator. If you or anyone has learned something that will help me do and be these things, I don't want to compete with you for it. I want your cooperation. I want you to be a model, a mentor, a teacher, an example, a resource. Isn't that what you want, too? Keep this in mind the next time you're around people who seem to have come a bit farther down the road than you have.

8. *Affirmations help you honor your word to yourself.* Affirmations and visualizations can't work for you if desire and commitment are missing. If you don't care much about achieving your goals, don't bother to write them or visualize them. Without a strong spirit of intent supporting and driving them, you'll be wasting time. Words without commitment and truth backing them are verbal static. Without truly reflecting your head and heart, whenever you speak them they will diminish your credibility, in your own eyes and in the sight of others.

It takes time and experience to get wise to ourselves and our own unconscious games. When you set a goal and are regularly affirming and visualizing it but still seeing no results, it's a cue to look inside yourself and ask some tough questions. Is this goal something you really want, or is it something you think you should want? Is it coming from within yourself or from pressure other people are exerting? Are you committed to doing it, to the work, time, and energy it will take? Or do you expect it to happen more or less all by itself, without any undue effort on your part?

As you continue to refine your affirmations, you'll stop using words you're not sure you mean. And when you give your word to someone else or to yourself, you'll take it seriously. Your credibility will be so high that when you affirm something, your words will have enormous impact. And you'll take your promises to yourself just as seriously as you take the ones you make to others. If you want to coach, mentor, and inspire others, there's nothing more important.

Flick Back, Flick Up

It isn't always easy to imagine feeling confident and comfortable in new situations. It isn't always easy to invest our affirmations with the emotional intensity they need to be effective. The flick back, flick up technique can help at those times. Here's how it works.

Let's say you're preparing to give a talk to a large group of people you've never met. Public speaking has always made your knees knock and your heart pound. It's definitely outside your comfort zone, so you've set a goal to deliver a logical, convincing, high-impact presentation. You are affirming your confidence, comfort, and poise, but you're having trouble summoning up feelings to go with the words.

Using the flick back, flick up technique, you simply review your past for occasions when you felt comfortable, confident, and poised talking to someone—anyone at all. The image that comes to you is one of you and your best friend talking. You feel comfortable, free-flowing, relaxed. You can easily visualize that experience, and it feels just like you want to feel in the intimidating situation. So you put yourself into the past for a few moments (flick back), inviting the memory of that confident, comfortable feeling into your mind and body. Then, you change your mental picture to the new situation (flick up), holding on to those feelings, and create an appropriate affirmation: "It's as easy for me to talk to a large group of strangers as it is for me to talk with my best friend."

Putting Your Affirmations to Work

Once you have written out your short- and long-term goals, decided how you'll track your progress, and created written affirmations to help you experience yourself behaving in new ways, what's next? It's time to put your affirmations and visualizations to work for you. Here are my suggestions for how to do it:

1. *Twice a day, every day.* Make the affirmation process a regular, twice-daily part of your life, like brushing your teeth, only more fun.

It doesn't take long. Each session should only take a few minutes, depending on how many affirmations you're currently making.

Try spending about 30 seconds on each if they're about changing your attitudes or habits or enhancing character traits you already have. Plan on taking a little more time if you're working on external changes, such as a new income level, or on changes that are complex. Between 3 and 15 minutes per session is about average. I usually have between 25 and 30 affirmations that I am visualizing on any given day, so it takes me about 30 minutes. I recommend that you develop a routine and, if possible, repeat the process at about the same times every day.

Morning and evening seem to work best. When you do it doesn't matter as much as developing a regular time and place and giving the process your undivided attention. Arrange for privacy and quiet, and choose a time and place that will allow you to work with your affirmations without interruption.

2. Read, picture, feel. Record all of your affirmations on 3 x 5 cards, in your daily journal, in a computer file, or anywhere that gives you easy access. Read the first affirmation and picture the images the words evoke. Hear the sounds, smell the smells, taste the tastes. Feel the emotions that accompany these images, and imagine all of it as if it were happening to you right now. Again, it should take no more than 20 or 30 seconds to complete this process for each affirmation.

As you visualize, imagine the scenario from the same perspective you'd have normally. That is, you won't see yourself as if you were in a movie, but you'll see the event as if your eyes were the lens of the camera. If your affirmation is "I'm as comfortable talking in front of a large group as I am talking with my best friend," you'll repeat those words. Then, you'll visualize yourself easily and comfortably giving a talk in front of a large group. You won't see yourself from the audience's point of view. Instead, you'll see the audience, the podium in front of you, the sides and back of the room, etc.

3. Repeat to imprint. This process of incorporating imagined images into your subconscious version of reality, or "imprinting" as it is sometimes called, takes time. As a rule, it requires many repetitions, sometimes several hundred, before the goal makes "a take" in your subconscious and your internal picture changes. Once it does, it is recorded firmly and solidly, not easily erased. So don't be discouraged if you don't see change happening immediately—it's worth the wait and the persistent effort. Sometimes, though, you'll see significant changes almost immediately.

Remember, it's the dissonance, the discrepancy you're causing by changing your beliefs about reality, that generates the drive and energy to close the gap. So, when you open your eyes after visualizing and affirming the new, and you see yourself surrounded by the old, don't be surprised if you feel out of kilter. Now that you're changing on the inside, now that you've repeatedly visualized something new, you're going to feel dissatisfied with the old. The wider the gap or discrepancy between the two, the greater the discontent you're likely to feel. It's that discontent, the sense that things aren't right, that will energize you to make the pictures match.

Sound like work? Absolutely. But it's some of the best work you'll ever do. It helps you to stop feeling like a victim and start feeling capable and powerful. It helps you to develop self-discipline and self-control, two old-fashioned sounding qualities that may be more essential in the late '90s and beyond than ever before. It helps you to enjoy more meaningful, satisfying relationships and a more relaxed, harmonious family life. And it helps you to respond to the stream of everyday events with accountability, adaptability, resiliency, and integrity.

Sometimes Once Is Enough

It is certainly possible to affirm something with such power and determination that once is all it takes. Have you ever made an affirmation, a vow like that? Perhaps a positive vow in negative circumstances? Do you remember Scarlett O'Hara in *Gone With the Wind*, digging in the desolate fields of post-war Tara for a few stunted vegetables to feed her family and saying, "I swear, as God is my witness, I will never go hungry again!"

She didn't know much about how to create a positively worded affirmation, but Scarlett's will was so strong and her vision so powerful that it didn't matter. Her inner picture of what was good enough for her was so unshakable that even when the war brought her life crashing down around her, current reality didn't stand a chance.

I still remember the vow I made after my father died and my grandfather turned his back on us when we desperately needed help. "I'll never, ever be like him," I swore. "No matter what, I'll always take care of my family and be there for them!" I didn't know anything about affirmations then, but I knew I would keep my word to myself, because I'd seen too many broken promises, and I would lose self-respect if I didn't.

So don't lock on to the idea that change always has to take a long time. When your spirit of intent is strong and your commitment absolute, a single, one time affirmation can cause you to change forever, just like that. Marriage vows, for example, are made in a moment but can change the behavior of two people for a lifetime!

For most of us, most of the time, though, change happens gradually, in increments, so be patient with your efforts and persist in them. After the one time affirmation of the vows, a marriage relationship will require many compromises, adjustments, and personal changes by both partners over a long period if they intend to live out their vows.

What If You Can't Visualize?

Some people find it easier to visualize than others, simply because they have more practice doing it or because they are naturally more visually oriented. Others have great difficulty seeing things in their mind's eye, particularly if they have a physiological impairment. If you think your predominant mode of perception or learning is more auditory (hearing-centered) than visual, try concentrating on the sounds of your affirmations.

Hear yourself adjusting the microphone, the soft hum of the air conditioner in the room, your words flowing smoothly and expressively, the laughter at your jokes, the clapping as the audience enthusiastically applauds your talk. Listen to the thumping rubber-soled shoes of your aerobics class pounding the wood floor, hear the instructor calling out the moves, your own heart pounding, the puff and whoosh of your breathing.

If you believe that your predominant mode of learning or perception may be kinesthetic (having to do with movement), pay special attention to the orientation of your body as you imagine yourself in your affirmation. Focus on feelings, both emotional and physical, and on your sense of touch far more than on sights or sounds.

If you have trouble visualizing but have no idea why, try shifting your focus to any of your other senses while you imagine the affirmation's scenario. Pay attention to the feelings you experience. If you can generate a greater emotional reaction while focusing on sounds, stick with sounds. If aromas do it for you, pay attention to what your nose knows. Your object is emotional response, not strict adherence to a formula.

Sample Affirmations

Following is a list of affirmations that may be helpful as you learn to write your own. Some will seem to best fit your work situation, some focus on your personal life, others may apply to both. If they feel right, please use them, adjusting my language until it sounds like something you would say.

- I like and respect myself because I am a worthy, capable, and valuable person.
- I enjoy my life and my warm relationships with other people.
- I have a positive expectancy of success in all I do, and I see all setbacks as temporary.
- I take pride in my performance and enjoy doing my best in every situation.

- I express myself clearly, and I know that others respect my point of view.
- I look for ways to praise and support myself and others.
- I am effective and efficient, especially in stressful situations.
- I take full accountability for the results of all my decisions and actions.
- I take time to enjoy my successes and reward myself for accomplishing my goals.
- When it comes to my own life, I am the expert, and I accept only positive, constructive feedback from others.
- It's easy for me to demonstrate warmth and love to my family in ways that are meaningful to them.
- I am firm yet fair with those I supervise, and I enjoy helping them to bring out the best in themselves.
- Because I am well organized and efficient, I achieve a great deal on a daily basis and am proud of my accomplishments.
- I quietly do helpful, meaningful things for others without expecting anything in return. The good feeling I get is ample reward!
- I have an excellent memory with clear and easy recall.
- I am fair and just in dealing with all people.
- I am an attentive listener, and I value what others have to say.
- It's easy and fun to write and visualize my affirmations twice a day, every day.
- I enjoy making my affirmations daily because of the positive results I get.
- Because I sincerely care about my customers as people, I enjoy helping them fulfill their wants and needs.
- I feel calm and relaxed in potentially stressful situations, and I see all challenges as opportunities.
- Continuous improvement is a way of life for me. I am always looking for ways to grow both personally and professionally.
- I enjoy living a healthy lifestyle because of the energy and feeling of self-empowerment it gives me.
- I am an optimist. I expect the best from the future, appreciate what I have today, and use the past to learn and grow from.

PART TWO

Coaching and Mentoring Others

Introduction

By far, most of the successful people I've known have had the benefit of at least one coaching or mentoring relationship. When the subject comes up, they are invariably eager to talk about their experiences, because it brings back such good feelings. Some of these relationships lasted much longer than others and some were far more influential, but all of them were important and, at their best, truly inspirational. In my experience, coaching and mentoring represent a progression, something like this:

We begin with a strong foundation of personal mastery, the basics of which were covered in Part One. We can't effectively help others to grow until we have become good at growing ourselves. Coaching, an activity that often focuses on building specific skills, is the next step—moving beyond ourselves to share what we've learned with others. Taken one step further, mentoring expands and deepens the helping process, encompassing larger areas of our personal and professional lives.

But what exactly is a mentor?

Many people think that good mentoring is simply a matter of being a role model, but there's more to it than that. Role models are wonderful, especially when they model personal virtues as well as success. They're generally well-known people who shine for us like distant stars, saying, in effect, "Look at me. I rose to the top, I made it. So can you!" We may have some things in common with them, such as a childhood lived in poverty, a physical disability, or a particular talent, skill, or ability. We may even adopt their clothing or hairstyles as our own, hoping that some of whatever they have that makes them so special will rub off on us—that we can narrow the gap between where *we* are and where *they* are.

Like distant stars, though, role models aren't usually people we can get close to. If they're famous, we can go to the library and read their biographies, and maybe we'll feel motivated to emulate them even more as a result. We can watch them on TV or in the movies, read about them in magazines or in textbooks in school. Still, no matter how much we know about them, they are seldom in a position to know anything about us and what makes us unique.

This distance between us is one of the reasons why role models are far less effective than coaches or mentors when it comes to influencing our behavior and inspiring us to achieve our highest potential. Another reason is that, while watching someone else model success for us is useful, if we can't see the behaviors that got them there, and, most importantly, if we can't see *ourselves* being and doing those things, no meaningful or lasting change in us is going to take place.

What does a good mentor do that a role model doesn't? Think about it for a moment. Who have your best mentors been? What did they do for you? I'm willing to bet that they were people who could see more in you than you were able to see yourself at the time. They saw you not only as you were, but also as you could be. They had a vision for you that was probably bigger than any you had for yourself. They weren't blind to your shortcomings and flaws, but they didn't focus on them. Instead, they helped you believe in your own strength, ability, and potential for growth. They inspired you and helped you to see possibilities for your life that you may not have seen without them.

Because your mentors had credibility in your eyes, you gave sanction to their visions. Then, whether you did it out loud or silently in your thoughts, your self-talk followed suit: "Yes, that *is* possible for me. I *could* do that. I *am* like that." Your beliefs about yourself changed, and you began to act like it.

Great coaches and mentors are so unshakably convinced that we have great things in us—their vision of what is possible for us is so clear and powerful—that they wind up convincing us, too.

Mentors can be virtually anyone—parents or grandparents, older brothers and sisters, teachers, neighbors, favorite aunts or uncles, supervisors or employers, members of the clergy, professional counselors, even colleagues or friends. We can have more than one mentor at a time, and we can be mentor to more than one person at a time. Our mentor may be older, younger, or the same age as we are, though traditionally a mentor is older and wiser. He or she may be the same gender, race, or ethnicity—or not. Who our mentors are isn't important, except in terms of their character, but the importance of what they do can't be stressed enough.

All of us need encouragement to stretch and grow, to go for our dreams, sometimes to allow ourselves to dream at all. We need support as we learn to be confident of our decision-making capabilities, and we need guidance as we take risks that may or may not bring success. We need to be around people who believe in us so that we can more fully believe in ourselves. This enduring belief in our own capabilities, more than anything else, is the gift that mentors give. What better way to give back to the world than to become mentors in turn?

Part One was designed to help you raise your self-esteem, boost your self-efficacy, and achieve higher levels of happiness and fulfillment. Part Two presents the information that will enable you to become a highly effective mentor or coach. It focuses on how to use what you know to help others grow. What you'll learn will work equally well no matter who you are mentoring: It will be useful whether you're grooming an employee to become a manager, taking an apprentice under your wing, or coaching a Little League player on the way to a great career. If you have children or grandchildren or are working in some capacity with young people, all the concepts you'll read about will be helpful, but those in Chapter 11 will have special value.

Even if you're not currently coaching or mentoring anyone and never expect to do so, Part Two will enable you to gain fresh insights into all of your relationships. It will help you talk and listen to others in ways that strengthen the trust between you. And it will help you talk to yourself in ways that enrich the most important mentoring relationship you'll ever have—the one that goes on all the time, whether you know it or not, with yourself.

CHAPTER SEVEN

The Mentoring Relationship: Does It Work? What's in It for You?

Why Coach or Mentor?

T he value of a coaching or mentoring relationship for the person being mentored (the protégé) is obvious. At every stage of personal and professional growth, effective mentoring has a positive, facilitative effect. In the following diagram, the actions described in the circle are based on the processes discussed in Part One, and are carried on continuously. As shown, mentoring can be introduced at any point in the process.

> "It is high time that the ideal of success should be replaced by the ideal of service. . . .
> Only a life lived for others is worthwhile."
>
> Albert Einstein

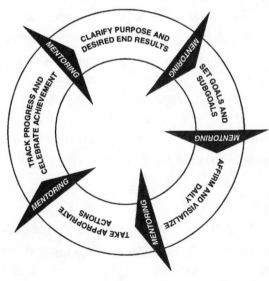

From the protégé's point of view, mentoring is clearly a great deal. Among the benefits are learning the ropes from someone who's been there, one-on-one coaching by an expert, increased self-efficacy and self-esteem, improved levels of goal achievement, sound advice, and continuing support and guidance from someone who genuinely cares. But what's the payoff for the coach or mentor? Why should anyone want to commit a significant outlay of their precious time and energy to helping someone else grow? Here's how I see it:

- **Enhanced self-esteem**

    It feels good to be recognized as someone with something to teach, something worthwhile to give. Have you ever asked someone for their opinion or advice and found them unwilling to give it or offended that you asked? Probably not, because it boosts our self-esteem when others seek out and benefit from our thinking and experience. When someone wants our guidance, it suggests that we are admired and respected. If it's clear that we aren't being flattered to serve some hidden agenda, we enjoy the feeling.

- **Fulfillment of your own developmental needs**

    As psychologist Erik Erikson pointed out, the developmental challenge for people in their middle or later years is one of generativity: They want to leave part of themselves as a legacy for the next generation. Perhaps this longing to influence the future is another aspect of our almost universal desire to have our lives mean something beyond the boundaries of our own personal existence. Perhaps it's the natural consequence of feeling ourselves drawing closer to death. In any event, it's a wonderful way to reinforce the link between past and future generations and to keep our sense of our connectedness active and alive.

- **Giving back**

    For those of us who have known the great blessing of having someone who was willing to be there for us when we needed it, someone who saw something special in us and helped us to stretch and grow, the desire to give back is strong. Deliberate, thoughtful, selfless mentoring of another person is a fitting and very satisfying way to express your gratitude and pass the blessing along.

- **Revitalized interest in your own development**

   Socrates once said that "we teach what we need to learn." In a vital, active, ongoing mentoring relationship, you may find your assumptions and beliefs challenged, your energy renewed, your mind doing fresh work with old ideas. Preston Munter, professor of psychiatry at Harvard Law School, thinks that very often a mentor exchanges wisdom for creative energy. In my own experience with mentoring high-performance people, I find myself relishing the exchange of ideas and stimulated by the task of articulating my beliefs and experiences in an clear, interesting, relevant way.

- **Increased self-awareness**

   The mentoring relationship is, by its very nature, a close and personal one. It is also a helping relationship that poses, if you take it seriously, some important questions that can enable you to expand your own self-awareness. (I am indebted to psychologist Carl Rogers for his thoughts on the dynamics of helping relationships, which I have adapted for our purposes here.)[1]

Are you secure enough to be open and honest with your protégé about who you are? Are there some aspects of your past or present life that you are unwilling to share? If so, what are they, and why do you keep them private? Are you willing to share failures as well as successes? Mistakes as well as smart moves? Tragedies as well as triumphs?

Are you willing to allow your protégé to be and express who she or he really is, even if that is very different from who you are? Can you be comfortable with those differences instead of threatened by them? Is the value of diversity something to which you pay lip service, or can you live it out?

Do you feel that your protégé must follow your advice and conform to your standards of behavior? Do you think that he should mold himself after you? Be dependent on you? Make no important moves without consulting you?

Can you honor and attend to your own feelings and needs at the same time you honor and attend to hers? Can you say no to unreasonable requests for your time, energy, or assistance, firmly but gently?

Can you be honest with yourself if certain aspects of your protégé's personality or character provoke your envy or disapproval?

Can you avoid judging your protégé as a person, and do you fully accept that the control of and accountability for who he is and what he does is his alone?

Can you be sensitive enough not to communicate judgment in your body language, tone of voice, or facial expression, even when you are avoiding it in words?

Can you see your protégé as a whole person, unfinished and in the process of becoming, rather than someone who "is" a certain way, fixed and unchanging?

Finally, can you allow your protégé to struggle through a crisis or transition without your having to take the wheel and provide solutions or answers? Can you confirm and validate her capability for creative inner development and ability to learn and grow from all of life's experiences?

Of course, not every mentor is going to approach the experience from this high level of self-examination. Sometimes, mentoring relationships just happen, without thinking much about it. And sometimes they work very well that way, particularly when the people involved are operating from a relatively high degree of self-awareness. But I believe that when you increase the amount and quality of consciousness you bring to an activity or a relationship—any relationship—its quality will inevitably improve. By consciousness, I mean a deliberate and deep awareness of what is going on with self and others; thoughtful articulation of purpose, goals, needs, and desires; commitment to frequent, open, honest communication; and a strong, even passionate commitment to the relationship and to the well-being, growth, and development of both people in it.

Consciousness may also mean awareness and acknowledgment of your sense that something has gone wrong; that communication is no longer frequent, open, and honest; that commitment has faltered. In that case, there may be need for a discussion of what it would take to repair the damage and whether such repair is mutually desired. It may even mean terminating the relationship. But it is far better to do so consciously, with as much understanding and control as possible, than by a rift or a puzzling drift apart that leaves a residue of rancor or self-doubt behind.

I hope I've convinced you, not only that mentoring is a worthwhile and satisfying endeavor for both parties, but also that it is best done with carefully considered intentions and a high degree of consciousness. Now, let's move ahead and look at the mentoring process itself—how it evolved, what it is, how it works, what makes a mentor credible, and some specific ways that you can use the material presented in Part One to help you help coach, mentor, and inspire others to greatness.

A Nutshell History of Mentoring

Everyone needs a helping hand from time to time. Sometimes we seek out that help, sometimes it comes unbidden, and sometimes we have to manage without it. The quality and quantity of the help we receive can make a great difference, for better or worse, in our lives. This has certainly been true for me. There are many kinds of helping relationships. Parent-child, doctor-patient, counselor-client, teacher-student, older-younger sibling, clergy-parishioner, friend-friend, to name just a few. But while all of these, at least when they are at their best, involve one person helping another, not all involve coaching or mentoring.

The mentoring relationship is a special way of helping that has ancient roots and modern offshoots. Mentoring is probably as old as human civilization, but perhaps the most well-known historical mentoring takes place in Homer's *Odyssey*. Around 1200 B.C., as Odysseus, king of Ithaca, was getting ready to leave home for the Trojan War, he asked his wise and trusted counselor, Mentor, to serve as protector and guardian to his household. During the ten long years it took for Odysseus to finally return home, Mentor becomes teacher, adviser, friend, and surrogate father to Odysseus' young son.

There was nothing unusual about a long-term mentoring relationship in ancient Greece. Close family friends or relatives were routinely paired with young males in an attempt to provide ongoing personal guidance and a worthy model to emulate. Similarly, both informally and through the guilds that began in the Middle Ages, professional "masters" with a high degree of expertise in a particular craft or trade took on young apprentices. These youngsters, who were often chosen because they had demonstrated a particular talent or interest, became part of the master's household for many years, with the goal of eventually becoming masters themselves. In many cases, they took over the master's business when he retired. If he died, the apprentice often married the widow and assumed responsibility for the household.

Since the mid-1970s, formal, structured corporate mentoring programs, particularly in large organizations but more and more frequently in medium and smaller ones, have become fairly common. As businesses become increasingly complex, competition more intense, and cost containment critically important, mentoring offers an appealing, inexpensive way to help develop skilled workers and managers. Formal, facilitated mentoring programs have also been widely and effectively used in the fields of education and social service for some time.

Does Mentoring Work?

Absolutely. From a myriad of professions, vocations, and avocations—medicine, law, business, politics, art, architecture, music, writing, education, psychology, social work, sports, the military, and many others—a wealth of testimony supports the idea that mentoring has great value for both mentor and protégé. In *Beyond the Myths and Magic of Mentoring*, Margo Murray says:

> A list of those who publicly acknowledge the value of their mentoring relationships resembles a Who's Who of the professions, business, sports, arts, and social activism. . . . No matter how minimal or extensive, this individual attention almost always had positive results for the protégé, such as increased professional recognition or job effectiveness. For the mentor, a sense of accomplishment came from having made a contribution to the growth of another human being.[2]

If you're doubtful or need more proof of mentoring's effectiveness, spend some time at the library, as I did while researching this book. Here is a small sampling of what I found.

- Several major insurance companies, including industry giant Cigna, are using mentoring programs to improve their new agent retention rates. They expect these programs to also help them lower new agent development costs and maximize the leverage of existing agency resources. (*Edward M. Berube, "Mentoring Is One Approach to Agent Retention Issue," Best's Review, Life-Health Insurance Edition, January 1996, vol. 96 no. 9, p. 82-3*)
- At the Douglas Aircraft Company, a structured mentoring program is an important part of its culture. The aircraft manufacturer is convinced that mentoring can help develop a better pool of managerial talent and technical jobs, and that it can be an effective means of spreading knowledge

throughout the entire organization. (*Adrianne H. Geiger-DuMond and Susan K. Boyle*, "Mentoring Takes Off at Douglas Aircraft Company," *Management Decision, September 1996, vol. 34 no. 5, p. 35*)

- Among guidelines presented in the journal *Human Resource Management* for firms that are downsizing, mentoring is cited as an effective means of assisting early career employees better manage their careers. (*Daniel C. Feldman*, "Managing Careers in Downsizing Firms," *Human Resource Management, Summer 1996, vol. 35 no. 2, p. 145*)
- A study reported in the *Journal of Management Studies* states that career-oriented mentoring has a significant positive relationship to number of promotions received and career satisfaction. (*Samuel Aryee, Thomas Wyatt, and Raymond Stone*, "Early Career Outcomes of Graduate Employees: The Effect of Mentoring and Ingratiation," *Journal of Management Studies, January 1996, vol. 33, p. 95*)
- A mentoring program at the University of Miami that pairs students up with real-world business men and women is getting overwhelmingly positive results. Now in its fifth year, more than 200 students participated in 1995. (*Allison Turner*, "Mentor Program Introduces Students to Life in Real Business World," *South Florida Business Journal, July 22, 1994, vol. 14 no. 48, p. 15A*)
- "Mentoring Drives Productivity Higher," says the title of an article published in *Managers Magazine*. It goes on to say that among salespeople followed by this three-year-long study, sales to both new and existing clients were higher for those who had mentors. (*Tod A. Silverheart*, "It Works: Mentoring Drives Productivity Higher," *Managers Magazine, October 1994, vol. 69 no. 10, p. 14*)
- Professional builders can keep their upper and lower management personnel from the attacks of corporate headhunters through fostering personal mentoring relationships, according

to *Professional Builder* magazine. (*William H. Lurz*, "How to Keep Corporate Raiders Away from Your Best People," *Professional Builder, December 1994, vol. 59 no. 13, p. 33*)

- Symbiosis Corporation, a medical products firm, offers a program that fosters loyalty and productivity through pairing employees with mentors. (*John H. Sheridan*, "Mentors Build Morale," *Industry Week, June 19, 1995, vol. 244 no. 12, p. 82*)
- Mentors have always played a significant role in the preservation of the stability of the electric utilities. Women managers in this industry consider the practice of mentoring one of the main reasons behind the rise in the number of women employed in electric utilities. (*Lorelei K. Harloe*, "Opportunity Through Mentoring," *Electric Perspectives, September-October 1995, vol. 20 no. 5, p. 80*)

I'll stop there, although I found many more studies, reports, and articles verifying the effectiveness of both informal and formal mentoring relationships not just in business, but also in social service organizations, schools, and elsewhere. They support what has been proven in the laboratory by Dr. Albert Bandura and others: Human beings tend to imitate behavior they see in others, especially when that behavior is rewarded. That, in a nutshell, is why mentoring works.

Our mentors are usually people who have achieved something that, consciously or not, we'd like to emulate, and they are in a position to help us do it. They reward us with their attention and approval. They see potential greatness in us, often far more than we can see ourselves, and they are so convinced of the truth of their vision that they convince us, too. They are proud of us when we live up to our potential, help us to get back on track if we give in to laziness or self-doubt, and expect us to do our best all the time.

Sure Enough! The Power of Self-Fulfilling Prophecies

This is a good place to talk in more detail about the power that expectations—our own and other people's—have in our lives. A self-fulfilling prophecy is just what it sounds like, and the mechanics of it are fairly straightforward: First, an event is predicted (expected). Next, some action or behavior takes place *because of the expectation*. Finally, as a result of the action or behavior, the predicted event occurs. It's important that you understand how self-fulfilling prophecies work, because if you just look at the name it might sound like something occult or magical is going on, and that is absolutely not the case.

Here is a classic example called "The Last National Bank." The bank starts the day as a solvent institution, but a rumor is spreading around town that it is about to fail. This prophecy leads people to act, and they rush to withdraw all of their deposits. Until they believed the prophecy, they were wrong—the bank was safe and sound. But when they believed it and acted on their belief, the prophecy came true. The run on the bank drained its resources and—sure enough!—it failed.

Some people believe that wars are often caused by the same principle. Although most of us hate the idea of war, we nevertheless expect that wars are going to continue. Our expectations shape our behavior, and we engage in preparations for war, although we call it "defense." Both our behavior and expectations are communicated, either overtly or subtly, to possible opponents, who then engage in their own preparations. The opponent's behavior confirms our initial expectations and leads to even more preparation, setting in motion a mutually reinforcing cycle of preparation for war that eventually—sure enough!—brings about the war itself.

These are negative examples, but the principle works in a positive direction, too. Let me tell you about "Sweeney's miracle." This is a true story that took place some time ago at Tulane University, where James Sweeney taught industrial management and psychiatry.

Sweeney was also in charge of the Biomedical Computer Center, and he believed that he could teach anyone to operate a computer. Now, it's important to understand that this happened long before the days of user-friendly, point-and-click programs. Operating a computer at that time was a complex, intimidating business.

To prove his point, Sweeney chose George Johnson, a poorly educated former hospital porter who worked at the computer center as a janitor. In the mornings George cleaned and swept, and in the afternoons he learned about computers. He was making good progress when word circulated that to be a computer operator, you had to score at a certain level on an IQ test. When he took the test, the results showed that George shouldn't even be able to learn to type, let alone operate a computer, and hospital administrators told him to get back to work, full-time.

But Sweeney was neither convinced nor discouraged. He threatened to quit if George wasn't allowed to continue his studies, and he got his way. At last report, George was running the main computer room and was responsible for training new employees.

You can see from this example that self-fulfilling prophecies can have extremely positive results. Can you also see how important the determination of the person making the prophecy is, if contrary expectations (the IQ test and the administrators' doubt) are not going to outweigh the power of the original prediction?

What we expect to happen influences our behavior. Our behavior influences the likelihood of our expectations being realized. It's that simple. It's also true that one person's expectations about another person's behavior can create a self-fulfilling prophecy. This is an extremely important concept to grasp and put to work for you if you're interested in becoming a better coach, mentor, parent, spouse, teacher, boss, etc.

Why Sugar Pills Can Cure

You've probably heard of the "placebo effect." A placebo is a substance or procedure that has no medicinal value. If your doctor gave you a sugar pill to treat your symptoms, but you believed you were receiving effective prescription medication, you would be taking a placebo. (By the way, this wouldn't happen unless you volunteered to take part in a controlled, scientific study; otherwise, it is unethical.) If you did nothing else differently, but, after taking the sugar pills for a while, your symptoms decreased or disappeared, you would be experiencing the placebo effect.

The placebo effect is all about the power of expectations, which are far more potent than most people think. In the previous example, both your doctor's expectations and your own would come into play. In fact, your doctor's expectations would probably have a strong effect on yours. In a controlled experiment done nearly thirty years ago, one group of doctors was trained to communicate confidence to patients about the effect of a drug they were given, while a second group communicated doubts. The doctors who seemed confident had much better results from the same drug than their doubtful colleagues did.[3]

Another early study showed that the drug morphine gave better results than a placebo, but only as long as the doctors knew who was getting which. When neither patients nor doctors knew which substance was being given, morphine did no better than the placebo. These doctors did not intend to communicate their expectations to the patients; nevertheless, they did. As a result of these and other studies, drug trials are no longer considered valid unless they use double-blind techniques where neither researchers, doctors, nor subjects know who is getting what.[4]

Even when placebos are given openly, attitudes and expectations have a powerful effect. In one notable experiment, doctors gave placebos to a group of patients, telling them in no uncertain terms what they were getting. Their exact words were, "Many people with your kind of condition have also been helped by what are sometimes called sugar pills, and we feel that a so-called sugar pill may help you, too. Do you know what a sugar pill is? It's a pill with no medicine in it at all. I think this pill will help you as it has helped so many others. Are you willing to try this pill?" Only one patient in this study refused to take the pills. She did not improve, but the others did! The study concluded that the doctors' attitudes—their enthusiastic "selling" of the sugar pills to the patients—were a critical factor in their effectiveness.[5]

We are still a long way from understanding exactly what happens in the body to produce symptom improvement and even, sometimes, cure as a result of a placebo. But it seems certain that the process is not purely physical. It seems to originate with a change in expectation and belief—a change that results in less fear and more hope.

Less fear, more hope: just four little four-letter words, but when they are vividly felt as emotion, they are behavior-changing, life-changing, world-changing. No wonder that the hope or fear we experience in our hearts and minds changes our body chemistry. No wonder that patients who feel hopeless recover more slowly and die sooner. No wonder that a dark view of the future can speed up the course of certain illnesses, such as some forms of cancer, and cause debilitating depression, even death.

The Pygmalion Effect

The Pygmalion effect is named after the mythical king of Cyprus who carved and then fell in love with a statue of a woman, which the goddess Aphrodite brought to life. Psychologists and social scientists use the term to describe the powerful influence that one person's expectations can have on another. In *My Fair Lady*, professor Henry Higgins was convinced that he could transform the barely educated cockney flower-seller, Eliza Doolittle, into a refined, elegant lady who could mingle comfortably in high society. He was so sure that he convinced Eliza, too, and she lived up to both their expectations.

We have already given you one well-documented real-life example ("Sweeney's miracle") in which the powerful beliefs of one person had an equally powerful effect on the behavior of someone else. There are many, many others. One of the most famous, perhaps, is the experiment originally done at Oak School. Teachers there were led to expect improved academic performance from certain "special" students, who had actually been chosen at random. Researchers gave IQ tests to all the students at the beginning of the year, at the end of one semester, after a full school year, and after two full school years.

The children who had been selected as special were no different than any of the other students, yet they showed significantly greater gains in IQ scores. What do I mean by "significant"? Well, all of these kids showed IQ gains; that's expected at their age. Nineteen percent of the kids in the control group (the ones who weren't selected as special) gained 20 or more total IQ points. But 47 percent of the "special" children gained 20 or more total points![6]

So what was happening at Oak School? The Pygmalion effect. In fact, the book that was written about the experiment at Oak School is called *Pygmalion in the Classroom*. It's the same thing that happens all the time in effective coaching and mentoring relationships—at the office, on the job, at home, on the playing field, in the studio, and, of course, in the classroom.

The challenges we take on, the goals we set for ourselves, are to a great extent determined by our self-efficacy—our own estimation of our ability to succeed. The greater our self-efficacy, the harder we are likely to try, and the more we will sustain our efforts in the face of difficulties and obstacles. Because what we can do depends at least in part on how hard we're willing to work, it's no surprise that people who believe in themselves tend to do better than those who don't.

Good mentors are Pygmalions, just like those teachers at Oak School. They think we (their protégés) are special. They help us to believe in ourselves. They boost our self-esteem and self-efficacy. They help convince us that we have what it takes to succeed, which affects how hard we try, which tends to produce success, which further boosts our self-esteem and self-efficacy—and on and on we go, in an upward spiral of belief and achievement.

My First Pygmalions

I don't know where I'd be today if it hadn't been for the influence of people I looked up to who believed in me, especially those who were there for me when I was a kid. Sometimes I imagine the worst: I see myself as an aging, alcoholic football coach in some two-horse town, mad at the world because I couldn't help anyone, even myself, to be a winner. And then I think of Mr. Anderson and Evan Thomas, who were among my first Pygmalions.

Mr. Anderson was a sixth-grade teacher who was also the physical education coach for my grade school. He was the only male teacher in the whole school and a wonderful role model and mentor for me. He was a genuinely good person, a strong person, and he noticed me when I was only in the third grade. He routinely put me in charge of my whole class at recess, a big responsibility that he was accountable for himself, so he made me feel like a strong and capable leader. After all, if Mr. Anderson trusted me to be in charge, I figured I must deserve it and be good at it.

When he organized team sports, he would sometimes put me in to play instead of more experienced, older players, even when those guys would protest. So, again, I reasoned that I had to be worth it. Whether I was or not before he noticed me doesn't really matter. What matters is that Mr. Anderson had credibility in my eyes, and he made me believe I was someone special—an extremely competent team player and leader. So, more and more, I made sure that I behaved like it. I was determined that I wouldn't disappoint him or let him down. He went out of his way to set up experiences for me that built and reinforced my own belief in myself, and I will always remember him for that. Just as I will always remember Evan Thomas.

Evan was three years older than I, and we grew up in the same miserably poor neighborhood. Now, none of the kids where we lived had much of what you'd call adult supervision, parental or otherwise. Because of the heavy production demands of World War II, those parents who were lucky enough to have jobs were putting in as many hours as possible, often working extra swing or graveyard shifts. Older kids were pressed into service to care for younger ones because no one had the money to pay sitters, and sometimes "older" meant eight or nine or ten years old. As a result, we were used to running wild most of the time, staying out long after dark, playing war in the woods, shooting our homemade "guns" at each other, and almost hoping for the adventure of real trouble to come along. But Evan was different.

He was physically, mentally, and morally strong. He was a Native American, but he didn't set himself apart from the rest of the kids, and we thought of him as one of us—but somehow better. He did some of the same dumb things that we did, but there was something about him that made you look up to him. Even kids who were his age or older knew he was special. He wasn't conceited. He had a heightened awareness and a powerful personal presence that you just had to respect. I'm sure Evan knew that the others paid a special kind of deferential attention to him, but he wasn't bigheaded about it. So you can imagine how it felt to have him notice me, to single me out and care enough about what happened to me to give advice. He told me to avoid certain people because they weren't good for me, and I listened.

Evan was a fullback, a starter on the high school football team. I had always wanted to play football, too, so he had double the cred-ibility in my eyes. But when I reached the ninth grade, I was still small for my age, so I went completely unnoticed by the coach among the hundred or so who showed up for team tryouts. With all those bigger guys wanting the same thing I wanted, there didn't seem to be any reason not to quit trying—I was sure I'd never make the team. But Evan wouldn't hear of it. "Here's what you need to do," he told me. "Don't let that coach out of your sight. You just go and stand by him every day, and you tell him you want a uniform. Tell him every single day until he gives it to you."

But that didn't work. So Evan went to Plan B. "OK," he said. "Now you go to the *head* coach and tell him you want a uniform." I would never have dreamed of doing this on my own. But if Evan thought I was good enough to deserve a uniform, I figured it must be true, and it gave me hope and courage. So I did what he suggested, and my persistence paid off, because the head coach told the freshman coach to go ahead and give me a uniform, and that's how I made the team.

The first time I ever went out with Diane, my wife, we went on a double date with Evan and his girlfriend. I was going to take Diane on the bus, but that wasn't good enough for me, according to Evan. "You'll go with us in my car. I'll pick you up, and then we'll drive over and pick up Diane," he told me. "But what if this girl you're going out with doesn't want us along?" I asked him nervously, remembering that they were three years older. "Don't worry about that," Evan said. "If she doesn't like it, we'll just leave her home. You're my friend." Again, he made me feel special and important to him, at a time when it mattered. I like to think that Diane would have fallen in love with me and we would have been married even if I had showed up for our first date on roller skates. But I sure felt a lot more confident and debonair arriving at her front door in a car chauffeured by my most excellent friend and mentor, Evan Thomas.

I heard that Evan died from a brain tumor about fifteen years ago. He had been in his forties at the time, considerably younger than I am now. It bothered me a lot to hear that he was dead. More than anything else, it disturbed me that I had never been able to tell him, as one adult to another, how much his friendship and support had meant to me when we were kids. Last May, I decided to try and find his mother. Maybe it was too late to tell Evan, but I could at least talk to his mom. So I drove across town to the old neighborhood, and, amazingly, the Thomas house was still there.

When Mrs. Thomas answered the door and heard me say that I had been a friend of Evan's, it was clear she didn't remember me at all. I was just some blue-eyed stranger with a fancy car parked out in front. When I told her my name, though, her eyes lit up and she said, "Ah—millionaire Tice!" Of course, that wasn't the way I thought of myself at all, especially at that moment when I was surrounded by so many vivid reminders of my distant past. I felt awkward and out of place for an instant. Then I realized that it was perfectly natural for her to think of me that way and that it might even lend more credibility and impact to what I had to say.

I told her what a fine person Evan had been. I explained how deeply he had influenced me and how important he had been to my growth, my character development, and my ultimate success in life. I told her that his attention and concern had meant the world to me at a time when I was very much in need of those things, and I told her how proud I had felt to have been Evan's friend. I told her I would never forget him, and I never will.

Great Mentors with Clay Feet

Mentors have enormous power. But it's not power over anyone or anything. It's not the kind of hypnotic, put-yourself-in-my-hands power that is used to dominate another and glorify oneself. Rather, it is power *to*: to cause, to accomplish, to facilitate, to create. Great coaches and mentors have an empowering rather than a commanding force that others may partake of and share in but never feel belittled or controlled by. They are people we look up to, but not as models of perfection, godlike in their pronouncements, infallible in their wisdom. Sure, they need to be mature and capable in a general sense, and they should be models of success in something that is significant to us. If a mentor hasn't figured out how to make good use of his own potential, how in the world can he help us do so? Mentors must be able to work with us from a position of personal strength and security.

Great mentors must also be unafraid of their own emotions, vulnerabilities, and weaknesses, and they must never operate from an "I'm up, you're down" stance. They aren't interested in commanding or controlling situations or people. Instead, they strive to understand, and, even though the final decision and accountability may be theirs and theirs alone, they routinely share the information-gathering and decision-making processes with others, particularly those who are close to them or those with different points of view.

What great mentors *do* control, though, is themselves. Their time, resources, communications, creativity, and imagination are used deliberately and thoughtfully to achieve worthwhile goals, to help others, and to further causes in which they believe. Do they ever lose control, waste time, make mistakes, or veer off course? You bet they do. One of the most endearing things about effective mentors is that they don't try to hide their clay feet, to appear perfect. They accept their own shortcomings, flaws, and imperfections with a sense of humor and equanimity, while constantly and visibly working to improve. In so doing, they tacitly give us permission to do the same.

Before we move on, I want to briefly address the question of why it's a good idea to accept our flaws and shortcomings in the first place, just in case there's anyone who may be feeling a bit confused. After all, this is a book about personal mastery, isn't it? It was written to show you how to make the most of your vast inner potential and to help others to do the same, so why am I talking about the importance of accepting your faults or weaknesses? Well, first of all, *accepting* something isn't the same thing as *liking* it. You can accept that you often have a very short fuse around your father or feel terribly uncomfortable in social situations or are drinking too much in the evenings at the same time you are working to change it. In fact, *unless* you accept it, you are going to be powerless to change it.

Self-acceptance is the bedrock of self-esteem. You can choose to change something about yourself, your behavior or your life, without condemning it, labeling yourself as wrong or weak or inept, and without ever entering into an adversarial relationship with yourself. Listen to what Carl Jung said about self-acceptance: "We cannot change anything unless we accept it. Condemnation does not liberate, it oppresses. Acceptance of oneself is the essence of the moral problem and the acid test on one's whole outlook on life."[7]

Read those wise words once again. As you do, consider the idea of accepting the current reality of something—accepting that this is the way it is right now—without having to judge it or label it as right or wrong, bad or good, righteous or sinful. Better words to use when you are looking at your own behavior might be "useful" or "not useful," "productive" or "not productive," "in line with my goals and values" or "out of sync with my goals and values." Whether you are in a mentoring relationship or simply trying to use more of your own vast potential, understanding and acceptance of both self and others is an absolutely critical first step.

Coming up in Chapter 8, we'll focus on the characteristics—and character—of great mentors. We'll find out why we admire them, why we're willing to listen to them, and why we want to be like them.

CHAPTER EIGHT

Character and Credibility: Why Should I Listen to You?

Become the Architect of Your Own Character

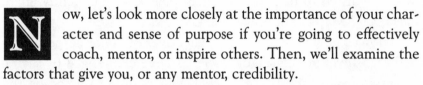

Now, let's look more closely at the importance of your character and sense of purpose if you're going to effectively coach, mentor, or inspire others. Then, we'll examine the factors that give you, or any mentor, credibility.

Before you can successfully mentor anyone, you need to have credibility in their eyes. I believe that it's also vitally important that you be of good character, meaning that you possess and demonstrate a high degree of integrity and ethical/moral strength. It isn't always necessary that you be liked, although good rapport and a high level of mutual respect certainly make the mentoring process more fun and will probably help it last longer. But it's absolutely essential that you be

> *"Do but set the example yourself, and I will follow you. Example is the best precept."*
>
> Aesop, *The Two Crabs*

believable and trustworthy in the areas where you want to offer guidance and exercise influence. Otherwise, why would anyone want to listen to or learn from you? And if your character is shaky or questionable, it doesn't matter what you say or do to disguise it— you'll be training someone to perpetuate your weaknesses.

I have seen the truth of this in my own life any number of times, and I'm willing to bet that your experience backs it up: Instructing, preaching, lecturing, or advising others about how to live doesn't carry nearly the weight that a good example does. Your actions are *always* more influential than your words. It doesn't matter how good what you say sounds to others. If it's not in line with your behavior, they'll eventually see through you. What matters, most of all, is what you *do*.

When the chips are down, the people we coach and mentor don't do what we tell them to do. Instead, they do what they have seen their role models and mentors do, or what they have seen their parents do, or what they have seen people in similar situations do. They do what we all do: observe and imitate. They model themselves after other people's behavior, not after high-sounding words. Will they listen to talk that will help them do it differently, more effectively? Maybe, but only if the talk walks.

I don't know how many top executives of major corporations and high-level public sector leaders I have challenged by saying something like this: If you expect your people to embrace the process of continuous personal and professional improvement, you should expect no less from yourself. You must demonstrate a zest for continuous improvement in every aspect of your own life. That means you actively seek out positive change, welcome it when it arrives even though you didn't invite it, and, as much as possible, direct it. The same is true for parents, grandparents, spouses, employers, teachers—anyone who's in a position to influence others, and that really includes all of us.

You may not like the idea that what you do has a more powerful effect on others than what you say. Maybe you'd like to continue to do as you please in private while living an exemplary public life and talking a good game. Maybe you believe that you can fool people into seeing only what you want them to see or that you don't need to concern yourself to any great extent with your own integrity, growth, and development because you're doing very well, thank you. You may not enjoy feeling like a raw beginner, so you work at perfecting the skills you already have and avoid venturing into new territory. Perhaps you never develop written goals yourself, but think other people should. Or maybe you've gotten out of the habit of asking for feedback, even though you know it's important, because you'd like to continue to believe that everything is just fine as it is.

If you seldom give serious thought to the shape, content, balance, and meaning of your life, or if you rarely measure the size of the gap between what you say you believe and what you actually do, you can't be more than dimly aware of areas of imbalance or needed change in your life. If you sense that this may be true, don't waste a second either defending or blaming yourself. Instead, carve out some time for contemplation, assessment, and planning for personal change before you think about coaching or mentoring someone else.

At the risk of stating the obvious, I also want to say that, while it's a good idea to have fundamental issues of your character fairly well thought through (the role in your life of integrity, honesty, loyalty, self-discipline, responsibility, courage, compassion, kindness, etc.), being a mentor doesn't mean that you have your act completely together—no faults, flaws, problems, struggles. It doesn't mean that you are or pretend to be a flawless person. But it *does* mean that you are consciously, actively developing as a human being.

So work at generating positive changes in many areas of your life, and do it openly, but without making a big deal about it. Let the people around you see you doing things differently, even when your efforts are imperfect. Wait for an opportunity or create one; then, tell them about your goal: *"I'm determined to become a better listener."* Share where you're making good progress: *"So I'm reading a book about interpersonal communication, and I've been listening to some great audio tapes in my car."* Share where you're falling short, too: *"Interrupting other people while they're talking is a old habit that's hard for me to break."* Outline your change strategy: *"Right now, I'm working on raising my awareness of how I participate in conversations, and I'm using affirmations and visualizations to make change easier."* Ask for their support, as specifically as possible: *"It would sure help if you could let me know on the spot if I slip and cut you off before you're finished."*

If others see you taking your own growth and development seriously (but not, for heaven's sake, somberly!), they're more likely to take their own efforts seriously, too.

The Value of Virtues

For some time now, we've been hearing a lot about the importance of values, particularly those that are often called "traditional," and that's fine. But it's important to understand that, in and of themselves, values aren't necessarily good or virtuous. Just as a color can have many different shades, depending on how light or dark it is, there is also a broad spectrum of values, and not all of them enhance character.

If you prize the adrenaline rush of perceived physical danger and think everyone should try bungee jumping at least once; if you believe a family means only a mother, father, and their children; and if you think recycling is a waste of time and effort, we may not share the same values in those areas, but that's all right. There may be other things that we value upon which we can agree and even base an amiable relationship.

If, on the other hand, we don't see eye to eye on the importance of qualities such as sincerity, honesty, responsibility, kindness, courtesy, dependability, self-discipline, loyalty, ethics, and integrity, it's not fine—at least it isn't with me. These are some of the values that are often called virtues, and they are the mainstays of good character. If you don't believe these things matter much in today's world, then, frankly, I question your ability to meaningfully coach or mentor anyone or to live in a meaningful way yourself. If you do believe they're important, I hope you live your belief. They're important enough to me and to the coaching/mentoring relationship that I'm going to list a few of them here.

My Personal List of Character-Building Virtues

Sincerity. Mean what you say, say what you mean, and be silent when you have nothing to say or when silence would be most eloquent.

Honesty. Do the work of searching out what's true for you, and share what you discover with others. Don't mistake opinions for facts, and remember that the opposite of a profound truth is often another profound truth.

Kindness. Help others, whether you know them or not, in countless small ways without expecting gratitude or returned favors. Be particularly and persistently kind to those who seem angry, weak, sad, or withdrawn. Avoid creating a "help strikes again" situation by being sensitive to circumstances where help is truly not wanted.

Courtesy. Courtesy is a form of kindness and the beginning of compassion. Its prerequisites are self-respect and respect for others, the ability to put yourself in the background and an active imagination that can really feel what it's like to be wearing someone else's shoes.

Dependability. Do what you say you'll do. If something absolutely unavoidable and out of your control prevents that, apologize, explain immediately, and do whatever you can to make it right. Honor your word to yourself with equal rigor.

Self-Discipline. The word "discipline" comes from Latin roots that mean "to learn." Self-discipline means that you serve as your own teacher, learning from your mistakes and controlling your behavior so that you can grow and develop in optimal ways. Stop doing things that you know are harming you, and start doing thing that help you to thrive.

Integrity. Know what you believe and live accordingly. Very simply, walk your talk.

Ethics. Take the moral high road, even when you don't have to. As Jiminy Cricket said, "Always let your conscience be your guide."

As you can see, virtues have to do with character and morals, with the spirit of truth and goodness rather than the letter and loopholes of law. Virtuous people are concerned about doing the right thing, even when it isn't required, even when no one is looking, even when it means that they'll never be applauded or noticed. They don't think kindness and consideration are for wimps, they are assertive rather than aggressive, and they get a lot of quiet pleasure from behaving well and helping things go well for others.

As a rule, virtuous people don't think of themselves as special, but they are. Often, they demonstrate their virtues in small ways. They're the ones who don't try to beat out the older, slower driver (who saw it first) for the only open parking spot. They don't borrow things and "forget" to return them, even when they know it has long ago slipped the lender's mind. They don't think twice about letting a child or elder or anyone with an unwieldy armload of parcels go ahead of them in the checkout line. They don't believe it's a dog-eat-dog world in which they need to gain the edge so that they won't get eaten.

Instead, they have generous spirits because they operate from a "my cup runneth over" belief system, no matter what their economic status may be. They give the most valuable gifts it is possible to receive: their undivided attention, encouragement, sympathy, understanding, laughter, compassion, forgiveness, and patience. If you are coaching or mentoring someone—anyone—these are parts of yourself you need to be able to offer freely, and you won't be able to do it if they're in short supply. Nurture the growth of these qualities in others by giving them generously to yourself.

Yes, that's right, to yourself. Be patient with yourself. Be understanding, compassionate, forgiving, and encouraging. Control your self-talk and dwell not on your shortcomings, but on your strengths and desire to grow. Give yourself the benefit of the doubt, laugh at your foibles and failings, and, above all, pay *attention* to yourself. Don't sweep your feelings under the carpet. You don't have to vent them inappropriately or even share them if you'd rather not, but you do need to be *aware* of them. Don't shove your desires out the back door, declare your dreams to be meaningless, or cast your yearnings overboard. It's not necessary to act on them all, but in your dreams, desires, and yearnings lie important clues to your complex and fascinating nature. Listen to them and learn from them. Like charity, virtuous behavior begins (but never ends) at home.

The Power of Purpose

The world is full of people who are definitely in motion, but they're not exactly sure where they're going or why. Sometimes they're moving so fast and are so caught up in a flurry of day-to-day activities that they never take time to ask—let alone answer—these critical questions. They feel like something's missing, but they're not sure what. I believe that the emptiness they sense is due, more than anything else, to a lack of purpose.

Some people think that purpose descends on you, rather like the calling that spiritual leaders feel as a directing force from God, but, since they never quite hear that call, they drift. Sometimes they drift in fortunate directions. More often they follow the path of least resistance and end up doing whatever they see others doing, blindly obeying their parents' wishes or simply latching on to the first acceptable thing that comes along. They marry, have children, work at a job, have hobbies and friends they enjoy, but they don't really put their hearts and souls into any of it, and they don't feel particularly fulfilled or enthusiastic about their lives.

While it's true that some fortunate folks seem to have a distinct sense of purpose from an early age, for most of us it's not that simple. We have to deliberately decide on a purpose, whether for a lifetime or less, through a process of conscious soul-searching. This process may be difficult or lengthy. It may take place after we've already become adults and, in some cases, long after we've made some major life decisions. Sometimes it happens that we don't choose our purpose until quite late in life, but our choice is no less important or meaningful because it comes at an advanced age.

For me, the seeds were planted much earlier, but my conscious choice was made during a three-and-a-half-day religious retreat that I attended while in college. I went, not because I had any strong desire to deepen my relationship with God, but for all the wrong reasons. I went because a good buddy of mine, a fellow football coach named Tommy O'Brien, was going, and I had hoped to spend the weekend with him drinking beer and drawing football plays. Tommy said he wanted to participate in this retreat instead, and I was amazed. How could he possibly prefer to do something boring like that instead of talk football with me? When I asked him if I could go along, he told me he thought I wasn't disciplined enough in some ways to handle it—not to challenge me but because he knew me very well. He knew I was physically tough, but he also understood that I had no significant spiritual source of power fueling me—my strength was mainly self-generated and primarily self-interested.

I went to that retreat anyway because Diane was in Europe with her sister who was having her first child at the time. I had nothing better to do, since Tommy clearly intended to bail out on me. Besides, I wanted to show him that I was tougher than he thought. I wanted him to see that anything he could do, I could do, too. How hard could it be? After all, I figured, it would just be a bunch of priests and laypeople talking about God and the church. Piece of cake!

So, when the time came, I went, but I dragged myself there half-heartedly. I left my house at the last possible minute, sure I was going to be late. I told myself that if I hit even one red light on the way I would turn back, because Tommy had said that it was very important to arrive on time. Remarkably, every traffic light was green—every last one of them, and this was a forty-five-minute drive, at least. So I got there just in the nick of time, and they let me in.

Well, it turned out to be a tough three-and-a-half days, all right, but not in the way I had expected. The retreat forced me to examine every belief I had about who I was, why I was alive, why I was doing the things I was doing, and the nature of my relationships to God and other people. It was time for me to put up or shut up about being a Christian.

During that retreat, I created a vision for my life that was far more compelling, expansive, and full of exciting possibilities than anything I had previously been able to imagine. The retreat challenged me to live in a way that would transform my work and the way I related to others into a continuous prayer of gratitude and praise. What's more, it convinced me that I could do it. I came away with a such a clear sense of direction and purpose that it has served as the rudder of my life ever since.

Expressing Your Mission

In his book, *The Seven Habits of Highly Effective People,* Stephen R. Covey recommends the writing of a personal mission statement as a way to articulate your purpose. He suggests separate mission statements for each major life role (spouse, parent, child, plant manager, scholar, mentor, Christian, sibling, neighbor, etc.). He also suggests that families try collaborating on the creation of a joint mission statement to express their unique purpose and responsibilities toward each other.[1] I like this idea.

There's something extremely valuable about the process of putting a concept (such as the overall purpose of an organization, or a life, for that matter) into a few well-chosen words, especially when those words are written down, maybe even framed, displayed, and viewed frequently. If you take the task seriously and apply yourself to it with an open mind, determined to settle for nothing less than getting it just right, something almost magical will happen.

When you finally wrestle into language the power and purpose that drives you—your highest aspiration—you bring that purpose much further into consciousness. You give it substance, weight, and some degree of permanence by moving it from a shadowy existence in your thoughts out into the world, via the process of focused consciousness and descriptive language. You cause that which was vague and blurry to become sharper and much more precise, that which was dim to become full of light.

Can you imagine how your life might change if you were to start each day by reflecting for a few moments on your personal mission statement? What if you began each day with a mission statement invented on the spot for that day alone? What if you were to enter into each activity of the day with a few words that would trigger a mental picture of how you want to behave and the results you want to achieve?

We're talking again, of course, about affirmation and visualization—the most powerful tools I know (see Chapter 6) for shaping the form and content of our lives, especially when they're used to support and clarify a virtuous and inspiring mission, purpose, or intention.

A Mentor's Spirit of Intent

Why do you want to be a coach or mentor? Do you have someone special in mind with whom you'd like to work? Are you already coaching or mentoring someone, maybe more than one person? Why are you doing it? Were you pressured into it, or did you take on the responsibility freely? Do you have enough time available to do a really good job?

What, specifically, is your picture of a coach or mentor like? How closely do you already resemble that picture? What would have to change for a better match? How about your picture of a protégé? Are you looking for a superachiever to help along? Maybe you'd rather work with someone who is having so much trouble that you'll seem like a savior. Do you long to be looked up to? Do you crave the power and authority coaching might give you? Are you looking for the closeness and intimacy mentoring might provide? Or is it not about your needs as much as a sincere desire to be of service?

In Chapter 7, we examined some reasons why you might want to consider coaching or mentoring, and we listed some significant benefits for both mentor and protégé. But taking priority over any benefits you might personally receive as a mentor must come a good fit with your overall purpose in life and a sincere desire to see your protégé grow.

Does that mean that it's wrong to feel good when you do good—to derive real pleasure from it? Not on your life! In fact, I sometimes wonder if that glow of good feeling we enjoy when we've truly been of service might be God's built-in mechanism for making sure our species survives.

However, I believe that it *is* wrong to mentor someone only to feel good about yourself. I also believe that it's wrong to become a mentor in order to gain power or respect or admiration. Don't gallop headlong into a mentoring relationship, or any relationship with such enormous potential to affect another person, without first fully considering what your purpose is, where you are in your own personal development, what your concerns and doubts may be, and what you have to lose and to gain.

The Role of Retreat and Self-Examination

If your life is too busy to allow you to retreat into contemplation and self-examination from time to time, you are doing yourself a great disservice. You can't remain in touch with your own soul if your life is filled with racing thoughts and a constant flurry of activities from morning to night, day after day, year after year, no matter how meaningful they may seem. You can't claim personal mastery if you're unable to stop the runaway train of your mind for more than a few seconds.

If you believe that your thoughts are really under your control, try this simple experiment. Sit in a quiet place and try to focus your attention on one thing—anything at all—for five minutes. Just five minutes. One hundred percent attention. Unless you're a regular meditator, you'll probably have great difficulty with this seemingly simple task. The more you struggle to prevent unwanted thoughts from entering your awareness, the more you'll find them pressing to come in.

If you are a churchgoer, how much of the time you sit or kneel in the sanctuary is actually spent worshiping, giving thanks, and opening your heart to allow communion with your creator? How much is spent thinking about things that have nothing to do with your ostensible purpose for being there? Without special care to prevent it, the same thing is likely to happen to the way you spend your entire life.

In his book, *The Heart Aroused*, poet and corporate consultant David Whyte tells of a workshop he conducted some years ago with a group of managers at AT&T:

> We were looking at the way human beings find it necessary to sacrifice their own sacred desires and personal visions on the altar of work and success. Out of this a woman wrote the following lines. She read them slowly from the back of the room, unaware how stricken we all were by the silence she created.
>
> > *Ten years ago . . .*
> > *I turned my face for a moment*
> > *and it became my life.*[2]

What a courageous act, the creation of this small but enormously important poem! What a self-empowering thing to do! For it is only when we are willing to take the risk of looking honestly and unflinchingly at the current reality of our lives—admitting that we may not have made the best use of our gifts, acknowledging that we may have lost touch with our vision or soulfulness or sense of purpose—that we can begin, if we choose, to recapture it and set things right. The willingness to risk is critical, make no mistake about it. As Whyte explains:

> We know intuitively that the first sip of intoxicating revelation is bought at very great cost. As if in preparation, the strategic part of our mind has already done a thorough cost-benefit analysis and is advising us not to go through with the bargain.
>
> We experience a form of internal sticker-shock, that the price of our vitality is the sum of all our fears, that the price of our passion and commitment involves the shattering of deep personal illusions of immunity and safety.[3]

On the surface, your reasons for not taking the time to plumb your own depths may be about being too busy, but on a deeper level they may reflect anxieties and fears. Anxiety about confronting the fact that there is, indeed, something vital missing. Fear of not knowing how to "fix" it. Worry about feeling out of control or operating without all the "answers." Unwillingness to experience, even for a short time, the sting of regret or the pain of deep sadness. Fear of what others may think if you admit to your feelings. Fear that they may not understand or even want to hear about them. Reluctance to acknowledge, even to yourself, that you may have unwittingly taken a wrong turn somewhere "and it became your life."

If they're present, it's a good idea to allow these entirely normal anxieties and fears to rise to the surface without judging yourself as somehow deficient for having them. Unless you can accept them as nothing to feel guilty about and then move beyond them to the deeper truths they may be masking, you will be like a timid traveler:

Imagine going on an extended holiday in some vibrant, colorful, exotic land but spending all your time shopping in the resort's boutiques and eating all your meals in the dining room at the Holiday Inn! You may have a pleasant enough experience, but it will be a tepid and shallow sort of pleasure, because your activities and encounters are so carefully confined to the safe and superficial. Like a reticent traveler, you won't be able to serve as a very effective or interesting guide for others, either, because you've been unwilling to take the risk of moving outside your comfort zone to know yourself and your environment in a deeply authentic way. You can't show someone else how to live life fully if you're unwilling to do it yourself.

The Three Pillars of Credibility

What gives a mentor credibility? What makes someone else want to listen to and learn from her or him? Depending on the specifics of the mentoring relationship and the personalities of the individuals involved, there may be various reasons for perceiving someone as credible, but three factors are always central. It isn't necessary that all three be present, and sometimes it isn't possible. Often, just one will do. Two are better, and all three make you a "who-said" of the highest magnitude. (A "who-said," by the way, is anyone with sufficient credibility to completely satisfy us when we ask, "Oh yeah? Who said so?")

1. You are seen as a "similar other." Most of us have a natural tendency to gravitate toward and relate most comfortably to people who are "similar others." In other words, people who are like us in some way or ways that we deem significant. They may be very different from us in significant ways, too, but our perception is that we are more alike than different. This makes it easier to believe that they can understand us and our needs and easier to see that what they have to say is relevant to our situation.

In the early '60s when I first started out as a high-school football coach, I had credibility with my players because I had, of course, spent many hours out on the gridiron. They knew that I understood firsthand the challenges and frustrations they were facing. I was an ex-player, a similar other, someone they wanted to listen to. Years later, when I quit teaching and coaching to begin the work I do now, some of my first personal and professional growth seminars were presented to audiences consisting largely of coaches, players, and their families. One of the reasons for this was that they saw me as a similar other, so I had credibility with them.

The concept of training teens to be peer counselors, which many high schools have successfully adopted, has worked well partly because it is based on the similar other credibility factor. When it comes to dealing with personal problems, teenagers are often far more willing to talk with and listen to another teenager than they are to a parent, teacher, or adult therapist, whom they may perceive as being out of touch with the experience of being an adolescent.

2. You have achieved relevant personal success. If you have personally achieved a considerable measure of success in a particular endeavor, you'll be seen as highly credible by others who want to succeed in similar endeavors. The fact that you are an expert business manager won't cut any ice with the guy who wants to learn how to put a truck chassis together faster, the new mom who needs to build her confidence and competence in parenting skills, or the real estate agent who'd like some help improving her closing rate. It will probably earn you rapt attention, however, from a business administration student, small business owner, or budding entrepreneur.

Simply being older or having "been there" isn't enough. You need to have "been there" *successfully,* and your success needs to mean something not only to you, but also to the person you'll be mentoring. For example, you may feel well qualified to give child-rearing advice because you've raised five kids to adulthood. But the first-time mother I mentioned a moment ago may not be impressed unless she knows that your offspring have college degrees and good jobs, if that's what her vision is for her own child.

3. You have mentored/coached others to success. Maybe you can't pitch a no-hitter or slam-dunk a basketball yourself, but if you've coached people such as Nolan Ryan or Michael Jordan, you'll have instant credibility with any ballplayer, coach, or fan in the world. Perhaps you seldom take to the stage yourself, but if you taught Jodie Foster or Tom Hanks their craft, you'll have tremendous credibility with anyone determined to make a mark as an actor.

As I've said, when I started out coaching football, I had some credibility with the kids on the team because I was an ex-player, a similar other. But I hadn't been a really exceptional player or achieved any special recognition, and I had been too physically small to play some positions. As my coaching techniques improved, and I learned more about how to help my players motivate themselves, set and achieve goals, and raise their internal standards, my teams began to amass outstanding win/loss records. Some of my individual players started to accomplish phenomenal things, too. That gave me much more credibility, because it addressed the third pillar: I had effectively helped others to achieve success.

After I left football and became a successful educator in the human potential field, I worked with many professional coaches, helping them to dramatically improve their win rates and even turn last-place teams into winners. By that time, I had earned a lot of credibility in the world of athletics because of the first and third pillars. Bit by bit, as word about the effectiveness and long-lasting impact of my educational concepts spread, I began to be asked to work with people who had nothing to do with sports—people from business and industry, government, school systems, corrections, social service agencies, etc., and I developed credibility with them in the same way—little by little, over time.

For example, when I wanted to take our educational programs to the men and women locked up in federal and state prisons, as well as to the staff of those institutions, I was aware that Lou Tice would probably have precious little credibility with the inmates. I just wasn't a similar other. They wouldn't give a rip how many pro football teams, *Fortune* 500 corporations, or four-star generals I had worked with. But they'd care a lot that I had never been arrested, let alone committed a violent crime, and had never experienced even a day of the regimented, bitterly hard life behind bars.

So I teamed up with a man named Gordy Graham, an extremely bright, very tough, energetic ex-convict I had personally coached. Gordy had gotten tremendous value from our curriculum and wanted to use it to help those who were still "on the inside." It made perfect sense. That way, the prisoners would hear what I believed they desperately needed to hear from a man they would see as credible—a man whom I had mentored (third pillar) who was both a similar other (first pillar) and who had achieved the kind of personal success that would matter to them (second pillar): Gordy was a free man with an interesting and challenging job, earning good money, working with the system instead of against it. And he was doing all of this because he had learned how to control what went on inside his head, instead of constantly trying to control other people or manipulate his environment as he had done in the past.

Even today, when one of my company's representatives goes into an organization for an initial consultation, one of the first things the leaders want to know is, "Who else like us have you worked with? What kinds of challenges were they facing? How were you able to help them succeed?" They want to know why they should listen to what we have to tell them, why they should see us as credible.

Acquiring Credibility Insurance

When Alex, my oldest granddaughter, was three, I asked her mom to bring her downtown to Seattle's magnificent Fifth Avenue Theater, where I was presenting a three-day seminar to a sellout crowd. My request had nothing to do with ego. I wanted Alex to see her grandpa in front of that audience as a kind of "credibility insurance."

You see, I was pretty sure that someday, something would happen to severely shake her self-confidence (as it does to all of us). Someone would say something intended to hurt or demean her, and she'd be filled with doubt about herself. I knew my response would be to remind her of the truth: that she is a wonderful human being—incredibly intelligent, capable, and beautiful, inside and out. But I wanted my positive images of her to have as much impact as possible. I wanted Alex to experience and remember that her grandpa who thinks so highly of her is also someone to whom a great many people want to listen, and that when it comes to human behavior, anyway, I really do know what I'm talking about.

Of course, demonstrating your clout with others ("All these people listen to me, so you should, too!") isn't the only way or even the best way to acquire credibility insurance. It presented itself to me and I used it because it's a natural part of my everyday life, and it makes sense in that context. As far as I'm concerned, actively and thoughtfully building and strengthening your own character is the best credibility insurance you can have.

If you want others to see you as trustworthy, offer your opinions and share information respectfully, keep your commitments, and never betray a confidence. If you'd like to be perceived as a person to whom others can open their hearts, take pains to maintain a non-judgmental stance, and ask questions that serve to empower and clarify instead of giving advice that directs or attempts to control. If you want to be thought of as courageous, don't wait for a national emergency, an injustice that needs challenging, or a life-threatening illness to fight. Stand up and speak out for what you believe on a daily basis, even when you're a minority of one. Take the risks you need to take in order to keep on growing—intellectually, emotionally and, every now and then, physically. Challenge yourself before you challenge others. You don't have to endure privation or put yourself in danger. Just make it a habit to regularly and routinely expand the outer limits of your comfort zones and your consciousness.

We own ample credibility insurance when we live authentically and enthusiastically, when we enter into the dance of relationship with spirits high and colors flying, taking full responsibility for development of our own character, skills, abilities, talents, and latent potential. We earn endless dividends when we look for ways to share what we have learned with others, while holding ourselves open to new perspectives and insights that may modify our understanding, even when it means that some of our most cherished assumptions may have to be retired.

Beyond simply being credible, though, we become downright magnetic when we can listen to and enter into dialogue with others (and with ourselves) in ways that stimulate and facilitate rather than suppress and impede the flow of natural creativity and problem-solving ability. We'll take a look at some effective ways to do this in Chapter 9.

CHAPTER NINE

Active Listening, Straight Talk

Communication and Change

C ommunication between a coach or mentor and a protégé, or between any two people, for that matter, is not about one person trying to get an idea into another person's head, as I once thought. Communication is a complex interaction that depends upon time and place, feedback, feelings, background and history, and the intricate web of our relationships with each other and with ourselves.

I've heard it said that in any person-to-person communication, there are at least six people involved: The person you believe yourself to be, the other person's beliefs about who you are, the person you think the other person believes you are, and the three corresponding perceptions that apply to the other person. Whew! Small wonder that the process of understanding and mastering the art of interpersonal communication isn't simply a matter of moving from A to B to C.

> *"Treat people as if they were what they ought to be, and you help them become what they are capable of being."*
>
> Goethe

Whatever the purpose of our communication, at its best it involves active listening, honest expression of thoughts and emotions, and the changes in our relationships with self and others that result. Without the possibility of change, the communication process is sterile, lifeless, without meaning. When you tell me something I didn't know about you, it may change how I perceive you, how I feel about you, how I conduct myself around you. If I tell you something you didn't know about me, the same thing can happen.

We are now relating to each other differently, even though the difference may be subtle. In the process, each of us may discover something about ourselves that changes our self-concept slightly and, as a result, our behavior in the world. Communication is important stuff. It behooves us to know something about how to do it effectively.

In this chapter, which is about how we listen and talk to each other, I'll explain what "active" listening is, and we'll see how it can improve the quality and depth of our relationships, especially those with people we are coaching or mentoring. We'll also look at some simple techniques for expressing thoughts and feelings that bring out the best in self and others. We'll discover how to avoid creating defensive reactions, and we'll talk about how to ask questions and give advice in ways that promote strong relationships and help solve problems.

The information in this chapter will enable you to dramatically and positively impact your ability to help yourself and others target and achieve meaningful goals. It will also provide you with powerful tools that can break down the walls that keep you from understanding your fellow human beings and build solid bridges in their place.

What Is Active Listening?

Most of us have never really learned to listen. As children, we learned to talk, to express our desires, thoughts and feelings, to describe, explain, persuade, gossip, complain. As we grew older, many people helped us to improve our speaking skills, usually by correcting our mistakes, directing our efforts, and providing examples we could imitate. Sometimes we even took classes called "speech" or "debate" so that we could learn to better express our thoughts and feelings. But we had little or no guidance when it came to developing our ability to fully and comprehensively listen.

It's not that we can't hear or don't have the manners to keep quiet when someone else is talking. Active listening involves much more than just letting information wash over us. It even involves more than attempting to understand the meaning of the message we are hearing by using our brainpower to analyze it, connect it with what we already know, draw conclusions from it, and remember it later—all valuable skills, to be sure.

Active listening certainly involves use of critical thinking skills, such as recalling related issues, questioning, agreeing, disagreeing, and reaching logical conclusions. But its *primary* purpose is to understand the meaning of the message *from the speaker's point of view*. Whenever you listen actively to another person's comments, your reason for doing so is to understand—to enter as much as possible into the world of the person who is speaking, to listen with your heart and gut as well as with your ears and brain.

To listen actively means that while you're taking in what's being said, you're not busy evaluating, judging, blaming, labeling, interpreting, thinking about how you're going to respond, speculating about where the conversation is likely to lead, considering whether you appear to be paying attention while your mind is drifting to the telephone call you need to make. Instead, you are focused entirely on using the verbal and nonverbal clues you're receiving to understand and appreciate where this person is coming from, how he feels about what he is saying, why he feels that way, and what the meaning of his words are to *him and his life*.

How do you know if you're listening actively? How can you tell if what you *think* someone means is *really* what they mean? Most people simply assume they know. They hear someone say something, and then they quickly consider what it might mean and select what they believe to be the most likely interpretation. When you're an active listener, you go farther than that. You check to make *sure*, rather than presuming you know what is meant. Psychologists call this kind of assumption checking "reflective" listening, because it reflects back to the speaker your best guess about the meaning of what you've heard. It asks for confirmation, denial, or adjustment, if necessary, and it can be delivered either in the form of a question or as a simple statement.

For example, if someone says to you, "I wish I were more assertive," there are any number of things it could mean. Possibilities include, but aren't limited to: "I'm feeling invisible in my department at work." "I have a hard time saying no to requests for my time." "I have trouble expressing my opinions." "I feel that I'm being treated like a servant by my family." If you're listening actively (reflectively), you might decide, based on what you know about the speaker, that the second possibility is what was meant. You could respond by saying something such as, "Are you saying yes when you really want to say no?" The reply you receive may let you know that you're on target ("I sure am! My schedule is so full that I feel like I'm running from one thing to the next all day, every day!"). Or it may tell you that you're off base ("No, I'm doing OK in that sense. But I feel as if I'm always apologizing for myself.").

When you listen actively, you're also listening empathetically, and the message you send by doing so is critically important. You're saying, "I hear you. I understand how you feel." This is a message that builds trust and enables greater openness and equality of relationship. It also gives the speaker a chance to hear herself think, to "live in the question" for a moment and see what other thoughts, feelings, and responses emerge, before you jump in with a response, a change of conversational direction, or a prescription to try and fix things.

How to Be an Active Listener

Here are some things you can do to become a world-class active listener. They aren't difficult, but, as with any new behavior, it'll take some practice before they begin to feel like second nature. Try writing some affirmations and using visualization to speed up the process. I've suggested some affirmations here, but they'll be more effective if you use mine as models for creating your own.

1. *Make a sincere commitment to become an active listener.* Bring your desire to listen more effectively into your consciousness several times a day. Remind yourself why you want to acquire or sharpen this skill and what it will do for you and those you care about when you've mastered it. *(When someone else is talking, I listen closely and actively at all times. It enriches both of us when I understand what's going on inside the speaker, as well as the content of the message being sent.)*

2. *Take a few moments to prepare yourself to listen.* Eliminate distractions and potential distractions. Turn off the TV; have your calls held or answered elsewhere; close the book or newspaper you were reading. If possible, move to a comfortable, private place. Put away your mental clutter, too. Remove your preoccupations, worries, or daydreams to a set of mental parentheses. You can easily retrieve them later. Focus your complete attention on the communication that is taking place, no matter how long or short it is likely to be. *(I eliminate distractions from my outer and inner environments to help make active listening easy for me.)*

3. *Wait patiently until the other person is finished speaking.* Don't interrupt. Your first task is to be certain you understand what's been said and how the other person feels about it. If you're not sure you understand, try a statement or question that seeks more information ("Would you tell me more about that?"), rather than trying to clarify or interpret what you've heard. Jumping to conclusions too quickly or being impatient to arrive at a solution can lead to difficulties down the line when you realize you didn't have the complete picture. *(I patiently give everyone a full hearing, just as I want them to do when I am speaking.)*

4. *Place your analytical skills on reserve.* Don't mentally linger over one idea even though the speaker has gone on to another. Keep up with the flow of information, unless you're beginning to feel lost and need clarification. Avoid shifting your focus to yourself

in order to plan how you'll respond when it's your turn to talk. Your intention as an active, empathetic listener is to understand, not to critique, analyze, advise, or argue. After you're certain you fully understand, you may choose to look more critically and logically at message content—or you may not. *(While I am listening in order to understand, I temporarily suspend all critical judgments.)*

5. *Notice nonverbal clues.* Not all communication comes to us through language. In fact, most of the messages we send one another are in the form of nonverbal signals, or what is commonly called body language. Posture, gestures, tone of voice, sighs, muscle tension, and facial expressions often convey more to an observant listener than what is actually being said. Pay attention to these important signals, and learn to read them. *(I notice and respond to actions and body language as well as to words.)*

6. *Check your assumptions to make sure you have understood.* Reflect back to the speaker your understanding of the full message he has conveyed. "You're feeling overwhelmed and a little frightened by your new supervisor." "You don't know what to do about your son's intention to quit school." "You're really excited about this business opportunity in China." "I get the feeling that you're reluctant to talk about this to me." "I hear a lot of sadness in your voice when you talk about this move you're planning." Wait for confirmation or correction, and indicate when you have understood. "OK, I think I understand what you mean now. You're not feeling sad so much as tired and frustrated." "I see. It's not that you're reluctant to talk with me. You're worried about confidentiality." *(Because I want to understand as fully as possible, I check to make sure I have interpreted a communication accurately.)*

Roadblocks to Active Listening

There are many ways to respond to something you've just heard. But responding isn't the same thing as listening. In *Parent*

Effectiveness Training, Thomas Gordon outlines twelve responses that interrupt the listening process and alter the direction or progress of the communication flow. They are:

1. Ordering, directing, or commanding
2. Warning or threatening
3. Giving advice, making suggestions, or providing solutions
4. Persuading with logic, arguing, or lecturing
5. Moralizing, preaching, or telling someone what they "should" do
6. Disagreeing, judging, criticizing, or blaming
7. Agreeing, approving, or praising
8. Shaming, ridiculing, or labeling
9. Interpreting or analyzing
10. Reassuring, sympathizing, or consoling
11. Questioning or probing
12. Withdrawing, distracting, humoring, or changing the subject

Gordon doesn't think that these responses should never be used, nor do I, but there is a proper time and place for them. Some, such as shaming, ridiculing, blaming, labeling, or moralizing, have no place in any well-meaning exchange under any circumstances. But it's important to realize that while you're responding in ways that seem helpful, supportive, and positive—praising, approving, sympathizing, or reassuring, for example—you're not actively listening.

In addition, many of these twelve responses imply that there's a power imbalance in the relationship—a one-up/one-down situation where one person knows best what the other should do or can evaluate the worth of what the other is saying. Even when this is true to some extent, as in the relationship between parent and child or employer and employee, it never feels good to be in the one-down position. The goal of good coaches and mentors is to eliminate imbalances and empower their protégés to decide for themselves what's true or not and what's best for them to do.

The Power of Strategic Questions

Have you ever noticed that you tend to pay more attention to questions than to simple, flat-out statements? That's because questions start us thinking and encourage us to use our minds constructively and creatively. They "hook" us by offering a chance for participation in a dialogue, rather than asking us to simply listen and take in information, as statements do.

If you want to help others solve their own problems and make their own decisions, strategic questioning is an essential skill. In addition to being a straightforward way to stimulate thought and gain necessary information, asking questions is a good way to introduce a new idea or different point of view, gain cooperation, reduce anxiety, clarify vague statements, and build intimacy in a relationship.

Open and Closed Questions

Most questions are either open or closed. Closed questions are best for gaining specific information, but they tend to stop the dialogue flow. They can be answered with a yes or no, or other simple, factual response. Here are some examples of closed questions: "Did you get to the meeting on time?" "Who's responsible for getting the reports we need?" "When will you be ready to leave?" "Have you called the dentist's office for an appointment?" "Did you say that you could paint the kitchen on Friday?" Closed questions can confirm what you already know or suspect, save time when you're in a hurry, or get a conversation back on track. But they limit the other person's involvement and don't require much in the way of creative thinking.

Open questions, on the other hand, encourage conversations to continue and invite people to open up in ways that closed questions can't. Often, an open question will begin with "what" or "how," but other words will work, too. For example, "How do you feel about your new teaching assignment?" "What was it like when you lived in Japan?" "Could you tell me more about your relationship with your boss?" "How could you have done that differently?" "What do you think about the new accounting system?"

Closed questions can be transformed into open questions, simply by changing the way you phrase them. With a little practice, you'll become very good at it. Here are some samples and some you can try converting yourself.

Closed: Could you have gotten there on time if you had really tried?
Open: What could you have done to arrive on time?
Closed: Can you operate a computer?
Open: Tell me about your computer skills.
Closed: Do you like your new boss?
Open: How do you feel about your new boss?
Closed: Do you have a hard time making that long drive every day?
Open: _____
Closed: Are you and your brother still not speaking to each other?
Open: _____
Closed: Did you enjoy the luncheon speaker?
Open: _____
Closed: Did you have a pleasant weekend?
Open: _____

Dangerous Questions

One brief note of caution. I have found that it's not as useful as it might at first seem to ask open-ended "why" questions. Little kids do it all the time, especially once they realize it can drive their parents crazy. With adults, however, it can be dangerous, because it's so easy for "why" questions to sound judgmental or critical ("Why did you tell your mother we'd come over tomorrow?" "Why are you in such a hurry?" "Why can't you do it like you've always done it?" "Why in the world do you like football so much?").

Even when your "why" question means that you sincerely want to know the reason for something, you have to be careful to avoid a tone of voice, facial expression, or gesture that implies disapproval or impatience. Even if you're careful, you can end up putting the other person on the defensive, anyway. So think twice before you ask a "why" question. Make sure you really want to know the answer and aren't just masking a criticism. Then monitor your nonverbal signals and body language to remove critical or negative indicators.

Two special kinds of open questions are extremely useful, especially when you're in a coaching or mentoring relationship and want to deepen the level of conversation. These are "feeling" questions and what I call "visionary" questions.

Feeling Questions

Feeling questions ask for an emotional response. Asking "How do you feel about that?" will often give you a very different kind of answer than asking "What do you think about that?" Even when someone has no opinion about a particular topic, they may still feel something about it. Exploring feelings is an important part of any helping relationship and an essential part of any quest for expanded personal development.

If you ask a feeling question and get a thinking response, you can always ask again, this time clarifying the kind of reply you're seeking. For example, "How do you feel about your department's reorganization?" may get you a response such as, "I'm sure it will be more efficient this way; after all, a lot of thought went into the planning." You may then choose to say something like, "I'm sure that's true, but I'm wondering how you're feeling about it, personally— how it's affecting you." You may then hear a response that goes a bit deeper: "Well, I have to admit that it's been hard to get used to all of the changes. Sometimes I feel pretty confused and nervous because I'm not sure yet how I fit in, or even whether I fit in."

Visionary Questions

Visionary questions are especially useful when there's a problem to be solved or a change to be made. These questions ask for a shift in perspective from the *problem* (how things are now) to the *solution* (how your listener would like things to be). They are a good way to determine and define objectives, even though the means of achieving those objectives may not yet be clear.

The time for visionary questions is usually after both parties have a clear understanding of the perceived problem—after the relevant aspects of current reality have been expressed and satisfactorily explored. These forward-thinking questions are a way of saying, "What will it look like when you no longer have the problem?" "What will it be like for you when the difficulty no longer exists, when the changes you want have been accomplished?"

Visionary questions are the first step toward setting goals, writing affirmations, and using visualization techniques to help achieve goals. They establish the desired end result, define an ultimate target to shoot for, and paint a word-picture of exactly what it is we want to be, have, and accomplish. They keep hope alive while encouraging optimism, building motivation, and promoting positive thinking.

For example, suppose you've been talking with your protégé about her career. You've established that she's feeling trapped in a dead-end job, frustrated by what she considers menial responsibilities, and angry that no matter how hard she tries, her efforts to move upward within the company have been discouraged. You've explored in some detail her position within the organization, her work history, and her feelings of escalating anxiety and stress. Then you ask a visionary question: "Tell me, without considering how it might come about, what would it be like for you if you didn't have these problems? What might you be doing? How would you feel? What would be different?"

After a little encouragement, something like the following emerges: "Well, sometimes I can imagine myself going back to school. Maybe part-time, at nights. I used to want to be a teacher, and I think I could still be a good one. If I were working toward a teaching degree, I guess I wouldn't mind my job so much. I'd have an end in sight, something to look forward to. Actually, this might be the perfect job while I was going to school, because I do it well and there are no huge responsibilities to worry about."

Instead of jumping in to "correct" her attitude or prematurely suggesting that she should start searching for another job, you've asked her to look inside herself to discover her own vision, to listen to the whispering of her heart's desire, to find the direction in which she'd move if she didn't feel so trapped. When we do this, the door to the trap very often unlatches and begins to swing open.

In some circumstances, it can be hard to answer visionary questions. Folks who are feeling hopeless, helpless, or worthless will have a hard time imagining a better life, a self-directed future from which they get real satisfaction and fulfillment. As a coach or mentor, it's your job to help them understand how they came to feel as they do. Then you need to help them realize that they can change their feelings and their circumstances. Along these lines, there is a great deal that you, as coach and mentor, can do.

You can reconnect them with their own strengths by asking them to remember and tell you about past successes. You can reflect and affirm the positive qualities you observe in them. You can talk about the importance of learning to take charge of self-talk, beliefs, habits, and expectations. You can share what you know about self-fulfilling prophecies and how they work in everyday life. You can explain how to use affirmation and visualization techniques and why they are so powerful. You can guide them toward the books, lectures, classes, seminars, and discussions that will reinforce their efforts to grow. You can help them see that, once they can control what goes on inside their minds, they can begin to exercise a much greater degree of control over what goes on in their everyday lives. And you can show them, by anecdote and personal example, that even when you have very little to say about what happens to you, you have *everything* to say about how you respond—and how you respond makes all the difference.

Avoid Defensive Pushback

Defensive behavior is what happens when someone perceives or anticipates a threat. "Threat" can mean virtually anything that feels uncomfortable—disapproval, domination, ridicule, loss of status, loss of affection, appearing thoughtless or inconsiderate, punishment, and so forth. Many times, although the threat is perceived, it isn't consciously examined or debated, and the effort to defend against it isn't conscious, either. Instead, the whole business happens just outside of consciousness and often has a circular or spiral effect: a perceived threat produces defensive behavior, which engenders defensive listening, which produces verbal and nonverbal signs that defenses are up, which further raises the defense level of the first person, and on and on we go until nothing constructive at all can be accomplished. It's a kind of negative self-fulfilling prophecy.

It's not easy to avoid appearing to evaluate or judge what someone is telling us. Even the simplest question can carry a message that produces defensiveness. A friend of ours tells a story that perfectly illustrates this point. One day, years ago, his family was startled by a series of extremely loud noises. Apparently, their next-door neighbor was working on a truck that was backfiring badly. He looked around for their five-year-old daughter, who had been in the room just a moment ago, and when he didn't see her, he called out "Marcie, where are you?" From the hallway came her uncertain and clearly defensive reply: "Right here, Dad, and I didn't do it!"

We go on the defensive whenever we feel that what we say isn't being taken at face value or when we think that another person is trying to control, manipulate, judge, or evaluate us. We may also adopt a defensive position when we believe that others are only pretending to be interested in us or don't believe we measure up to their standards.

If coaches and mentors are open about their agenda, it goes a long way to dissolve defensiveness. For example, what happens if I really believe that you shouldn't under any circumstances quit your job and go back to school, but I pretend to be neutral while cleverly guiding you with logical arguments toward coming to that decision yourself? You're likely to sniff out my motives and resist just to retain your autonomy. But if I'm honest with you about what I'm thinking and ask you to let me explain my reasons, you'll be more inclined to give me an open hearing.

Better yet, you'll have no reason to feel defensive if I acknowledge my own biases and put them aside in order to approach the issue from a collaborative stance—collaborative meaning that I work with you to define and analyze the problem *from your point of view,* determine costs and benefits, and arrive at a solution you feel comfortable with. This way, I'm allowing you to set your own goals, examine your own feelings, evaluate the options according to your own values, and make your own decisions. By doing so, I have helped you to be more fully empowered.

It's also important that I don't feel superior to you because of my position, power, wealth, physical characteristics, intellect, achievements, etc. If I feel that you are inferior to me in any way, it won't be possible for us to enter equally into a collaborative, problem-solving relationship. You'll probably pick up on my superior feelings and, rightfully, resent them. Of course, certain differences in ability, power, appearance, status, talent, and other characteristics do exist. But, if I see these things as relatively unimportant when it comes to what goes on between us, and completely unimportant when it comes to what really matters in life, you'll sense it and will have no need to be defensive.

One final note about reducing defensiveness. Don't be too sure of what you "absolutely know for certain" and "the right way" to do things. If there's anything that puts us on guard, it is someone who is so dogmatic, so sure that they know what's what, that they have to have their way, win the argument, and convince us that they know "the truth." So let your protégé know that you're willing to investigate, try on other points of view, and experiment with your own attitudes, behaviors, and ideas. See problems as puzzles to be solved rather than issues to be debated. Explore rather than expound. Process rather than pronounce.

If you are a coach or mentor who is genuinely interested in your protégé's well-being, and if you honestly want to develop and grow yourself, you'll enter into the mentoring relationship with an open mind and heart. You'll be willing to share what you know and to learn, as well. When you communicate this open attitude, no offense will be taken, and no defense will be necessary.

If It's Broken, Don't Fix It—Offer Power Tools

It's not your responsibility to solve other people's problems. In fact, as a coach and mentor, it's your job *not* to do this for your protégés. It weakens them and tends to make them feel dependent, less than competent. Instead, try to create an environment within which others can work out their own solutions. Provide support, encouragement, and useful information. Then, listen actively to their assessment of the situation, and reflect back to them the best that they are and the best that they can be.

As I write those words, I have a vivid mental image of Father James McGouldric, one of the wisest, kindest, most truly selfless people I have ever met. While Diane and I were attending Seattle University, Father McGouldric was teaching there. He must have been in his late 70s or early 80s then, a Jesuit scholar who had served for a time as the University's president. He had Ph.D.s in psychology, philosophy, and theology, and he had a photographic memory. But his wisdom came from a supremely loving heart as much as an uncommonly keen mind.

Father McGouldric didn't notice color, wealth, privilege, or power. Instead, he saw the face of God in every human being. He felt so close to his creator that he didn't care much about what other people thought of him, but he was deeply concerned about where he stood with God. He talked out loud to himself whenever he felt like it, often chuckling delightedly at his own private jokes. As a result, many of the students considered him too eccentric to take seriously.

For Diane and me, though, he was a profoundly affecting and influential mentor. He took a personal interest in us, helping us learn how to raise my brothers and our adopted children, helping us understand what children needed and what it took to be good parents, helping us figure out how we could do everything we needed to do and still manage to stay in school. We would often have long discussions about what it meant to live well, to be a Christian in the twentieth century, to use the talents of our minds and the labors of our bodies to glorify God, and to try to make the world a better place.

Does that sound corny in this day and age? I hope not. It sure wasn't corny when Father McGouldric talked about it. It was exhilarating and deeply meaningful. You see, he didn't always agree with the dictates that came from Rome, and he didn't have pat, prefabricated answers to our questions and dilemmas. But he had a wonderful way of talking us through them so that we could make up our own minds. More than that, he helped us feel that we were capable of rising to the challenges we were facing. He was always affirming our strength, intelligence, and determination, and reminding us that we had tremendous personal and spiritual resources to call upon. And if Father McGouldric, as brilliant as he was, believed those things about us, well then, we wanted very much to act like it. And, of course, the more we acted like it, the more true it became.

Remember what we learned about Pygmalions and self-fulfilling prophecies: When you see the best in people and consistently reflect it back to them, they're much more likely to live up to your expectations. James McGouldric reflected the best in us back to Diane and me.

More recently, Iain Kennedy comes to mind as someone who really knows how to bring out the best in people. Iain is a big, burly Scot who'll probably say, if you ask what he does for a living, that he "fixes companies." During the past few years, he led the work force to record-breaking accomplishments at Northern Telecom's radically downsized manufacturing plant in Northern Ireland. If you ask him how in the world he's able to boost output and profits while reducing defects and waste with a drastically reduced workforce, he'll say, "It's not me that does it. It's the people themselves who work the miracles."

But I know Iain Kennedy to be a tireless, exceptionally creative leader. He understands the importance of providing an inspiring common vision and a work environment that not only allows, but encourages and supports personal excellence and continuous improvement. I think it's equally important that he truly cares about his employees as unique human beings, and they know it. While he was at Northern Telecom, he avoided his wood-paneled office, preferring to spend most of his time on the shop floor. As a result, he knew most of his work force personally. He knew their names, what their job responsibilities were, how they felt about their jobs, and, very often, something about their personal lives, as well.

Iain brought in my company's *Investment in Excellence* program for the folks at Northern Telecom because he knew they would benefit enormously, as individuals and as a group. He invited spouses to participate, because he wanted the benefits to affect personal relationships and home lives. He also offered them training in assertiveness (so they wouldn't feel timid about interacting with supervisors), communication skills, and team building (aboard a three-masted sailing ship!). When it was time to tell others about their accomplishments, Iain took a backseat and let his people do the talking. But he praised them to the skies both in and out of their presence, and they did the same about him. To me, at least, these "miracles" are not surprising.

Affirm the Greatness You See

The most powerful thing any of us can do for others is help them to access their untapped potential, to nurture and grow the best parts of themselves—those aspects that are hopeful, brave, persistent, inquisitive, hardworking, creative, resilient, kind, assertive, thoughtful, resourceful, and so forth. In the more than twenty-five years that I've worked as an educator, I've been able to ask some of the world's finest behavior scientists to tell me how much potential human beings actually have. Their answers varied, but boiled down to the same thing: No one knows. Every one of them agreed, though, that we haven't even begun to approach our limits.

Potential, remember, means *possible*—capable of being, with a capacity for development, but not yet in existence, or only partially so. If we can help others to value and believe in themselves, help them to feel supported in their choices, no matter what the outcomes may be, we are helping them to grow into their own greatness. In *Managing from the Heart*, a wonderful parable about leadership that I highly recommend to anyone in business, one of the characters puts it this way: "All the Joes hope they have potential greatness. They carry that hope around in their hearts like a little plant. When somebody else sees it and mentions it, it's like pouring water on the plant to make it grow. When you affirm the greatness inside people, you empower them. They stand straighter. They walk taller."[1]

Saying that we shouldn't try to solve other people's problems, stand between them and the rightful consequences of their actions, or fix their lives for them doesn't mean that we should do nothing but actively listen and help them to see themselves in positive ways. As coaches and mentors, we may have a measure of experience and wisdom that allows us to offer much more.

For instance, through skillful questioning, we can help our

protégés to clarify the elements of a problem or decision they are thinking through. We can help them to identify and evaluate their options and create scenarios for various courses of action, imagining the outcomes of each. We can point out possibilities they may have missed and suggest alternatives to which they may have built scotomas. We can share our own strategies and the results of similar experiences that we have lived through, both successful and unsuccessful (sometimes our failures, mistakes, and aborted attempts can teach far more than those times of relatively smooth sailing).

After we're sure we understand the situation, we can propose certain constructive actions or behavior changes, as long as we accept that our protégé is free to agree or disagree, to accept or reject our proposals, and as long as we don't disapprove or feel disappointed if our ideas are questioned or rejected. We can help our protégés examine and adjust their self-talk, especially their affirmations and visualizations, and know themselves better. And we can help them review and evaluate the consequences of decisions they have made—what worked and what didn't, what new decisions need to be made as a result.

When and How to Apply Pressure

Assuming that our protégés need guidance (why else would we be mentoring or coaching them?), there may be times when we'll need to be directive. This is certainly true in athletic coaching, but it's also true in many other contexts. You have to know when to demand action and when to ease up; when to explain, interpret, and predict and when to let the course of events speak for themselves; when to schedule use of a particular strategy and when to allow a period of relative freedom.

Sometimes there may even be an element of deception, like when the boxing coach allows his student to hit him hard for the first time or the mother lets her child beat her by a slim margin at checkers. There is, of course, no guidebook for mentors or coaches that will tell you exactly what to do when. The art of good timing is acquired as a result of personal experience and learning to trust your intuition. No one can teach it to you.

Nevertheless, one or two general rules of thumb apply. If you are directive or apply pressure too early in the relationship, before a high level of trust and mutual respect have been established, you may see the relationship go out the window. You have to earn the right to tell someone what to do once in a while. On the other hand, if you move too slowly or not at all when directive action is what's needed, you may lose credibility or find yourself dealing with a thoroughly bored or restless protégé.

Just as athletes are required by their coaches to make their way through certain step-by-step progressions that will allow them to improve their skills, so a mentor must sometimes challenge a protégé to dissolve scotomas, let go of old ways of doing and seeing, take calculated risks, push a little harder, stretch comfort zones, and move forward into unfamiliar new territory.

After all is said and done, all the pros and cons examined, all the feelings discussed and possible consequences evaluated, sometimes you just need to say: "Look, I really don't think you should take that job. I know you, and I know that company, and it's not for you." Or "Frankly, unless you learn to listen without judging and to express your love in ways that mean something to your spouse, I don't think you're going to make much headway with healing your marriage." Or "My sense of things is that you're not taking graduate school seriously. Otherwise you'd find a way to get to class on time, and you'd make it your business to do the required reading." Or "It's time for you to get off the fence and take the plunge as an independent contractor. You may fail, but I don't think so, and it's worth the risk."

The Gift of Receiving

There's something else we can give to those we are coaching or mentoring, and it's extremely important. I'm talking about our willingness to let them give to us. We *feel* good when we can *do* good. Giving builds a generous spirit and self-esteem. If we cast our-selves exclusively in the role of coach, teacher, mentor, benevolent bestower of precious gifts, we rob our protégés of this pleasure. The message we send is that they have nothing we want or need, and that is a devaluing message. Besides, it's not true.

Sometimes it's hard for us to feel comfortable in the recipient's role because we've been taught that it's better to give, and that it is somehow an imposition, shameful, weak, or morally wrong to ask for or accept assistance, praise, or gifts. Just the opposite is true. When we open our hearts so that we can receive graciously and apprecia-tively from others, it enhances our well-being and theirs, too. Even when the gift we are given is a simple compliment, too many of us habitually tend to deflect it, shrug it off, ignore it, or even deny it out of a misguided desire to behave modestly or humbly. A smile, a light touch on the arm, and a sincere "Thank you!" gives the other per-son the pleasure of having caused us, for a moment, to feel good.

Do you know anyone who *always* has to pick up the dinner check, *always* has to buy your movie ticket, *always* has to pay your way into the ball game, no matter how much you'd like to have a turn? It feels pretty uncomfortable after a while, doesn't it? What about the friend who is constantly ready to listen to your troubles and frustrations, perennially eager to help you out when you need help, but never seems to want or need your counsel, never asks for a favor, never wants to accept your gifts or tokens of appreciation? Wouldn't you feel better about the friendship if you were allowed to give something back that was received with real appreciation?

Children, old folks, the unemployed, and people who find them-selves in dependent circumstances have special needs to give. In his book, *Priceless Gifts*, psychologist Daniel Sugarman tells the story of a sensitive, psychologically aware woman who puts her ninety-year-old grandmother to work for her. The grandmother lives in a senior hous-ing facility where the focus is on doing as much as possible for the res-idents. But during the two or three visits a year when she comes to stay with her granddaughter, her services as an expert cookie maker are in great demand. The granddaughter lets her know that she really needs her help in preparing for a luncheon or other special event, and, as the old woman mixes and bakes the cookies, they talk. What a wonderful gift this wise woman is giving in allowing her grandmother to give and feel useful! What a wonderful gift she is giving to herself as she strengthens this important relationship![2]

The late Sir Alec Dickson, who founded Britain's Voluntary Service Overseas (after which our Peace Corps was modeled) and Community Service Volunteers, believed that everyone, no matter how difficult their present circumstances or painful their history, has something of value to give. Alec and his wife, Mora, loved to tell stories about their volunteers. Many of them were people who might just as easily have been on the receiving end of a helping relationship. But the point of Alec and Mora's anecdotes was always that the opportunity to give in a meaningful way benefited not only the recipients, but also the volunteers themselves. It allowed them to gain tremendous self-confidence and a new sense of self-worth.

In Paris, the natives, deservedly or not, have a reputation for coolness, even rudeness to foreigners. But I have heard that the words "*J'ai une probleme . . .*" ("I have a problem . . .") preceding an inquiry will earn a tourist instant attention, interest, and genuine friendliness. This makes perfect sense to me, because I believe that the desire to be of real service, to connect with each other in meaningful, useful ways, exists within us all. When we are approached as if we have something important to contribute (in this case, a problem to help solve), even the most distant of us is likely to respond.

In Chapter 10, we turn to the often misunderstood concept of motivation. You'll find out what works, what doesn't, and why. Then, I'll tell you why you can't really motivate anybody to do anything unless you understand some little-known facts about how our minds work. Finally, we'll talk about how self-efficacy affects motivation, and I'll show you how to raise your own self-efficacy as well as that of the people you're coaching or mentoring.

CHAPTER TEN

Inside-Out Motivation

Why We Don't Do What We Have to Do

hy does your spouse eagerly run five miles every other day, rain or shine, but you practically have to threaten him to get him to mow the lawn? Once he does agree to do it, how come something "urgent" always seems to come up that requires his attention elsewhere? Why is it that your best friend never seems to lose any weight, even though she's been on a diet for as long as you've known her? Why is it like trying to herd cats to get your employees to show up at mandatory staff meetings on time? Why did your twelve-year-old daughter bring home As and Bs from school last term, but now can't manage anything better than a C? Why does it take weeks for your office manager to get a few annual performance reviews finished, when she whizzes through the more complex quarterly financial reports in half the time? Why is it that you've been meaning to start working out for a year now, but somehow you haven't gotten around to actually doing it?

> "Where the heart is willing, it will find a thousand ways, but where it is unwilling, it will find a thousand excuses."
>
> Bornean Proverb

People can do just about anything if they are highly motivated, and there is plenty of evidence to support that statement. Even in cases where lack of ability, access, or means may at first appear to be formidable obstacles, these can eventually be overcome if motivation is strong enough. But what does it mean to be motivated? Are there different kinds of motivation, as well as different levels? Are superachievers and peak performers born that way, or is it something that can be learned? Can you, as a coach or mentor, influence the motivation your protégé feels to do certain things? And can you do it in a positive, nonthreatening way?

In this chapter, we'll look at why people behave the way they do. We'll see what causes us to enthusiastically take on some challenges and doggedly avoid others—why we sometimes resist and drag our heels and sometimes jump in with both feet and persist until we get the job done. And we'll see how to help ourselves and others control what goes on inside our minds in order to feel more highly motivated and accomplish more of what we want to do in life.

Let's start by agreeing that motivation is *an incentive or motive that causes you to behave in certain ways or to take, or fail to take, some action*. Now, let's look at two of the most common, and most important, kinds.

Constructive Versus Restrictive Motivation

When you are motivated in a constructive way, you feel excited and enthusiastic about doing something you really want to do or achieving something you really want to achieve. You're convinced that you are moving forward in a positive direction, toward a result you truly desire. Nobody has to remind you to do it, persuade you to take the next step, or list the benefits for you. It's motivation in the form of a nice, juicy carrot dangling out in front.

Restrictive motivation, on the other hand, drives you from behind with a stick. When you're motivated restrictively, you are doing something only because you want to avoid something else: failure, rejection, punishment, shame, ridicule, conflict, disgrace, loss, pain, or any other consequence you see as negative or threatening. You aren't taking action because you really want to, but rather because you feel that you have to . . . or else. You aren't moving toward an outcome you desire as much as you are trying to move away from an outcome you want to avoid.

Restrictive motivation is based on some form of fear, and, like most of us, you are probably all too familiar with how well it works. Your parents, teachers, coaches, spiritual and political leaders, even the neighborhood bullies who terrorized you when you were a kid discovered long ago that pain and fear are great motivators. They could get you to do what they wanted for as long as they could convince you that you had a good reason to be scared of what would happen if you didn't. If you were persuaded to believe in those reasons for a long enough time and with a strong enough emotional investment, you could even end up doing what they wanted long after they were no longer watching, sometimes long after they were dead and gone. But you do it only because you believe you *have* to (ought to, need to, should, must) . . . or else.

Except that something very interesting tends to happen whenever you believe you have to do something. It's called pushback, and it's exactly what it sounds like. When you feel coerced, manipulated, or pushed into doing something, you resist, rebel, and push back. Or you procrastinate, practice creative avoidance, become easily distracted and unable to concentrate. Or you do the job badly, making careless mistakes, breaking equipment. Or you get sick or accidentally injure yourself. You probably aren't doing these things deliberately, but conscious intention isn't necessary. Your creative subconscious can take care of it for you very nicely.

That's why something else always seems to come up when your spouse is scheduled to mow the lawn, and it's probably why you can't find your staff when it's time for the weekly meeting they *have to* attend. It's also why your best friend doesn't lose weight, in spite of constant dieting, and why you have a hundred reasons for postponing your workout program. If it's not something you really want and freely choose to do, you'll either find a way to get out of it altogether, or you'll do it halfheartedly or sporadically, and the results will reflect your efforts.

Restrictive motivation disappears as soon as the threat of negative consequence is removed. The mice play when the cat's away. Production on the shop floor runs in slow motion or develops major problems when the tyrannical, hard-nosed supervisor is out of town. Dishes pile up in the sink, and the garbage overflows when the superfastidious, controlling roommate is out of town. The kids raid the refrigerator and put the dog in the clothes dryer while the baby-sitter is talking to her boyfriend on the phone. As soon as the pressure is off, we tend go back to our normal behavior instead of that which has been imposed upon us from the outside.

I have found this to be a key factor in the less than satisfactory results of many Total Quality Management (TQM) programs. TQM means new ways of doing things, new responsibilities. It means change, with a capital "C." And whenever change is imposed from the outside, resistance and a tremendous desire to get things to somehow change back can be expected. When a TQM program is implemented, people who think they are already doing the best they can hear the message "not good enough" carried on the winds of change. They're not looking at the fact that they have virtually unlimited potential for doing and being more than they presently are. Instead, they're feeling the pressure and stress that inevitably come from someone else telling you that you had better change, had better do things differently, if you want to measure up.

An ideal TQM implementation would change the workers' internal picture before, or at the same time as, the external standards change. It would give them the education, tools, knowledge, and skills that enable them to empower themselves. It would give them the information that allows them to change, and it would give them the opportunity to change—willingly and wholeheartedly—their own picture of what's good enough for them. To many managers' surprise, most people, when given this opportunity and information, do choose to make that change. In fact, they often set higher standards for themselves than the managers would have set for them. What's more, they not only achieve their goals, but often surpass them.

Life in the Restrictive Zone

There is a special kind of restrictive motivation that can be extremely stifling and negative. It's called *inhibitive motivation*, and the words that alert you to it are *I can't . . . or else.* Instead of all the things you *have to* or *must* do, inhibitive motivators are concerned with all the things you'd *better not* or *can't* do.

It's safe to say that all of us have been raised with at least a few inhibitive motivators nipping at our heels. Some of them were clearly necessary to keep us and other people safe—to see us through to adulthood alive and in one piece: We'd better not cross the street without carefully looking both ways, better not play with matches, can't drive the car until we're old enough for a learner's permit, can't go to school only when we happen to be in the mood, can't lash out with a baseball bat whenever we feel furious. Some of the inhibitive motivators that affect our behavior today make good sense, too. We don't indulge ourselves with all the ice cream and fried foods we want because of the damage it will do to our blood vessels, not to mention our waistlines. We don't drive with bald tires or bad brakes. We don't carry on a conversation while the film is running at the movie theater. And we don't let our dog run wild in the neighbor's flower garden.

Unfortunately, though, many of the "better nots" we internalized when we were kids had a lot more to do with our parents' desire to control us than they did with safety or good sense. Some of us learned that children should be seen and not heard, and that if we want to avoid trouble, we'd better not speak our minds or express what we really feel. Some of us were taught, not that it's important to try our best to be punctual, but that we can't ever be late. Not that it's useful to be able to look on the bright side, but that we'd better wear a smile at all times, or else. Not that it's beneficial to bring up children in a two-parent family, but that anything else is unworkable and doomed to failure, period. Not that good nutrition and a balanced diet are important parts of overall good health, but that we must never enjoy a soft drink or eat anything that even looks like junk food. The list is endless.

As we grew older, though, many of us learned to question these inhibitive motivators and discard those that were no longer useful or that weren't backed by a reason we could understand and agree with. Having parents who really wanted us to learn to think for ourselves was a tremendous help. They would answer our "Why?" and "Why not?" questions and wanted to avoid dumping a bunch of unnecessary restrictions on us just so they could feel more powerful.

Some of us were not so fortunate. Guilt, shame, and fear of the consequences if we stepped out of line took away many of our choices. If we didn't rebel later on, and sometimes even if we did, we grew up to be rigid and dogmatic, and we developed "restrictive zones" by the score. Whenever we violated our own inner rules of conduct, we felt anxious and upset. But we also felt that way whenever *someone else* violated those hard and fast rules. Gradually, over time, we took on a job that I call "Captain of the World"—we became petty tyrants who thought we knew just how everyone else should behave and were constantly fuming because they refuse or fail to do it.

"Look at those people, walking in after the concert has already started. What an annoyance! Don't they know you're not supposed to do that!" "Do you see how long that kid's hair is? Boy, if I were his father, he'd get a haircut pronto, and none of those tattoos, either, or he'd be looking for another place to live." "Didn't anyone ever tell her that you don't *type* thank-you notes? They have to be handwritten! She might as well have not have sent one at all if she doesn't know how to do it correctly!" "His desk looks like a tornado struck it. What a mess! Why doesn't he put his work in file folders and store it out of sight, the way I do? He can't be very efficient." "Can you believe the getup on that woman at church? Is she color-blind? It looked like she was decked out for a night on the town. I think I'll say something to her if she shows up next week. Someone certainly should."

Constructive Conversions

Have-to's restrict and create pushback. Want-to's motivate and create drive. So how do you build more want-to's into your life and eliminate those pesky have-to's? How do you help other people to do it? Well, you start with self-talk. You start, as always, with what's going on inside your head and heart. And with the realization that, with very few exceptions, have-to's are cop-outs—lies we tell ourselves to avoid taking responsibility for painful choices we have made.

I vividly remember the time I worked with a famous distance runner who was training for the Olympics but had been experiencing a serious problem. He had heard about the successful work I've done with other college and professional athletes, so he thought I might be able to help. As he explained it, no matter how well he was running, when he reached the final quarter-mile or so of the race, he began to experience severe pain in his lungs. He had been thoroughly checked out by a doctor, but there was nothing physically wrong, and he wondered if there was anything psychological he could do to beat the pain.

"There may be something," I said. "But first, tell me what you think about when you're running a race. What goes through your mind, particularly as you hit that last quarter mile?" "I don't think," he replied. "I block everything out. But when I reach the last quarter mile, my lungs start burning so badly, I have to talk to myself to get through it. So in my mind I tell myself, 'Keep going! You have to keep going! You have to finish this last quarter mile! You have to keep running!'"

"OK," I said. "I've got the answer, but I don't think you're going to like it. When you get to that last quarter mile and you feel like you have to keep running, just stop right there, move over to the side of the course and sit down." He looked at me as if I had just told him to unfold a pair of wings and fly for the last quarter mile. "That's ridiculous," he responded. "If I stop and sit down, even if I slow down, I'll lose for sure." "That's right," I said. "But I guarantee you, your lungs will stop burning."

"But why do you think I run in the first place?" he asked me. "I have no idea," I replied. "Why don't you tell me?" His face grew serious and fierce as he drew himself up and squared his shoulders. "I run for my family, for my village, for my country! My family made many sacrifices to send me to college in America, and I want them and everyone back home to be proud. If I win a gold medal, it will bring great honor to my family and my village. When I return home I will be very respected and rich."

I said, "Then stop complaining, man, and run! You're not running because you *have* to. No one's forcing you to run. No one's holding a gun to your head. It's *your* idea, your *choice* to race. Forget your lungs, and remember why you're running in the first place. Think of how happy you'll feel when you win, and focus on that. Imagine the proud faces of your family and the people in your village when you win that gold medal. Focus on that! You don't *have* to run, you *get* to! And when you're moving into that last quarter mile, remind yourself, 'I don't *have* to do this, I *want* to do it! I *love* to do it! I *get* to do it, and I'm going to win!' And you'll just eat that race alive!"

That's the way to keep yourself motivated, to stop simply existing and start truly living your life! It's also something to keep in mind when you're trying to help someone else with a motivation problem. Some time ago, I read a report that fascinated me. It said that enthusiastic people have so much vitality because it takes only about one-tenth as much energy to do something enthusiastically as it does to force yourself, dragging your psychic feet and resisting your own efforts. By the way, our English word *enthusiasm* comes from a Greek term that means "to be inspired by a god." No wonder we feel so much lighter, energized, more creative and practically tireless when we are operating from a want-to, choose-to, get-to, love-it point of view!

What do you believe you have to do, like it or not? What are the shoulds and ought-to's that you keep putting off? Do you think you ought to lose twenty-five pounds? Do you believe you should stop smoking? Do you feel you ought to spend more time with your family? Do you have to make sure your kids eat a good breakfast every day? Must you have dinner at your in-laws' every Saturday? Do you have to drag yourself out of bed five days a week at 6:00 A.M.?

If you'd like to have fewer shoulds and have-to's and more want-to's and get-to's in your life, and to help others feel that way, too, try this experiment. It's designed to help you get a handle on your self-talk and improve your self-awareness, accountability, and motivation level. Draw a line down the center of a page of lined paper. Then, on the left side of the page, make a list of all of those things in your life that you are not currently doing but believe you should or ought to do. List one per line, starting with the words "I should . . ." Following these, list all the things you have to do, starting with the words "I have to . . ."

Now, on the right hand side of the page, opposite every should or ought-to sentence you listed, write a new sentence that begins with the words, "If I really want to, I can . . ." So, opposite "I should lose twenty-five pounds," you have a sentence that reads, "If I really want to, I can lose twenty-five pounds." And opposite every have-to sentence, write a new one that begins, "I choose to . . ." So, next to "I have to get up every morning at 6:00 A.M.," write "I choose to get up every morning at 6:00 A.M."

Do you see what you've done? In the case of the shoulds and ought-to's, you have put the accountability for doing or not doing these things right where they belong—in your own hands. You are giving yourself an opportunity to look at what's really going on (Do you really want to lose those twenty-five pounds, or is someone else pressuring you into it?). At the same time, you have empowered yourself to take action when you are clear about what you want. You are telling yourself that you *can* do it, that you have the ability and the power, if you so choose and desire. With the have-to's, you are helping yourself to see that everything you do in life, with the exception of taking up physical space and eventually dying, you do by choice. You are, once again, empowering yourself, putting control of your life where it belongs and where it, in fact, really is all along.

Granted, some choices are easier to make than others, and some come with pretty stiff consequences if you don't make them. You don't *have* to make your mortgage payments, but if you don't keep your agreement to pay, they'll take the house away from you. So you choose to pay them. You don't *have* to go to work every day. You could go on welfare or try to make your home on the street, living on handouts from the food banks and missions. Or you could become a thief, taking what you want from others and running the risk of capture and jail. But you probably don't like those options, so you've *chosen* to work. And when you remember all those folks out there looking for a job—any job—or trying to make ends meet on a temporary unemployment check, you also remember that you *get to* go to work.

All of us have to make some tough choices sometimes, and I don't know anyone who hasn't made a few that they've come to regret later on. If you really don't like the way a particular aspect of your life is going, for heaven's sake and your own well-being, do something about it. Take steps to change it or something about it by changing your attitude and your behavior. If, now and then, no matter what you try to do, it looks like you're just going to have to bite the bullet and find a way live with it, it may help to remember the Alcoholics Anonymous Serenity Prayer: "Lord, grant me the courage to change what I need to change, the serenity to accept what I cannot change, and the wisdom to know the difference."

Self-Efficacy, Self-Regulation, and Motivation

In his book *Social Foundations of Thought and Action*, world-renowned efficacy expert Albert Bandura tells us that "people will approach, explore, and try to deal with situations within their self-perceived capabilities, but, unless externally coerced, they will avoid transactions with aspects of their environment that they perceive as exceeding their coping capability."[1]

In simpler terms, this means that we don't take on tasks we don't believe we can accomplish or that we think we'll perform poorly. We don't let ourselves try to acquire or even desire what we don't think we can have. Our desires, goals, and ambitions conform to our beliefs about what we can do, what we deserve, what's good enough for us. We adjust our activities to fit our inner pictures of who we are.

Let's back up a bit for a moment. As you remember from our earlier discussions, you have a self-image—an internal picture of who you are and what you're like. You have personal expectations or standards for yourself and ideas about what you can and can't do well. These expectations or standards grow out of your self-image. For example, if you see yourself as a good problem-solver, when a problem comes up, you'll tackle it confidently and expect to succeed. If you see yourself as an accomplished public speaker, when it's time to make a presentation, you'll be eager to show your stuff, instead of trying to fade into the wallpaper.

You are constantly evaluating yourself and your performance against internal standards. Then you react to your evaluations with rewards (self-praise) or punishment (guilt or self-criticism). If your self-image is poor and your self-efficacy is low, it won't shake you up too much when you perform badly. After all, there have been no surprises and your poor performance is consistent with your self-image. "That's like me," you think. "I've done it again." No big deal.

If your self-image is strong and your self-efficacy is high, you naturally expect a good performance from yourself. If you happen to do poorly, your system will be thrown out of order. "That's *not* like me!" you'll think, and you'll set about doing whatever you need to do to correct for the mistake. That's how all of us operate. **We self-regulate up (or down) to our own internal standards.**

We've already talked about what happens when high standards are externally imposed on people whose internal standards are lower: As soon as they can, as soon as the external pressure is gone, they return to behavior that reflects their own standards. The same thing happens if your self-image is poor and your self-efficacy is low, but for some reason you turn in a stellar performance. Again, the internal message is "That's not like me!" and your subconscious helps you adjust back down to your usual, comfortable level of mediocrity. You correct for the mistake.

Let me tell you a true story that will help you to remember this principle. Some time ago, I was visiting the Australian branch of my company and doing some public presentations. While I was there, I was asked to consult with the governor of the Northern Territory. I was told that they were having some problems with the Aboriginal people and were feeling very frustrated. Apparently, the government had built some new homes for the Aborigines. But, after they moved into their new quarters, they would tear off the metal roofs, carry them to the ground, and sleep under them.

While the governor and I were flying over the territory, inspecting the houses, we chatted casually about many things. At one point, I said to him, "Have you ever thought about moving into new quarters yourself? Of course, I've heard that your house is lovely by some standards, but considering your station and responsibilities, don't you think that you should really have something much better?"

The governor looked startled. "Well, no," he said. "Not really." "Oh, yes," I persisted. "Something much larger and more opulent. Indoor and outdoor tennis courts. A swimming pool. Two pools. Conservatory. Ballroom. Something, perhaps, on the order of Buckingham Palace." At this point, he gave me a look that clearly questioned my sanity, his chin lifted, and his spine straightened. "I am really quite comfortable where I am," he said. "My family and I are very fond of our home, and we would feel entirely out of place in a mansion such as you describe." "Yes," I replied. "And that's exactly how the Aborigines feel!"

Remember, **all meaningful and lasting change starts first on the inside and then works its way out.** You simply can't impose change from the outside and expect it to be welcomed or, even more important, to last. You can't build houses that seem like palaces to Aborigines, move them in, and expect them to successfully adapt, just like that. It doesn't fit their picture of who they are and how they live. It makes them uncomfortable, just as it makes any of us uncomfortable when our mental picture of how things should be doesn't match current reality. And, when our internal picture and current reality don't match, we consciously or unconsciously correct for the mistake.

Expectations That Motivate

Self-efficacy is related as much to what we *believe* about our ability to do something as it is about our actual ability to do it. Given roughly equal ability to perform a task, people with a strong belief in their ability and high expectations of success usually do better than those with weaker beliefs and lower expectations. Why should this be? Well, if you remember what we've learned about self-fulfilling prophecies and the way our minds work to make sure our internal pictures of reality match what's happening in our environment, it's not surprising.

First of all, people with high self-efficacy feel that they have more to say about what happens to them than people with low self-efficacy. They believe that, even though external forces beyond their control may be operating, their own actions and efforts will ultimately determine how things work out. And, as Dr. Albert Bandura points out, "People who believe that outcomes are determined by their behavior tend to be more active than those who perceive events more fatalistically."[2] "Being active," of course, means taking action. Trying harder. Persisting in the face of obstacles and difficulties. Bouncing back from failure or poor performance, increasing efforts, changing tactics, getting assistance if necessary.

In *Learned Optimism*, Dr. Martin Seligman tells the story of swimmer Matt Biondi, the young man who won seven medals in the 1988 Seoul Olympics. Biondi, whom everyone expected to "bring home the gold," began his performance with bronze and silver medals, disappointing himself and thousands of fans around the world. But Dr. Seligman, who was watching from his living room in

Pennsylvania, felt certain that Biondi would rebound from a situation that might easily discourage and depress someone else.[3]

Seligman thought so because, some time earlier, Biondi and his team members completed a questionnaire Seligman had designed to measure optimism, pessimism, and explanatory style (the way we explain to ourselves why things happen). The results had shown Biondi to be extremely optimistic, with a very strong belief in his own accountability and very high self-efficacy. Here, in Seligman's words, is how those questionnaire results had been verified in the pool, and why he felt so sure that Biondi was going to do extremely well, even after a less than promising beginning:

> [After the questionnaires were scored] we had then simulated defeat under controlled conditions in the pool. Nort Thornton, Biondi's coach, had him swim the one-hundred-yard butterfly all out. Biondi swam it in 50.2 seconds, a very respectable time. But Thornton told him that he had swum 51.7, a very slow time for Biondi. Biondi looked disappointed and surprised. Thornton told him to rest up for a few minutes and then swim it again—all out. Biondi did. His actual time got even faster, 50.0. Because his explanatory style was highly optimistic and he had shown us that he got faster—not slower—after defeat, I felt he would bring back gold from Seoul.[4]

In his last five events in Seoul, Biondi won five gold medals. Here is Albert Bandura again: "Judgment of self-efficacy determines how much effort people will expend and how long they will persist in the face of obstacles or aversive experience." In other words, our beliefs and expectations about how well we can do something affect how well we actually do it, because they cause us to try harder.

Encouraging High Expectations

Can a good coach or mentor help raise self-efficacy? Can he or she help create strong expectations of success, thereby affecting effort and ultimate performance? Absolutely. Do you recall Albert Bandura's prescription for building self-efficacy? He listed four components: (1) mastery experiences; (2) vicarious experiences (relevant, successful role models); (3) social persuasion; and (4) a positive physiological state and/or positive interpretation of physical inadequacies.[5] Let's look at them again, one by one, and see how coaches and mentors can play an important role in creating and reinforcing them.

Mastery experiences: Encourage your protégés to make their own choices and to view their activities and purposes as uniquely their own. Don't let your desire to guide, protect, care for or help rob them of their autonomy and rightful self-determination.

Henry David Thoreau once observed, "If I knew that a man were coming to my house with a conscious design of doing me good, I should run for my life." Don't do for your protégés what they can and should do for themselves. Instead, remind them of their past accomplishments, strengths, and successful solutions to knotty problems. Help them remember and affirm their own good judgment, their ability to run their own lives, to take full accountability for the results, to take risks, and to make—and learn from—their mistakes.

Vicarious experiences: If you're coaching or mentoring others, you've had the benefit of plenty of experiences they haven't. Share what you've learned from those experiences, from your own mentors, from your formal education, and from the school of hard knocks. Tell them about your successes and failures in situations relevant to their own. Talk about events that caused you to stretch and grow, decisions you made that paid off and those you lived to regret, things you'd do differently.

Let them see how you deal with current obstacles, frustrations, failure, and setbacks, as well as with opportunities and achievement. Let them know that you've come out on top, not so much because you've been lucky (though you may have been), but because of your own determination, resiliency, willingness to learn, and guts. Let them know you think that if you can do it, so can they.

Social persuasion: Assuming that you have credibility in the eyes of your protégé, you will definitely have clout in the social persuasion department. When you say, "I know you can do it!" it will mean something. When you say, "Hang in there, you've got what it takes to succeed in this business!" it will encourage. And when you say, "Everybody makes mistakes. The important thing is that you gave it your best shot. You'll do better next time," it will comfort and inspire. Self-confidence grows in the presence of those who have confidence in us. Self-efficacy grows around people who see us as competent.

I once heard the Reverend Dale Turner, pastor of a church in Seattle, tell a story about a little boy who considers drying dishes for his mom a great honor. One night, he had been drying a large meat platter, when it slipped out of his hands and shattered on the floor. Then there was a moment of silence, until his mother said, "You know, Robert, in all the times you've dried the dishes for me, this is the first time you've ever broken one. I think you've set some kind of world record!" Anxiety left the boy's face, and he grinned. Enough said.

Positive physiological state and/or positive interpretation of physical inadequacies: Empathy, reassurance, and gentle coaching are a great help in dealing with life's inevitable assaults on our bodies— extreme or prolonged stress, disease, injury, profound fatigue, disability, old age, even the approach of death. So is the conviction that, no matter what happens to us, our response to those circumstances, including management of our health care and environment, is still under our control.

A large and growing body of evidence indicates that our sense of control has numerous effects on our physical health. In *Anatomy of an Illness*, Norman Cousins describes how he failed his exercise electrocardiogram when he had to take it under rigid, strictly controlled rules but passed it easily when he was allowed to oversee the pace and environment.[6]

Yale psychologist Judith Rodin says, "Control is more likely to affect health than health is to affect control." Rodin and her colleague, Ellen Langer, are responsible for several studies supporting that statement. One of them, which took place in a nursing home, is especially interesting. The nursing home staff encouraged one group of residents to take care of themselves as much as possible. They dressed, fed, and groomed themselves and maintained their own environments. Another group of residents was cared for almost entirely by the staff. After three weeks, the men and women who were responsible for their own care were more alert, active, and happier. Not only that, after 18 months, only 15 percent of those in the self-management group had died, compared to 30 percent in the group that was cared for by staff![7]

Compassionate, interested role models who have dealt with similar physical difficulties are valuable, too. If you don't fit into that category, seek out and introduce your protégé to someone who does. But even if you've never faced this kind of challenge, you can still help with attitude adjustment support, stress management, and encouragement when it comes to positive interpretation.

In his exceptional book, *Who Gets Sick,* psychologist Blair Justice says that, "Our attitudes . . . toward the very subject of stress can influence our reactions when we are in trying situations. Our physiological responses will be considerably less intense if we see stress as an inevitable part of life and a challenge rather than something that is awful and must be avoided."[8] Mentors and coaches can help us adopt the "inevitable challenge" perspective. They can also help us keep spirits up and hope alive. Dr. Viktor Frankl, the eminent psychiatrist who survived confinement in a Nazi concentration camp, affirms that "those who know how close the connection is between the state of a man—his courage and hope, or lack of them—and the state of . . . his body will understand that the sudden loss of hope and courage can have a deadly effect."[9]

While we're on the subject of inevitable challenges, Chapter 11 is all about coaching and mentoring people who are facing substantial obstacles and formidable tasks. In it, I give you ten practical ways to get through tough times. You can use them yourself or add them to your repertoire of skills as a coach or mentor when the time comes.

CHAPTER ELEVEN

Mentoring Through Tough Times

Paths Without Obstacles Go Nowhere

Obstacles are part of any significant quest. No matter how diligently we set goals, visualize results, affirm a successful outcome, and maintain a positive attitude, no one escapes mistakes, setbacks, illness, pain, fatigue, failure, and loss. Carefully laid plans go up in smoke—sometimes quite literally. People we counted on bail out. Resources we needed to finish an important project dry up. A health or family crisis strikes. An earthquake, flood, or tornado puts us back to square one.

> "If I had a formula for bypassing trouble, I would not pass it round. Trouble creates a capacity to handle it."
>
> Oliver Wendell Holmes

When we look at the plight of people who are immersed in real tragedy, our own problems may seem trivial by comparison, and sometimes they are. Our problem-solving *experiences*, though, are not trivial. Solving problems and coping with crisis offer some of the most important opportunities for growth we will ever have. Of course, because our initial focus is usually on the threat, loss, or challenge, they probably don't feel like such great opportunities at first. But they are.

In the Chinese written language, the two characters signifying "danger" and "opportunity" are combined to create the one that represents "crisis." In medical terminology, a crisis is a turning point, a sudden change *for worse or for better* in a serious illness. But it's not just a crisis that encompasses these two seemingly opposite elements. Every problem, every adversity contains, along with the prospect of pain and loss, the seeds of an opportunity and the possibility of growth and gain. Some good can come from every bad situation. As a coach or mentor, it's important to understand that this is not "Pollyanna" thinking. It's the simple truth.

Armed with what you're learning here, you will be equipped to help others navigate their way through the dangers to discover and follow the path of opportunity. I don't mean that someday they're going to look back on every tough time and crisis in their past and think, "Well, that was certainly a blessing in disguise. I'm really glad it happened." That won't always be the case, and you wouldn't want to mislead anyone into believing it.

No matter how difficult or painful the experience, though, you can help them adopt a perspective that looks back and says, "As wrenching as that was, something good came from it. As hard as it was to get through, I did it, and I learned something important from it." If nothing else, you can help them realize that they're survivors, people with the ability to tough it out, to hang on and hang in until things ease up—a valuable character trait that often makes all the difference when it comes to positive end results.

During this past year, my mother died. Her death was not entirely unexpected, as she had been ill for some time and was getting on in years. Nevertheless, it was a hard time for me. Part of what made it so hard was the looking back that almost inevitably accompanies the death of a close family member. Such a big part of what I had to look back on when it came to my mother was painful. I've already told you some of that story: She struggled with alcoholism most of her life, and my brothers and sister and I pretty much raised ourselves. She was unpredictably violent sometimes, yet she also had a very warm, artistic, creative side and became a fairly accomplished writer and potter. I guess she really wasn't very well-equipped, psychologically, to be a mother, and that didn't change just because she happened to have children.

One of the condolence messages we received when she died came from Mary Martin, a long-time friend and business associate who lives in California. Mary is a wonderful, wise, highly successful woman, and her message meant a lot to me because it helped me to remember the opportunity that had blossomed from the adversity of my childhood. She reminded me that life with my mother may not have been easy, but it was an important part of who and what I had become. It had helped me to learn self-sufficiency, resiliency, mental toughness, and the value of persistence. It showed me that not only could I take care of myself, I could help others grow at the same time. It helped me realize that I wanted something very different for myself and my children. And it taught me that even people who can't stop themselves from hurting and from hurting other people can still bring beauty and value to the world.

Adversity: What You Make of It, What It Makes of You

Bad things happen to good people. The most important thing to remember when you or someone you're coaching or mentoring is going though a tough time is this: Even though it may be true that you have little or no control over the circumstance you find yourself in, you still have a choice about how you're going to respond to it. In the long run, if your goal is to be successful on your own terms, that response is what matters most.

For more than twenty-five years, I've been studying success. As a result, some of the most successful people in the world have been my students, and I, in turn, have learned a great deal from them. As I've mentioned earlier, I have also spent a lot of time in the company of some of the world's most respected research psychologists, talking about what makes some people succeed and others succumb, some rebound while others lie down for the count—the difference, in short, between people who make it and people who don't.

After all these years of study, experience, and research, I can tell you one thing with the utmost confidence: Everyone likes to think that they have what it takes to survive adversity and tough times, but when the chips are down, some people definitely do better than others. The secret of getting through tough times and achieving eventual success is *attitude*. That's it. And it's really not a secret.

People who survive and succeed don't have fewer problems than other people. They don't start out with greater brainpower or better looks or exceptionally loving parents or more money, either. As a matter of fact, they often start out having to work against formidable odds. But they have developed personalities that allow them more options. They have a strong, clear intention to survive and succeed, and to do it in good shape. They seem to have a way of looking at things, a way of seeing the diamonds of opportunity embedded in the mountains blocking their path. When problems or setbacks occur, they don't waste time complaining, and they don't dwell on the past or on what they've lost. Instead, they focus their energies on getting things to turn out as well as possible. They don't get mad at the world for not treating them better, but they do have an extensive menu of behaviors they can choose from, depending on the situation.

Stephen Hawking, one of the most remarkable figures of the twentieth century, is a perfect example. Hawking has Lou Gehrig's disease, a progressive illness that has taken from him his ability to walk or even move most of his muscles, care for himself in the most basic ways, and speak. Yet he has earned an international reputation as an extraordinarily brilliant and immensely popular theoretical physicist. At a lecture he gave in Seattle last year, he says that although aids like wheelchairs and computers can play an important role in overcoming physical deficiencies, the right mental attitude is even more important, and he urged disabled people to stop complaining about public attitudes and start taking action to change how they are perceived.

Hawking clearly understands that successful survivors are option-thinkers instead of black-and-white, either/or, one-way kinds of people. They believe (as Hawking does) that *they* are the ones who are ultimately in charge of their own destinies. They are stubborn in their refusal to give up on themselves or on their vision, persisting in spite of every conceivable mishap and misfortune, in spite of their own occasional bouts of uncertainty and even doubt. They also have a wonderful ability to laugh at adversity, because they know that even if they lose everything else, they will still have themselves. They can head confidently into the unknown, because they fully expect to find a way to make things work out.

The Role of Failure in Success

I consider myself very successful. The Pacific Institute, the company Diane and I started in 1971, now has representatives on six continents, and the seminars I once held in my basement for small groups of teachers and coaches now reach millions of people every year—many of them world leaders and top corporate executives. I believe that one of the main reasons I'm successful is the same one that made Ty Cobb, the greatest baseball slugger of all time, as good as he was.

If you look in the record books, you'll find that Ty Cobb's lifetime average was only .367. That means he got a hit only once out of every three times at bat. He *didn't* get a hit twice as often as he did. It's the same story, with slightly different numbers, for Babe Ruth. And for me. And, I'd wager, for virtually every other successful person in the world: We're not afraid to try because we're not afraid to fail. For us, the only real failure is in not trying at all.

Failure is always a choice. It turns out that people don't remember the two out of three times that Ty Cobb swung and missed, and they don't remember the many projects I started that, for one reason or another, didn't work out. Failure is only failure if you let it cause you to quit. If you choose to let it help you, it is information you can learn from. Even if things go wrong, even if outside influences you can't control force you to adjust your goals or your timetable, even if others see you as a failure, they'll be wrong. As long as you're determined to learn and grow from your mistakes, to use everything that stands in your way as a teacher, you'll never be a failure.

By now, many people know that Thomas Edison tried nearly ten thousand substances before he found the one that would function effectively as a filament for his electric light. Not everyone knows, though, that some time afterward, his laboratory in Menlo Park burned to the ground. All his records, all his notes and works in progress were destroyed. Even then, he refused to give up. He even refused to see it as a tragedy. Walking through the charred debris of his dreams, he was heard to say, "What a wonderful opportunity this gives me to start fresh!"

More than anything else, I believe it was Edison's attitude that brought him so much success. Sure, he was a bright, creative guy with a fondness for science, but so were lots of his colleagues and contemporaries. What he had more of than they did was vision, determination, dedication, and persistence. It's no different for me or you, or for those you are coaching or mentoring. When you intend to succeed, when you have a clear picture of exactly what success means to you, and when you're willing to do whatever it takes, no matter how long it takes, to get there, you may have setbacks but you won't fail!

Ten Ways to Triumph over Tough Times

If you have a reliable guide to follow, you can get through tough times. Here are ten effective, practical tips that will help those you are coaching or mentoring, or yourself for that matter, to get through a difficult period. They are useful in any situation, not just when the going gets rough, but they're especially good to remember in times of crisis or adversity.

1. Acknowledge and accept current reality. Denying that anything is wrong when we're feeling terrible is not a good idea. Bad feelings don't just go away on demand. Often, though, they do go underground when they are suppressed, causing big trouble.

Especially in the early stages of a crisis, powerful and painful feelings such as anger, grief, remorse, guilt, anxiety, disappointment, and sadness are to be expected. Covering up these feelings doesn't mean we are in control; it means we are in denial. Identifying and expressing painful feelings relieves some of the pressure and is the first step toward developing a strategy to manage them.

This is where the active, empathetic listening skills of a good coach or mentor can be invaluable. Encourage your protégé to talk about what the situation means and to express feelings that have been stirred up, no matter how negative or extreme. Listen without judgment, with the intention of gaining as full and complete an understanding as possible. Then, reflect that understanding back in your own words to make sure your understanding is accurate.

If tears are part of this process, let them come. Crying is sometimes seen as a sign of weakness or self-pity in our culture, especially when the person shedding tears is male. But if we aren't made to feel ashamed of it, a good cry can help us to feel better. In fact, recent studies indicate that crying in response to strong emotion releases certain chemicals thought to be members of the endorphin family—the body's natural pain-relieving substances.

2. Get help if you sense serious danger. Suicides happen. So do violent assaults on others, up to and including murder. While it's not likely that you'll ever find yourself in a mentoring or coaching situation where serious danger exists, it is possible. It's important to know what to do, just in case.

Most people who are considering hurting themselves or someone else provide clues to their intentions. When discussions reveal destructive thoughts or impulses, or if your intuition or instincts are telling you there's danger, take action.

If you think your protégé should be receiving help from a professional, express your concerns, explain the reasons for them, and suggest it. If you get a reluctant or ambivalent response, call your local crisis hot line or a qualified therapist for advice on how to deal with the situation. In the meantime, ask your protégé to agree to call you if things get worse or if acting on destructive thoughts begins to seem like a good idea.

3. Protect your health. There's something about coping with adversity that often makes taking care of our bodies seem unimportant. Exercise, rest, relaxation, and good nutrition are usually among the first casualties. Add to that the fact that unusual or prolonged stress can cause or contribute to physical deterioration, and you have a recipe for disaster. If our health goes down the tubes or we die of a heart attack as a result of coping with adversity, it won't matter how well we managed the rest of it.

If you doubt that stress can kill, listen to this. Heart disease is the number one killer of adults in our society. A major study done not long ago for the Department of Health, Education, and Welfare found that the best predictor for heart disease was none of the physical risk factors you might imagine (smoking, high blood pressure, high cholesterol, diabetes mellitus). It was *job dissatisfaction.* The second best predictor was what the researchers called "overall happiness."

During tough times, be sure to remind those you're mentoring or coaching that when we're exhausted, badly nourished, and on a nervous edge, it becomes extremely difficult to think clearly, make good decisions, and carry them out. It's amazing how much half an hour of brisk walking or swimming can do for an overloaded mind, so encourage maintenance of adequate nutrition and exercise. Discourage use of alcohol and drugs to get through.

If the situation includes having to care for or advise another person, remind your protégé that good self-care is a basic requirement if we want to be effective at helping someone else. Of course, the same goes for you as mentor or coach.

4. Get to the roots of the problem. If we're going to learn and grow from tough times, we have to be willing to face, and help our

protégés to face, what may be some unpleasant truths. Often, these lead us to revelations about ourselves, our perceptions, and our beliefs about reality. We may have to question our assumptions, seek out scotomas, and honestly examine our role in creating the situation:

"Am I really as safe a driver as I thought I was? Could I have avoided this accident?" "What, if anything, could I have done to prevent myself from getting this disease?" "Why was getting those divorce papers such a surprise to me?" "Did I honestly do my all-out best at that job?" "How could my child be using and selling drugs without my knowledge? Were there clues that I ignored? Have I ever even talked to him about drug use?" "If I had exercised more self-discipline, would I be in the financial mess I'm facing now?"

Of course, no one enjoys scrutinizing his own character for deficiencies. No one likes owning up to his conscious or unconscious role in creating difficulties. But, remember, doing these things isn't life threatening. In fact, it's often when we have the courage to face a painful truth, without laying blame on ourselves, judging ourselves weak, incompetent, or inferior, or otherwise giving ourselves unnecessary grief, that we really begin to grow in that area. Mistakes we've made in the past can only be corrected when we're willing to admit we made them. Mistakes that are denied can never be learned from.

5. Declare an intention and accept accountability. If you're coaching or mentoring others through tough times, here's a question you'll eventually want to ask: "What do you want to happen as a result of this experience?" Suggest that sufficient time be taken to develop a thoughtful answer, because it is critical. Given that they can't move backward in time and prevent the difficulty from happening, ask them instead to imagine moving forward into the future. Invite them to see themselves a year or five years from now, thinking back over this period in their life. Ideally, what would they

like to be able to say about it? What is the best that could conceivably come from it?

Once an ideal outcome has been identified, ask them to write it in the form of an affirmation and, after they do, ask if they are willing to accept accountability for bringing it into reality. Remind them that how we use hard times and what we learn from them are deliberate choices we can make. Suggest that they spend a few minutes each day repeating and visualizing the end result they intend to achieve, and remind them to mentally experience it as vividly as possible, as if it has already happened.

Here are some examples: "I learned some important things about myself from my divorce. As a result, I now enjoy a successful, loving, intimate relationship." "My struggle with cancer helped me to grow. I am now compassionate, resilient, patient, and fully accountable for deciding what's best for me." "Getting laid off motivated me to find a much better job—one that offers many opportunities to challenge myself and grow." "The death of my spouse really brought home to me the importance of friends and family. I now find many ways to express my love and gratitude to them on a daily basis." "My accident taught me to stop postponing the things I really love to do. As a result, I spend much of my free time traveling and perfecting my skills as an artist."

6. Control self-talk. When an intention concerning desired end results has been declared, and when that intention is being affirmed and visualized regularly, an excellent start at controlling self-talk has been made. But more can be done. For instance, at all times but especially during times of trouble, coaches and mentors must be on the lookout for either/or, black-and-white thinking and nip it in the bud.

Either/or thinkers don't see shades of gray. They want easy answers to difficult questions, so they see life and themselves in terms of winners or losers, good guys or bad guys, success or failure, right or wrong. They fail to realize that right and wrong depend on time, place, culture, and purpose, among other things. And they don't understand that no one is all good or all bad and that success and failure depend on how you define them, just as winning and losing do.

Either/or thinking drastically limits our options, and that's the last thing anybody needs when they're trying to steer a safe course through troubled waters. One of the marks of successful people is their ability to change tactics when the one they're trying doesn't work out. They're successful, not only because they see themselves as problem-solvers, but also because their minds hold an array of alternatives.

When you watch a good running back moving down the field in a football game, you're seeing a lesson in the exercise of option thinking. He is making dozens of split-second adjustments and changes of direction as he runs, constantly looking for openings in what may seem like an impenetrable line of opposition. The more options we have, the more flexible we can be, and the more flexible we are, the less likely it is that we'll break when the pressure is on. When we have options, we have choices, and when we have choices, we have power. Help your protégé (and remind yourself) to avoid either/or thinking. Instead, cultivate the habit of scanning constantly for alternatives—other ways to see things, other avenues to pursue, even if you don't use them. The practice sessions will stand you in good stead for the times you have to cope with the real thing.

Remind those you are coaching or mentoring to watch the kinds of questions they ask, too. High-quality questions lead us in high-quality, positive directions. But dead-end questions only serve to keep us stuck. For example, do you ask, "Why me, Lord? What did I do to deserve this?" or "What's the use of trying to live a good life, if this is what happens?" or "How am I ever going to get though this dreadful day?" or "When will this ever end?"

Or do you ask useful questions, such as "How can I manage my resources to make the best of this?" "Who can help me, and who can I help?" "Is there something here that I can learn that will make me a better person?" "What can I do to make at least some progress today?"

At any time, but particularly during tough times, it's important to avoid worry or fruitless rumination. Worry is a form of negative goal-setting where we're stuck in the problem, like a fly on flypaper. When we worry, our minds are filled with all the negative "what-ifs" we can imagine, our stress levels skyrocket, and our immune systems suffer. Since we move toward and become like that which we think about, what do you think we move toward when our thoughts play and endlessly replay all the terrible things that might happen? When we worry, we sketch a self-fulfilling prophecy. Why should we be surprised when life puts the finishing touches and frame on it?

Ask those you're coaching or mentoring to think of worry as interest paid on trouble before it comes due. By all means, encourage them to make an investment in introspection, analytical thought, cost-benefit comparisons, options analysis, goal-setting, and action planning. But explain that we throw away precious intellectual and emotional capital by worrying. If the worst happens (and it seldom does), you'll deal with it. For the present, though, suggest a shift in focus from worrying about the problem to visualizing a solution. World-class coaches and mentors help others to imagine what might be done to improve the situation and to vividly and specifically visualize and affirm the desired end result.

Help your protégés listen to what they say to themselves in terms of wants and needs, as well. All of us have legitimate needs. We need to have food and water, air to breathe, shelter and protection from extreme weather. Often, though, when we listen closely to how we talk to ourselves and others, we'll hear about all kinds of pressing "needs," which really amount to "have-to's": "I need to get that promotion." "I need you to be home with me in the evenings." "I need to quit my job and stay home with my children." "I need to get out of the city." "I need to pass the LSAT and get into Harvard Law School."

We'll also hear about the anxiety, tension, and stress that go hand in hand with these so-called needs, because, after all, what if we don't get what we need? It's a sign of maturity and self-discipline when we can upgrade most of our needs (have-to's) to wants or preferences. It's also a sure-fire way to lower our stress quotient. For example, suppose the promotion you "needed" so badly doesn't come through? You're totally devastated, right?

What if you shift the focus of your self-talk from "need" to "prefer"? Sure, you would prefer to have that promotion. You would prefer to have the recognition and salary increase. But you don't *have* to have it, you're not going to drop dead without it, and there are probably many good things about your present job. Maybe your desire for recognition and achievement can be met in some other way. Volunteer work, for instance. Maybe your desire for more income can be fulfilled, too. Or maybe the truth is that you've gone as far as you can in your company and would be better off looking for a job somewhere else or becoming an entrepreneur or independent contractor. Who knows, maybe going after what you really want may lead you to an exciting change of careers.

Reassure your protégé that learning to take charge of self-talk isn't difficult. Like building any habit, though, it takes a bit of time and persistence to acquire and assimilate. More than just about anything I know, it's worth the effort. Mastery of this single, critical skill can mean the difference between rising above tough times and sinking under your own weight.

7. Enlist support. How many of us—especially us males—are lugging around the restrictive myth that we should be able to handle tough times by ourselves? Maybe we're uncomfortable with our own human vulnerabilities, afraid of becoming (or being perceived as) dependent or needy, or maybe we were taught that wanting or needing help means we're weak or incompetent. Not so.

The truth is that people with good support systems tend to weather hard times a lot better than those who go it alone. Encourage the people you're coaching or mentoring to draw on their social resources. In times of trouble, it's OK to let friends, family members, mentors, and coaches know we could use some support, and it's a good idea to be as specific as possible about the kind of support we have in mind. If we just want someone to listen, it's fine to say so. If we'd prefer help with practical matters, such as child care, client follow-up visits, housekeeping, errands, or rides to the hospital, we'd do well to simply ask for it.

Assure your protégés that it's not necessary to wait for someone to offer help or to worry about imposing, either. It's nice to be needed, and if there are any doubts about this, review our discussion of "the gift of receiving" in Chapter 9. Remind them, too, that it's sometimes a good idea to seek out professional help from clergymembers, counselors, physicians, psychologists, etc., especially if we lack a good support system or if we could use more help than friends and family are able or willing to provide.

If those you're mentoring or coaching have strong religious or spiritual beliefs, it almost goes without saying that their faith will be of great assistance during hard times. Sometimes, though, in the face of tragedy or death of loved ones, especially the death or suffering of a child, we find ourselves questioning our beliefs, even questioning the motives of God. Discussing these doubts with a compassionate priest, minister, rabbi, or other religious leader is a wise idea. Ironically, it is often our darkest and most doubtful times that eventually lead us to a stronger, deeper faith than we have ever known.

8. Set goals and track progress. You have to know where you're going if you expect to actually arrive there, right? When someone you're coaching or mentoring creates a vision for the way they want to emerge from a crisis, they have begun a journey toward a specific destination. When they take accountability for making it happen,

they have taken a giant step forward. For a while, that may be all they feel up to. The dissonance that affirmations and visualization create may seem like too much. Before a great deal of time passes, though, you'll want to encourage them to start working on the action steps that will bring their vision into reality. That means setting some clear short- and long-term goals.

If I've just been through a painful divorce, and my ultimate goal is to enjoy a successful, loving, intimate relationship again, here are some goals I might choose:

Tell friends, family, and coworkers that I'm ready to begin dating. Ask them to help me meet suitable people.

Locate, sign up for, and complete a course in male-female communications or marriage and family relationships.

Join a club that reflects one of my interests or get involved with a social group and participate in its activities at least twice a month.

Call for information about the "Parents Without Partners" organization.

Walk or jog at least three times a week to reduce stress.

Start keeping a journal.

Write at least three affirmations that support these activities and visualize them happening (with lots of emotion) as I repeat them each morning and evening.

Here's a list that focuses on the end-result goal of finding a new and better job after having been laid off:

Update resume. (Locate a professional writer who can polish it and make it more attractive and persuasive.)

Investigate career-related classes at local universities and community colleges. Register for and complete one that will upgrade my skills.

Go through Rolodex and list people who may be able to help with job search. Call at least five each day. Ask them for other names. Make lunch appointments with those who are receptive.

Create profile of company I would ideally like to work for.

Check yellow pages and trade publications for companies that might fit my profile. Call these companies for name of person who makes hiring decisions, and send him or her resume and cover letter. Follow up in one week with phone call with the objective of obtaining a personal interview.

Check classified ads daily. Respond to those that sound interesting or for which I might be qualified.

Make appointments with all appropriate employment agencies.

Write ten affirmations to support myself in this process. Repeat them, while visualizing and feeling the appropriate emotions, at least twice daily.

Notice that all of these items call for specific actions and all are easy to measure or keep track of. Tracking progress is always a good idea. It helps us to see how far we've come and to know when to choose another option if one approach isn't working.

Rewards, in the form of self-praise or something more tangible, should be given whether or not we achieved the desired results. It's taking the action that's commendable and deserving of recognition. As the people you're coaching or mentoring check items off their goal lists, remind them to give themselves a mental pat on the back before adding new ones. Remind them to encourage themselves with positive self-talk, even if they're not feeling positive. Instead of "I didn't get a job today, I feel terrible, I'll probably never have a good job again!" suggest they try something like this: "I didn't get a job today, and I have to admit I feel a little shaky right now. But I have a good plan, I'm following it, and I will achieve my goal because I won't quit until I do!"

Propose that they credit and applaud themselves for every

single move they make toward the desired end result, using words that feel meaningful and powerful. Remember, change is seldom accomplished in giant leaps. Even if the changes they're making and the actions they're taking are small, enough of them, headed in the right direction, will get them there. Many centuries ago, a Chinese philosopher said, "A journey of ten thousand miles starts with a single step." Think about it. Not only does a ten thousand mile walk start with a single step, it is composed entirely of many single steps and ends with a single step, too. So, after they've taken the first step, remind those you're coaching to give themselves a pat on the back, focus their vision on the destination, and keep moving!

9. Know how to handle setbacks. What happens if those you're working with get stuck? What happens if they lose their motivation or momentum or begin to feel as if they're right back where they started? Well, first of all, recommend that they don't worry about it too much. Suggest that they take the pressure off by arranging a change or a rest. Everything in nature passes through cycles—periods of dormancy, rest, and renewal followed by activity, fertility, and creativity.

Every now and then, everyone can use a break. Discuss the benefits of doing something entirely different for a while. If they live in the city, they could take a long drive to the mountains or the beach. If they sit in front of a computer screen all day, they might trade in their mouse for a pitchfork and take a weekend to turn over the sod for a vegetable garden. If their work is physical, what about venturing into the abstract world of mathematics or spending a few days learning a computer program?

Then, suggest that they sit down in a quiet place and review the previous eight points. Is there something that's been missed? Do they have all the information needed to move forward? Are there risks they need to take that they're feeling reluctant about? Are there areas where they may be going through the motions, but really don't want to change? Are they operating from restrictive (should, have to, ought to) rather than constructive motivation (want to, like to, choose to)? Could they use help working through any of these eight points or additional support or input from anyone? Have they set unrealistic goals, too difficult to achieve or perhaps too easy? Would a more objective observer have a different point of view?

They might also want to ask themselves if they've been trying too hard for perfection, which can cost a lot in terms of mental health and harmonious relationships. People who can mobilize themselves in the face of tough problems are usually those who don't worry about being perfect, even though they're striving for excellence. They're happy to move ahead with a partial solution, trusting that they'll be able to invent the rest as they go along.

Perfectionists will sometimes try to tell you that their relentless standards drive them to levels of productivity and excellence that they couldn't otherwise attain. But sometimes just the opposite is true. Perfectionists often accomplish less because they waste so much time paralyzed by fear of failure. They won't start anything until they know how to finish it without any mishaps, and that's a mistake.

Even though they don't know precisely how they're going to do something, high-performance people keep their vision of the end result uppermost in their minds and forge ahead anyway. They believe that they'll get the help they need, find the resources they need, and figure out the how-to's as they go—and they usually do. If for some reason they don't achieve the exact outcome they wanted, they don't chip away at their self-esteem and self-efficacy by beating themselves up about it. They simply choose to learn from the experience and move on.

Setbacks or imperfect results don't mean that we aren't growing. On the contrary. For example, suppose a relationship I valued has fallen apart, and one of the things I've decided as a result is that I want to learn to be a more loving, respectful person. I've been working at developing these qualities, and my daily affirmations include the statement, "I really enjoy treating all people with respect and courtesy in every possible circumstance." Then, one morning as I'm driving to work, another driver cuts me off, glaring at me as if I had no right to be on the road in the first place. I respond automatically by making a very disrespectful gesture, calling him an extremely discourteous name, and then feeling terribly guilty. Should I just give up in disgust and say to myself, "Well, obviously affirmations don't work, so why bother?"

Not at all! You see, before I began trying to change and making my affirmations, I probably wouldn't even have noticed my disrespectful behavior as anything unusual. But because of my efforts toward change, my promise to myself, and my affirmation, I was instantly and uncomfortably aware that this isn't how I want to behave. Instead of abandoning my efforts, I can say to myself, "That's the old me talking. Next time, I intend to respond courteously and respectfully, no matter how I'm provoked!" And I keep on affirming it and seeing myself doing it, day after day, time after time, until the new behavior becomes second nature, and I no longer remember having been any other way.

10. Take a walk on the lighter side. A sense of humor is a tremendous gift, an ally that can help us rise above tough times. Laughter and pain are not incompatible. Remember the "in-your-face" humor of Hawkeye Pierce and the surgeons of M*A*S*H? Or Abraham Lincoln, who said, "With the fearful strain that is on me night and day, if I did not laugh I should die." People who use humor to help them cope can more easily let go of anger, fear, hostility, and a host of other negative feelings that hinder personal healing and keep us stuck in nonproductive ways of thinking.

Laughter is a vital sign of life that releases tension and produces a wide range of beneficial changes, psychologically and physiologically. It is the other side of darkness, a light in the wilderness of pain and confusion. I agree with Norman Cousins, who asserts in his book, *Head First*, "Of all the gifts bestowed by nature on human beings, hearty laughter must be close to the top." Cousins, who used laughter to help heal himself of a serious illness in the late 1970s, holds the only honorary degree in medicine awarded at the Yale University School of Medicine and sees laughter as a "metaphor for the full range of positive emotions."[1]

What if the people you're coaching or mentoring can't see the value of your "lighten up" advice? What if they respond with something like, "How can anyone laugh at a time like this? There's nothing funny about it"? That may well be true—right now. Tell them not to force it. But if a wry perspective or a chuckle begins to bubble up, tell them not to suppress it, either. And suggest that if they can spend some of their time with people who understand what they're going through and sympathize, who also tend to tickle their funny bone, they should go for it!

When they're ready, encourage them to seek out entertainment and engage in activities that lift their spirits: Adopt a couple of ten-week-old kittens. Borrow a cheerful four-year-old to take to the zoo. Walk for a few hours in a beautiful, natural setting. Get tickets to a concert or baseball game and invite a friend. Attend the local high-school's talent show. Go to see the latest Robin Williams film, or spend a couple of evenings watching classic Marx Brothers or Abbott and Costello movies.

The more prolonged and deadly our seriousness, the deader our lives are likely to become. A good laugh, especially when shared with another person who "gets it" and will laugh along with us, can relax and revitalize us and act as a catalyst for healing.

In the next chapter, we focus on a particular kind of mentoring—one that deserves special attention. Mentoring is all about leaving a meaningful legacy, and there is no better way to do this than to thoughtfully and lovingly prepare the children we care about for success. In Chapter 12, we'll talk about how to help kids be confident, optimistic, and adventurous. We'll talk about how to discipline in ways that teach instead of turn off, how to help children cope with adversity, and how to help teenagers steer clear of violence while making the transition from childhood to adulthood.

CHAPTER TWELVE

Mentoring Children

The Most Important Job on the Planet

You don't have to be a child psychologist to know that children who receive plenty of consistent, positive, affectionate attention from adults are more likely to thrive than those who don't. They are probably going to do better in school, feel more confident and capable, enjoy more harmonious relationships, and want to give something back to the world.

So how can we coach, mentor, and inspire the children in our lives so that they, and we, are better for it? How do we teach them what we know without trying to mold or control them? How do we encourage them to take risks and test their limits while still guarding their safety? How do we help them to see themselves as capable and valuable without becoming arrogant? How do we discipline them without doing harm and help them learn from disappointment and difficulty?

> *"Just as the twig is bent, the tree's inclin'd."*
>
> Alexander Pope

These are important questions that we will try to answer, at least in part, in this chapter. Please keep in mind that I am not a child development expert, although I have a couple of relevant degrees and a world of practical experience as a result of having raised eleven children. What I've written here is intended to serve primarily to create awareness for coaches, mentors, teachers, parents, grandparents, leaders of youth groups—and you, if you have children in your care. It will help you see how the concepts you have been reading about can be applied to help the children in your life be all that they can be—the most important job on the planet!

Understand Development, Appreciate Uniqueness

If there is even one child in your life, you owe it to both of you to learn something about child development and accepted child-rearing principles. Having been a child yourself, or even having been a parent, is just not enough.

Ask your librarian to help you find some books on the subject, or call your local community college and ask for a schedule of child development classes or some recommendations for independent reading. Make sure it's understood that you want *nontechnical* information. These books or classes will describe for you the stages that most children go through as a natural result of the growth process. Why is this so important? Well, when you know roughly what kind of behavior to expect and what kind of activities and experiences a child is physically, intellectually, and emotionally ready for, it makes coaching, mentoring, or parenting a lot easier.

Notice that, in the previous paragraph, I said "most" children and "roughly" what to expect. Even though all children go through the same general stages of development, each child is different, and will go through them at his or her own pace, in his or her own way. The importance of recognizing and honoring these differences can't be overemphasized. Brothers, sisters, even identical twins may differ greatly in the way they experience and respond to their environment, and what is appropriate and effective for one child may not be for another.

What Children Can Teach Us

As we attempt to coach, mentor, teach, and guide the children in our lives, remember that there is a great deal we can learn from them, too, if we approach them with open hearts, humility, and receptive spirits. In some ways, kids are the greatest teachers of all, because they do it simply by being themselves. And they start out with so much going for them!

When healthy children are very young, they are naturally

trusting. They are also relatively fearless, joyful, lively, and loving. They play happily together regardless of race, religion, sex, or ethnic background. They feel honest and confident, secure and venturesome, open and happy. When you realize that *all* of us started out that way, it's hard to escape the conclusion that if we let children help us to reconnect with these elemental parts of ourselves, the world could be transformed. I wonder if that's part of what Christ meant when he said we needed to become as little children in order to enter the kingdom of heaven.

Building a Strong Self-Concept

Nothing is more important than helping children develop and maintain a strong, positive self-concept, and there's nothing mysterious about how to do it. The foundation of a child's self-concept is built by how he or she is treated by adults. Children who receive plenty of respect, consideration, and genuine affection from the beginning see themselves as valuable and lovable, and it's easy for them to value and love others. Children who are constantly blamed, shamed, and criticized feel insecure, deeply flawed, even worthless. As a result, their relationships with others suffer badly.

This response to how we are treated begins at birth. Don't let anyone tell you that infants and toddlers are too young to suffer from the injuries done to them or that their emotional wounds do no lasting damage. Little children don't have the language skills to clearly express their hurt and confusion, but that doesn't mean it's not there. Emotional wounds are as real as physical ones, and, though they are harder to see, they are probably far more common.

Even the most conscientious adults may be unaware of the harmful effects of many long-accepted ways of interacting with children. It hasn't been that long since "spare the rod, spoil the child" was child-rearing gospel, and some grown-ups still think there's nothing wrong with humiliating or physically hurting kids "for their own good" or to "teach them a lesson." Of course, these are usually people who were themselves treated badly when they were young, and they end up unwittingly perpetuating the cycle of pain, abuse, and violence. It's hard to give when your hands are empty, and their own self-concepts are so deficient that they are unable to build anyone else's.

In fact, that's one of the reasons why I decided to organize this book the way I did. Before you can effectively mentor a child, or anyone else for that matter, it helps a great deal to have the information found in Part One at your disposal—to have used and internalized those concepts and principles yourself.

When you understand the significance of beliefs and expectations, you are much better equipped to help children create positive self-fulfilling prophecies. When you realize the power of a meaningful purpose and clearly stated short- and long-term goals, you can more readily help kids learn to set and achieve them. When you know how to use affirmations and visualizations to expand your comfort zones and create change, you can make it much easier for young people to do the same thing. And when you grasp the importance of high self-esteem and self-efficacy and know how to build them in yourself and others, you exponentially increase your ability to serve as a catalyst for the growth of a child.

Just as a writer can't convincingly create a character who is any wiser or more perceptive than he or she is, you can't mentor anyone to be a better, happier, more motivated, more self-respecting, more effective person than you are yourself. Charity—good will, affection, love, and acceptance—must indeed begin at home.

Preparing Children for Success

What makes certain kids turn out to be successful? Some people think it's in the genes: Some kids are born to succeed, others aren't, and that's that. I'm convinced they're wrong, and I'm glad I'm not the only one who thinks so.

More than twenty years ago, the great Japanese teacher, Dr. Suzuki, who taught over twenty thousand children to play musical instruments like virtuosos, had some words of wisdom to share with us. He said:

> People today are like gardeners who look sadly at ruined saplings and shake their heads, saying the seeds must have been bad to start with, not realizing that the seed was all right, but that it was their method of cultivation that was wrong. They go their mistaken way, ruining plant after plant. It is imperative that the human race escape from this vicious circle.[1]

Dr. Suzuki didn't think that only a few children were gifted. He believed that every child could be taught to be "superior." Talent, he believed, was no accident of birth, but rather a purposeful effort, a powerful creation.

The work of Dr. Benjamin Bloom of the University of Chicago bears this out. Dr. Bloom studied one hundred extraordinarily successful young athletes, musicians, and students, and found that most of these young prodigies didn't begin by showing signs of brilliance. Instead, most received careful attention, guidance, and support, and *then* they began to develop. The *belief* that they could be special came before any outward indications of great talent.

Even though genes certainly matter, my experience has taught me that our environment and our ability to choose what we want for ourselves matter even more. I believe that all children can grow up to succeed in some important ways and to make the most of their potential, if they are used to seeing others around them doing it, and if they are taught to believe they can do it, too. That's where good coaches and mentors come in.

Make sure the children in your life realize that when they see someone with exceptional skill or ability, they are probably seeing a person who has been carefully taught and who has worked hard, not someone who just "is" that way. Remind them that they have their own potential for greatness and that they can do similar things, if they're willing to take the time to learn and to practice self-discipline and persistence. Encourage and reward their efforts, even if they don't succeed, and never punish or ridicule poor performance, unless what you want them to learn is to avoid both you and the activity as much as possible.

Sending Messages of Love and Confidence

It's crucial that the kids you care about receive lots of positive, loving messages about who they are and what they're like. If they do, and if these messages are repeated often enough, they give sanction to them and store them in the neural pathways of their brains, where they become part of who they are. Then they begin to behave accordingly.

Often, these messages are nonverbal. For example, when a child speaks to you and you respond with interest and your full attention, you are, in effect, saying, "I think you're an important person. I value what you have to say." When you laugh with, but not at, children, you are saying that you enjoy them as people, and you're helping them to enjoy life and develop a good sense of humor. When you hold and cuddle them and give them lots of hugs and kisses, you're telling them, "You are lovable just the way you are."

Messages are also sent by what you say. Many times, as you try to shape children's behavior, you'll focus on what's wrong instead of what's right. You diligently point out their errors and shortcomings, intending to help them change for the better. But because we move toward and become like what we think about, and because the pictures in our minds today determine our tomorrows, this kind of criticism seldom does what you hope it will do. In fact, it usually does just the opposite, because the negative pictures it creates are part of the problem.

One of the ways I decided to reinforce the positive messages my grandchildren were already receiving is by means of a special audio tape. It started several years ago with one tape I recorded for my granddaughter, Alex, to play in her Walkman. I wanted to boost her self-confidence and reinforce her feelings of affection for her new little brother, so I talked a lot about what a creative, happy, helpful, loving, and much-loved kid she is. I played some special background music to help create a receptive mood, and I really put my heart into the message. Well, Alex just loved it! She took it everywhere, listened to it before she went to bed, while she was riding in the car, and pretty soon she had memorized parts of it and would say them along with me. It was a tremendous hit!

When other people heard about the tape, their response was incredibly enthusiastic, too. They all wanted me to make one like it for children they knew, but I told them it wouldn't help unless I was a part of those kids' lives. I suggested that they make a tape themselves, because a stranger's voice just wouldn't work. But somehow they just never got around to it.

I ended up making tapes for my other grandchildren and for a few close family friends' children, too. Still, I kept thinking about all the people I knew who wanted one and all the people I didn't know who *might* want one, and wondering what I could do to make it easy for them. Then one day, I stopped wondering and set a goal, enlisted some help, and, before long, my tape idea had become a new reality.

I call it *A Message from Your Heart* and it's a kit that includes a flexible, easy to customize, age-appropriate script, background music, blank cassettes, gift cards, and complete instructions that enable anyone to create an audio tape very similar to those I made. To order one or find out more about how it works, see the Appendix. If you'd rather try to make your own, go to it! Just make sure the language you use is right for the age of the child and that your messages are personal, relevant, affectionate, and positive.

Encouraging an Adventurous Spirit

The vast majority of us want to keep the children of the world safe and happy, to protect them from adversity, illness, and physical and psychological pain. Some adults, though, in their sincere desire to keep kids safe, try too hard. Overprotectiveness, instead of saving life, can end up suppressing it, because it prevents the development of an adventurous, efficacious spirit.

Too many of us go through life afraid of all sorts of things—heights, dogs, meeting new people, going barefoot, riding horses, traveling in foreign countries, germs, eating food we didn't prepare ourselves, driving on the freeway, you name it—because of fear-based conditioning received from overprotective adults when we were young.

Sure, we need to teach children to be cautious when it's necessary. But we also need to teach them to risk and test their own limits. When they're young, we need to be watchful and ready to haul them away from danger. But as they grow into the world, we must take care that we don't crush their spirits in our desire to keep them out of harm's way. If we can teach them how to take calculated risks and to live life fully, by our own example and through patient encouragement, we will be giving them a gift that will serve them well throughout their lives.

Kids Coping with Adversity

Nothing we can do will guarantee the kids we care about a trouble-free childhood. Many children suffer serious trauma or prolonged illness, death in the family, parental conflict, divorce or separation, natural disaster, and the like. Many others have to get through highly stressful events, such as problems with school performance or social relationships, a move to a new home or city, loss of a pet, bullying by another child, etc.

How can coaches, mentors, parents, and other concerned adults help? First and foremost, you can set a good example. This is always the most powerful way to teach attitudes or behaviors to a child. Children are terrific imitators, which gives you a great tool. If you fly apart in a crisis or become helpless or hopeless, depressed, or enraged when things go wrong or you're under pressure, the children around you will tend to respond similarly.

Please understand that I'm not suggesting that you mask your feelings or pretend that everything's OK when it isn't. This kind of well-intentioned denial is not an effective way to cope. Instead, acknowledge the difficulty and your feelings about it as calmly as possible. Then let children see you dealing with it in a positive, hopeful way. Let them know that bad things do sometimes happen to good people, but reassure them that you, and they, are not helpless when this happens, because you can choose how you want to respond.

"Turning the Channel" from Sad to Glad

One of the ways you can help kids get through stressful times is by teaching them how to deliberately relax their bodies. Even fairly young children can learn to tightly clench and then relax large muscle groups, making shoulders and hands, arms and legs "hard as rocks," then into "wet noodles" or "floppy socks." Because our bodies and minds are so closely connected, muscle relaxation usually causes mental relaxation.

Even more importantly, though, you can teach kids to control their thoughts. Help them, as we've already said, to acknowledge feelings, letting them know that it's OK to feel sad or mad or scared, and that everybody has these feelings sometimes. Then help them to learn how to "turn the channel" to happier, calmer thoughts and feelings.

Begin by showing them that they can deliberately create mental pictures whenever they choose. Ask them to think back to something sad or slightly painful—last week's skinned knee, for example. Help them to remember it in detail, something like this: "After you fell off your bike and skinned your knee, remember how we had to clean the dirt out with peroxide? You didn't like that because it hurt! After it was clean, we put some medicine on it. That stung a little, too. Then we put a big bandage over it, and we put a new bandage on every day, remember? Getting hurt like that wasn't any fun, and it doesn't feel good to think about it now, either, does it?"

Then ask them to revisit a happy time—a birthday party or

going out for ice cream or taking the dog to the park on a sunny day. Help them recall how it looked, sounded, smelled, tasted, and felt: "Do you remember how Brownie tried to catch those pigeons? He looked so funny jumping all around with his ears flapping! Can you see how he looked in your mind? Then you took off your shoes and socks and played on the beach for a while, right? Can you remember how the wet sand squished between your toes? The sun felt so hot we took our coats off, and then we sat by the lake and watched the sailboats and ate lunch. Do you remember what kind of sandwich you had? How did it taste? That was a good time, wasn't it?"

As the child responds, chimes in, and remembers along with you, reinforce the visualization experience with words: "That was great! You sure have a good imagination! And, you know, you can turn off sad or scary thoughts, like the ones about your skinned knee, and turn on happy ones like our day at the park, whenever you want to. Let's try another sad-to-glad picture, OK?" Practice with them and praise their efforts until you're certain they can do it on their own. Make sure they realize that they can change the pictures inside their minds whenever they feel sad or mad or scared about something. Make sure, too, that they know that if they want to, they can talk with you about any of their feelings at any time.

Setting the Stage for a Great Tomorrow

Here's a wonderful idea that parents and grandparents can use to help children to bring each day to a close on a happy note and move toward the future with positive expectations. After they are tucked into bed, take a few minutes for some relaxed conversation, during which you ask them to tell you about the *best* parts of their day.

Listen attentively and respond to what you hear with appropriate, affirmative comments: "You really know how to have fun, don't you?" "You went down the tall slide by yourself for the first time? That's great!" "I can just see you hitting that home run!" "Wow, a 95! Your spelling tests are improving all the time! All that studying is paying off." "I'm glad your teacher said your drawing was good. I really like the pictures you make, and I know you have a lot of fun making them." "I'm not surprised those kids asked you to sit with them at lunch. You're smart and funny and nice to be around."

Then, ask them to tell you what they're looking forward to tomorrow. Again, listen attentively and respond appropriately. If they have trouble coming up with positive images, a little prompting may be helpful. "You've been studying hard, doing all your homework, and paying attention in class, so I'll bet you'll feel pretty good when it's time to take that test tomorrow. What do you think?" "You're so creative—I can see you coming up with a really neat project to work on in art class tomorrow. That'll be fun, won't it?" "It sounds like you've had a really good time playing with your new friend today. Do you think that might happen again tomorrow?"

This is a variation of the "flick back, flick up" visualization technique we talked about in Chapter 6. It makes use of positive experiences from the past (flick back) to help us visualize and create similar positive experiences in the future (flick up). It helps children to acknowledge and focus on their skills and strengths, to expect good things to happen to them (self-fulfilling prophecies), and to develop an optimistic point of view. It may also help them to sleep better and start their day more enthusiastically in the morning.

Comfort Zones That Grow Along with Kids

This same visualization tool, slightly modified, can be used to help kids adjust to change and lower the stress associated with moving into new physical or psychological territory. As children age, good mentors, coaches, siblings, and parents help them to see themselves taking on new challenges and succeeding, feeling more and more comfortable in the adult world, growing into bigger and bigger responsibilities and freedoms as they grow into bigger tennis shoes.

Whenever I say that good mentors see more in us than we can see in ourselves and that they help us grow into that vision, I'm really saying that they help us to expand our comfort zones. They encourage us to raise our internal standards of where we belong, what's good enough for us, and what we expect to happen to us.

One of the best ways to do this for children is by repeatedly articulating your vision of who they are now and who they can be in the future: "Pretty soon, you'll be able to operate the computer by yourself. You sure catch on quickly!" "You like books so much, I can see that you're going to be a very good reader." "When you go to college, you'll do very well. You're learning good study habits and, more and more, you take the time to do first-class work on your assignments." "You really have what it takes to be an excellent student!" "You certainly have a knack for getting along with people." "What a fine drawing! You have so many special talents!"

In this way, you are also subtly helping children to visualize and affirm their own growth, set goals that challenge but are still within reach, and control their self-talk. As they move into new territory, you can help them remember their past successes, strengths, skills, and abilities and transfer them into the future, just as you did with the bedtime conversation described earlier. For example: "Remember the great reading you gave when you tried out for the drama club? Can you imagine yourself doing it again at this professional audition?" "Junior high school may feel strange, at first. But you made friends quickly when we moved here, and at summer camp, too. Can you see yourself doing it again?"

Three Steps to Effective Discipline

Discipline is a touchy subject for some folks, but if it's handled kindly, correctly, and appropriately, children can learn a great deal from being disciplined. After all, that's the whole point. The word *discipline* comes from various Latin roots, all having to do with learning. The goal of discipline is to teach kids how to control their own behavior so that they avoid unnecessary pain and move toward positive, desirable outcomes. In that sense, although discipline is most commonly a task carried out by parents, it may often be a part of being a teacher, mentor, or coach.

Step One: Express Appropriate Expectations.

The first step in effective discipline is to make sure your expectations are clear and appropriate. Let's face it, all adults who have meaningful contact with children expect certain things from them, and expectations that are unrealistic or unclearly expressed cause trouble. Expectations that are far too high guarantee failure and lead to an enormous amount of stress. Standards that are too low can lead to failure too, because they don't help children stretch their capabilities and develop a sense of competence and resourcefulness.

Make sure you talk to the kids you are parenting, mentoring, or coaching about what you expect from them, and make sure they understand what you've said. If you expect them to show up on time and dressed appropriately, make sure they know exactly what "on time" means and what is (and isn't) OK to wear. If you want them on their best behavior for a special event, tell them specifically what "best" means. If you want them to clean up after an activity, spell out exactly what "clean" looks like to you and what steps are involved, or you'll get their version, which is probably very different. If you expect them to be responsible about keeping up with their schoolwork, explain what behaviors and results you have in mind.

Make sure your expectations are realistic and appropriate for the child at his or her particular stage of development, too. What's right for one isn't necessarily right for all, and what was reasonable when you were growing up may no longer make much sense. Consider the circumstances, too. Expecting a five-year-old to sit through an hour-long church service without fidgeting or talking may be too much to ask. In a couple of years, the same child will probably be able to handle it. Expecting all As on a report card is unrealistic, while expecting a good-faith effort in every subject is not.

Step Two: Separate Behavior from Being.

In other words, don't confuse what a child is doing with who he is. Even when you're angry with them for misbehaving, make sure children understand that it's the behavior you have a problem with, not their character or personality. This can't be overemphasized: Respond to the *behavior* while remaining friendly and respectful toward the *person*.

This means that when a child draws a picture on a wall, for example, you don't call him a "bad boy," but you do tell him how you feel about it: "Walls are not for drawing on! I'm sorry that you did this and upset that I have to take time to clean it up. Next time, please remember this rule." You can require that he help you with the cleaning, and you can make sure he understands that, in the future, all nonstandard drawing materials have to be preapproved by you.

The same principle holds for those times when children are doing what we want them to do. Separate behavior from being. When she brings you your slippers without your asking, don't say "What a good girl!" Try something like, "What a nice surprise! Thank you very much!" Praise the behavior and smile at, or hug, the child. When you do that, the message you send is "You don't have to do or not do certain things to be valuable and lovable. I love you just the way you are!" Hugs and warm smiles tell children they are loved. Praised behavior tells them they are competent. It's a powerful combination.

Step Three: Be Compassionate, Consistent, and Careful About Timing.

It's probably obvious by now, but worth saying again. Never humiliate, shame, or physically hurt a child. By example and in words, teach the kids you are coaching, mentoring, or parenting that psychological abuse or physical violence are *never* acceptable ways to treat others. Simple statements of disapproval, removal from the situation, distraction, and time-outs work well as discipline for younger children. Clear, fair rules and loss of privileges or extra chores for rule violations are better for older ones.

Whatever methods you use, timing is important. The discipline should immediately follow the offense, or come as soon after it as possible. Clearly, some social situations will prevent this, but make sure the child knows he or she has broken a rule and that a time-out or penalty will follow as soon as possible. Follow through and make sure it happens.

Be consistent. Don't come down on a child for breaking a rule on Monday when you're feeling stressed, then let the same thing go without comment or consequences on Tuesday when you're back to normal. This doesn't mean that you can't occasionally change your mind if you believe you've been too tough or can't change no to yes after thinking it over. Modeling flexibility and thoughtfulness helps children develop these qualities themselves. But if you do this a lot, your rules will seem arbitrary and kids will constantly be trying to stretch or bend them.

Part of consistency is follow-through. Don't tell children not to do something and then overlook it. Breaking rules or disobeying instructions should have consequences that are clearly spelled out and, again, appropriate to the age of the child and the severity of the incident. If you say there'll be consequences, make sure you're ready to deliver them. Don't create rules you aren't prepared to enforce, and don't warn of consequences you aren't going to carry out.

Defusing Anger and Violence

In spite of frequent attempts to blame schools or our mayhem-loving media, I think that most children learn to be violent in their own homes, from adults who are close to them.

It happens when they are raised around adults who are violent or think it's OK for others to behave violently. I don't mean an occasional loss of temper, but rather a habitual flow of open hostility directed at others.

It happens when adults fail to set and enforce strict limits on physical expressions of anger. Kids, like everyone else, sometimes feel furious. They need to know that it's OK to feel angry and to express those feelings, but it's never OK to do so by hurting others.

It happens when their discipline comes in the form of painful or humiliating punishment. If you want kids to respect you and others, treat them with respect. It doesn't matter how old they are. Everyone, of every age, deserves respect.

It happens when there are no adults who will help them realize that the glamorized brutality they see in the media is, in real life, a painful and unproductive way to live. A good coach or mentor, even when in no position to be providing discipline, can be a tremendous influence in this respect.

It happens when adults fail to reinforce and praise positive behavior and provide safe outlets for angry feelings. This is another area in which coaches and mentors outside the family can do a great deal.

Our criminal justice system is aimed not at rehabilitation but at restraint and retribution, and by the time a violent kid gets that far, it's usually too late. How much better off all of us would be if we practiced the proverbial ounce of prevention, instead. And what a better place the world would be if every child had at least one loving, concerned, patient parent, mentor, or coach who was willing to teach better ways.

The Turbulent Teen Years

Adolescence presents special problems for those who are going through it and for those who care for them. I'm not going to go into those problems here, because that's another book, maybe a whole library of books. In any event, there's a wealth of good material available to help you better understand and deal with teenagers. I do want to make a couple of points, though, about our attitudes when it comes to guiding and mentoring these young people.

First, if you're parenting, coaching, or mentoring an adolescent, don't believe for a second that your guidance, limit-setting, and involvement are no longer as necessary as they used to be. There is plenty of data indicating that teenagers want and need adult interest and participation in their lives. In fact, it's amazing what teenagers can do when they feel supported by adults who really care, when they feel good about themselves, and when they have the tools they need to make good decisions and take action. I'm convinced that, given half a chance—and the things I've just mentioned—the extraordinary stories we occasionally hear of high-achieving, community-minded teenagers demonstrating admirable character and values would no longer be extraordinary.

Case in point: Not long ago, some teenage gang members paid a disruptive visit to the small town of Spruce Grove, Alberta, Canada. The media made a fuss, and the mayor responded by imposing a curfew to keep all young people off the streets. But it was the local kids who felt punished, not the outsiders who had caused the trouble and then disappeared. With encouragement from some supportive adults, the local kids met with the mayor and police officials to try to persuade them that the curfew should be removed, but their arguments fell on deaf ears.

At this point, they could have decided to give up, sulk or complain, get hostile, or feel victimized. Instead, they put their heads together to figure out what they could do to create a public image for themselves that was so overwhelmingly positive that the grown-ups would have to change their minds. One of their most active adult supporters and mentors, Pat Mussieux, told them about The Pacific Institute's education and how useful it could be in helping create desired end results. They decided they wanted to go through one of our youth programs and, soon afterward, they became very focused about setting goals and getting involved in their community in positive ways.

As a result of our education, these kids began to see themselves as powerful people who could make things happen—for themselves and for people in their town who needed help. They wrote visionary articles about their activities, dated 1998 to show the results they intended to achieve, and sent them to the local newspaper asking that their articles be published. After having been attacked in the media, they felt they deserved an opportunity for some positive coverage—and they got it.

As you might expect, the curfew was lifted. But that's not all. Spruce Grove teens raised $1,400 for a Christmas "Share Tree," providing gifts and groceries for needy families. They continue to be active in many worthwhile community projects and are determined to share the education that empowered them with Spruce Grove's public schools and with its adults.

Maybe you're thinking, well, sure, so what? Those are nice, middle-class kids living in rural Canada. The biggest obstacle they had to overcome was some mistaken perceptions. So, let me tell you another story. At Westwood High School in Florida, kids had to be in trouble to participate in our program. They had to be making poor progress with their grades, show poor attendance, be identified as potential dropouts, or have other serious behavior problems. In other words, they were teenagers who are often labeled (perceived) as "at-risk," which is often a polite way of saying "doomed to failure."

After going through our program and learning how to change the way they think about what they can and can't do and what they've been conditioned to believe about themselves and their environment, the changes were dramatic: Eighty-three percent improved their grade point average by at least .5, which equals half a letter grade (many improved by much more than that—.5 was the *minimum* improvement). Seventy-five percent improved their attendance by *at least* 10 percent. Not only that, there was an 88 percent reduction in discipline referrals, and 90 percent of these kids stayed in school instead of becoming dropouts as predicted.

I wonder what would happen if *all* children were exposed to this education from an early age, right along with history, geography, and the three Rs. What if they were taught to think of themselves as both powerful and accountable, to see themselves in terms of their incredible potential rather than through the distorted lenses of adults who have already made up their minds?

If Not You, Then Who?

Perhaps one day we may actually be able to answer these "what if" questions. I hope so, and I'm working on it. In the meantime, though, all children should have at least one adult who cares enough to take an active role in their lives. Even better would be an active, caring adult who also knows something about how children grow, how to help them build self-esteem and self-efficacy, and how to help them experience the unique pleasure and satisfaction that come from being of service to others. But many thousands of children have no one who meets even one of these criteria.

In too many instances, what they have instead are adults who run them down; abuse, neglect, or ignore them; blame and shame them; and teach them to expect little from themselves and even less from life. Unless something in this picture changes, these kids' chances of avoiding trouble and becoming productive, self-supporting individuals, family members, and members of society are slim.

You can change that picture. Organizations like Big Brothers and Big Sisters have far more kids who need guidance and companionship than adults who are willing to provide it. Boys and Girls Clubs are always glad to have volunteers. So are churches, city parks/recreation departments, and schools. Maybe you know some kids who are growing up without a dad or mom. Could you talk to their parent about how you might help on a regular basis? What skills do you have that you could share with a child? What do you really like to do that a child might learn to enjoy, too?

Unlike coaching, which generally goes on within the practice-and-play structure of an athletic team, successful mentoring of children usually takes place between bites of a burger, driving home from the movies, putting together an airplane model, or during the seventh-inning stretch. It grows out of the time you spend building and enjoying a fun, close, trusting, mutually respectful relationship, and it happens spontaneously as much as by design. You can't mold kids as if they were clay. But you can spend time with them, getting to know them, showing you care, letting them get to know you, having a good time, teaching and learning, sharing and growing, and hope that they'll see something in you they want to imitate.

If you do care (and I think you do, or you wouldn't have made it to the end of this chapter), I challenge you to become a long-term, committed mentor to at least one child who is not your own. Look around you for a child in need. I guarantee you'll find one. Maybe you'll find two or three or a whole community full. And then ask yourself, "If not me, then who?"

CHAPTER THIRTEEN

Passing on the Baton

We're Not in Kansas Anymore

I t was a few weeks before Christmas, 1993, and I was squatting on a bare wood floor with about seventy-five lively elementary schoolchildren spread out in front of me. Diane and some of our Pacific Institute staff members and friends were perched on pint-size chairs along one side of the room. An hour or so earlier, these kids, all wearing green sweatshirts imprinted with "Oakgrove Integrated Primary School," had been buzzing with excitement about the American visitors for whom they had prepared a special assembly. By the time I joined them on the floor, most of the assembly was over, and they had settled down a bit.

We were in Northern Ireland, in a small town called Derry (also Londonderry and L' Derry) for the third time since 1988. The previous day I had given a three-hour keynote address entitled "The Challenge of Change" at a national business leaders' conference. Today we were visiting three integrated schools. I was on the floor because I had been asked to talk with the children for a few minutes about self-esteem, tolerance, and diversity, and I wanted to get a good exchange going on their level.

> "The great use of life is to spend it for something that outlasts us."
>
> William James

Now, in Northern Ireland, the term *integrated* has nothing to do with race. An integrated school means that Catholic and Protestant kids are educated together, and in 1993, the concept was revolutionary. For some people, it still is. These progressive schools had been started a couple of years earlier by parents and community members who firmly believed that unless Protestant and Catholic children could get to know each other as human beings in an environment that taught and modeled tolerance, trust, and respect, the hatred and violence that had been tearing their country apart for so long would continue indefinitely.

In other words, they were being driven by something that most parents can readily identify with: an intense desire for a better life for their children. They believed in their vision of a peaceful future through integrated schools so strongly that they were willing to pool their resources to put up the money it would take, and none of these folks is affluent. When the start-up money was gone, they raised more. They formed a trust, located buildings, hired teachers, negotiated leases and contracts, purchased books and equipment, and began classes, all essentially on their own. And they used my company's video-based education to help create change—to learn to think differently, create an inspiring vision for the future, set and achieve meaningful goals and overcome obstacles, including their own blind spots and traditional negative conditioning.

Teachers and parents, in turn, had been consistently and creatively sharing what they had learned with the children. They deliberately coached and mentored these kids to nurture positive, life-affirming beliefs about their worth and potential and about the worth and potential of all people, regardless of religion, race, gender, class, or politics. They taught dignity, responsibility, tolerance, respect, and trust right along with math, science, social studies, and language skills. And as I sat on the floor of the Oakgrove Integrated School that December morning, the evidence of their success was obvious.

You could see it in the handmade posters all around the room—lists of "put-up" words such as "smart," "nice," "fun," "special," "neat," and "great" that make us feel good, and lists of "put-down" words to avoid because they cause shame and pain. You could see it in the songs, stories, and skits the children presented: upbeat, funny, appreciative of the wide range of talents and backgrounds in their classroom, proud of their own personal accomplishments. And you could see it in the way the teachers and pupils interacted. This was a very lively, cheerful, outgoing bunch of kids, but they instantly, respectfully responded to their teachers' friendly requests for attention and quiet.

As I talked with these little ones about the importance of self-esteem, mutual tolerance, and respect for others that day, it felt like I was preaching to the choir. I had to keep reminding myself that these kids with the shining, happy faces who were listening so matter-of-factly to what I had to say about diversity and giggling so delightedly at my silly jokes were growing up in a war zone. They had been born and raised in a culture that for decades had been torn by bloody civil war, a culture that for centuries had been steeped in mistrust and hatred, a culture that, at least in the past, had been agonizingly slow to change its ways. But these children were tangible evidence that change was coming, that it was well on its way and not to be stopped.

As I write this, little more than a year has passed since that day, but much has changed. There are more than forty integrated schools throughout Northern Ireland, most of them enormously successful and rapidly growing. The political powers-that-be have finally declared peace, though there are still violent flare-ups and the terms are still being hammered out. No longer do armed guards patrol shopping malls. No longer do firebombs routinely convey deadly messages of intolerance, retaliation, and death. And the same Pacific Institute programs that helped teachers, parents, and others in Derry to alter their beliefs and expectations and create positive change are now helping thousands of government employees, businesses, schools, and private citizens throughout Northern Ireland to do the same.

Our education has been in South Africa for more than a decade, too. Now, if you think I'm trying to give you the impression that we had something to do with helping to bring peace to these two long-troubled lands, you're right. Diane and I, as well as our friends and business associates around the world, are convinced that The Pacific Institute's programs did play a small but significant role in creating a receptive climate for positive change in Northern Ireland and South Africa.

It was no accident, either. Some years ago, we asked ourselves, "Who really needs this information? Where can it do the most good?" Then we looked around and decided where we wanted to go. After we had a clear vision of the end result we wanted, we set about figuring out how to do it and who could help. And we never gave up. We never said, "This problem is too big for us to waste our time on." We never said, "This is going to take much too long, so let's go somewhere else and do something that will give us quicker results." We now have similar visions that are taking us into Southeast Asia, Central America, China, and Japan to help the people there adjust to and learn to take advantage of the unprecedented, radical changes that are going on all over the planet.

The Dream Begins Inside a Single Mind

I'm telling you these things not to blow my own horn, but to challenge and encourage you to take an active part in solving some of the problems you see around you. I hope you'll use what you've learned from this book to empower yourself so that you can set an inspiring example. And I hope you'll use it to help others believe that they can make a difference. Because it's true—you *can* play a significant part in creating a better world. You can influence your protégés to play a part, too, and they can, in turn, influence others. And, one day, what do you know? We're living in a different reality!

Sure, society's problems can seem overwhelming. Sometimes it's as if everywhere you look there's a critical need or an ongoing human tragedy causing pain and suffering. You read about them every day in the newspapers, you hear about them on TV, and because you're just one person, maybe you feel pretty helpless when it comes to doing anything about them. Often, after sufficient time goes by, you get used to them and view them as unassailable, unsolvable, just "the way things are." But it's amazing how much one person who *doesn't* feel helpless can set into motion, cause, and make happen. I have hundreds of examples I could share with you. Here are three.

Let's start by returning for a moment to Northern Ireland. If it hadn't been for a man named Patrick J. Given, an Irishman by birth who has spent most of his nearly seventy-five years in Britain, things would look much less hopeful for a great many people in that part of the world today. Certainly the course and possibly the speed of my work there would have been far different.

Pat discovered our education in 1985 and delivered it personally to more than thirty-five hundred people at the South of Scotland Electricity Board, where he was working as Training Manager. After his retirement, Pat decided he wanted to devote his time to helping the people in his native land. His vision was simple: By the year 2,000, he wanted Ireland to become a model for the rest of the world of how to develop the potential of the individual. He knew that the Irish people have an abiding passion for learning, he felt certain that they were ready for political and economic change, and he believed that The Pacific Institute's *Investment in Excellence* program was the perfect vehicle to help them break the shackles of the past and build a new future.

Pat flew to Seattle to visit me in June 1987. I was struck and indelibly impressed by his intelligence, determination, selfless spirit of intent, and belief in the basic goodness of humanity. As we talked, it became clear that we shared a similar vision, and we both knew from personal experience the power of The Pacific Institute's education when it came to helping people bring a vision into reality. We knew that this education would not be a panacea for all the ills of Ireland, but we believed that it could serve as a solid foundation upon which to build a wide variety of remedies. It could help create the inner changes that would eventually produce the necessary outer transformations. Together, we agreed to launch an initiative that would eventually achieve our common goal of paving the way for peace and prosperity in Ireland.

During the next few years, Pat worked tirelessly, arranging many community meetings and delivering countless seminars in Derry. He was paid only for his travel and accommodation expenses. All other fees were used to create and develop an organization that could bring *Investment in Excellence* to more and more of the unemployed, the uneducated, community leaders, and to teachers, because, as Pat says, "they are the ones who hold the future in their hands."

Bit by bit, as the people of Derry reimagined their environment, old businesses were renovated, new businesses sprang up, and the city took on a fresh, vibrant, hopeful look. Debris and rubble from bombed-out buildings disappeared and flower boxes took their place, with some of the labor provided by people who had been convicted of the bombings. Men who had been idle for years went back to work. As of January 1996, well over four thousand people in and around Derry had graduated from the *Investment in Excellence* program. Leaders of many other communities had begun to sit up and take notice, too, as the positive changes taking place there received more and more publicity.

In December 1994, Diane and I made our fourth visit to Northern Ireland. This time, we were there to videotape a special version of our education tailored for the Irish people and to speak to a large group of citizens and community leaders who were coming together in Belfast to find out how they, too, could do what the people of Derry had done. As of September 1996, nine thousand employees within the largest, most influential department of Northern Ireland's government have become *Investment in Excellence* graduates. All of this and much more has come to pass because one man with strong self-efficacy—Pat Given—saw a need that touched his heart and decided to do something about it. Of course, it didn't stay a one-man operation for long. But that's the way it started.

Here's another story about what "just" one person can do. I am not personally involved in this one, but I find it inspiring and think you will, too. A couple of years ago, businessman Robert Young read a newspaper article explaining that some Native American elders were dying from the cold during harsh winters because of inadequate housing. It made him angry to learn that people could literally freeze to death in one of the wealthiest nations on earth. So, on the way home from a business trip, Young took a detour through the Pine Ridge Sioux reservation in South Dakota to see for himself. What he saw was appalling: grinding poverty. Scraps of boards and tree limbs thrown together to serve as dwellings, more like kids' tree forts than real homes. No electricity. No running water. Not much of anything.

Now, Young is not a Native American, but he wanted to do something to help. He started small, by "adopting" two Sioux grandparents. He sent money for their care, and gifts, too, on a regular basis. After a while, though, it didn't seem like enough. He wanted to do more. He wanted to address the problem in a broader, more meaningful way, and he wanted to do it personally, not through some government agency. So he talked to the people in charge at the reservation. In time, he was able to convince them that he was truly committed to helping and that his motives had nothing to do with desire for personal profit. Then he talked to friends and his business partner, telling them he was determined to build some decent houses for Sioux elders and asking if they would help.

He formed a foundation called Bigfoot Development, raised thousands of dollars, and, last I heard, was working to raise many thousands more. The Sioux families themselves will be involved in the construction of their houses. Robert Young and his partner will be swinging a hammer, too. And Young is thinking about taking his ideas and experience to other places that have similar needs.

I recently heard about Leah de Roulet, a Seattle social worker who has people all over the city collecting medical supplies that are then shipped to Russia. It all started when she and her husband visited that country a few years ago. An oncology specialist, she was invited to lecture at a hospital, where they were eager to hear about modern American methods. She talked with staff, took a tour, and was stunned by the dearth of supplies and equipment. They didn't even have latex gloves!

She returned home determined to help. Working alone at first, Leah began to collect useful items. It soon became apparent that she would need help and funding if her efforts were going to matter. So she began making phone calls, getting educated, asking for help. Before long, she had several volunteers working with her and some much-needed grant money. The project, which as far as I know still doesn't have a name, is presently funded as part of America's official aid-to-Russia effort, and one woman's commitment to be of service is making a big difference in the lives of many people she will never meet.

Who says one person can't change anything? And who says that one person can't hook up with another like-minded person, and then with another, and another? That is exactly how "grass roots" movements get started, and grass roots movements can be extremely effective. It's the mistaken belief that we are helpless and isolated that stops us and robs us of our strength. With a powerful purpose and a can-do attitude, anything is possible! That's right, anything!

As Powerful a Wiz as Ever Was

I have often used the metaphor of *The Wizard of Oz* in my seminars. I told you about one memorable, last-minute *Wizard of Oz* presentation in Chapter 2. I like it because it's a frame of reference that almost everyone in the Western world shares and because it so perfectly demonstrates the power of beliefs.

As you no doubt remember, one of the points the story makes is that Dorothy and her pals already had every personal quality they needed to do what they wanted to do . . . they just didn't believe it. But they *did* believe in the Wizard, and, like most good mentors, he could see more in them than they could see in themselves. He recognized that each of them possessed exceptional abilities, and, because he had credibility in their eyes, he was eventually able to inspire them to believe in themselves.

That's how it works in real life. As a mentor, parent, grandparent, coach, teacher, etc., you have far more influence over your protégés, your children, your students, your players—for good or for ill—than any wizard that ever was. You have the power of personal example, the charm of genuine caring, the strength of credibility, the accumulated magic of day-after-day, month-after-month, year-after-year, real-life relationship. You have the ability, through your expanding sphere of influence and power to inspire, to play a part in shaping the future.

How High Do You Want to Climb?

It doesn't matter whether we're talking about how a family functions, how a company functions, how a community functions, or how a society functions: What you as an individual do—or don't do—matters enormously in the greater scheme of things. And the messages you send to others about what they can and can't do matter tremendously, too.

Forget what you've been like in the past. Maybe you've been overcritical, perfectionistic, skeptical, distant. Maybe you've been too busy, too worried, too preoccupied, or too uncertain of your own abilities to help anyone else grow. Maybe you've even made it difficult for them to grow, not to mention making it difficult for yourself. OK. Maybe some or all of that was true, up until now. It doesn't have to continue to be true.

And it won't, if you're willing to take accountability for your past behavior and its consequences, do what you can to make amends where amends are needed, forgive yourself for your mistakes, and move forward. Just take care to develop a very clear vision of what you want to do for yourself and for others in the future. Then, support that vision with your self-talk, particularly daily affirmations and visualizations, and with short- and long-term goals. Remember, you don't have to know exactly *how* you're going to achieve them, at first. Just get very clear about where it is you want to go and why. I guarantee you'll find a way to get there. Or else you'll invent it.

Sir Edmund Hillary lost one of his team members in a failed initial effort to climb Mt. Everest. When he returned to London, some of the most powerful people in the British Empire held a banquet in his honor. Behind the speaker's platform were huge blow-up photos of the mountain. When he rose to receive the applause of the audience, Hillary turned his back to them, faced the photographs, and said, "Mount Everest, you have defeated me. But I will return, and I will defeat you. Because you can't get any bigger—and I can!"

It Takes Courage, Brains, and Heart

You, too, have the courage, brains, heart, and imagination to take on any personal, family, company, community, or social problem that exists—to put yourself on top of any mountain that you want to climb and to lend a hand to others who are below you on the path. If the terrain seems tougher than you are at times, if you're intimidated by it for a while, that's OK. You won't stay intimidated because, like Hillary, you can grow bigger than it is.

If you doubt that, just take some time to reflect on what you've managed to accomplish in the past. Look at what you've been through, and what you've survived. Look at what you've learned simply as a matter of course, and how much more you've learned because you really wanted to. Look at what you have helped others to learn. Look at what you have created, cared for, and maintained.

And just as you take on bigger and bigger challenges, so can you play an important role in helping those you coach and mentor to believe that they can achieve their heart's highest goals. You can help them feel supported as they take the risks they need to take in order to grow—because there is definitely some risk involved. Do you remember, in *The Wizard of Oz*, that wonderful scene near the end of the film when Dorothy is getting ready to leave Oz? Glinda, the good witch, tells her that she has always had the power to go home. She tells her that there wasn't ever really any magic in the ruby slippers. But there was big magic in Dorothy's *belief* in them.

What if Dorothy *had* chosen to go back to Kansas sooner? What if she hadn't been willing to set out alone down a peculiar, spiraling yellow brick road in a strange land filled with even stranger characters? What if she hadn't been ready to join forces with some very odd characters who obviously needed help? And what if they hadn't, together, had the nerve to take on a menacing, seemingly all-powerful adversary? Well, Dorothy would have gone home the same old Dorothy—unchanged, unchallenged, untested, no wiser. She would have unwittingly been running away from the greatest experience of her young life, and her pals would have stayed stuck in the ruts (and rust) created by their own negative beliefs. But Dorothy was a risk-taker, just as you are, just as you can help your protégés to be.

The Challenge of Diversity

It's easy for us to feel comfortable with people who are very much like we are, but "easy" is not how we grow. As we move toward the twenty-first century, all of us are going to be meeting and working with many people who look and sound different than we do. Some of them will speak English as a second language, with varying degrees of fluency. Some may not speak English at all. Some will be physically or mentally challenged. Some will have been raised in cultures that are radically different from our own, and they'll have different values, different lifestyles, different ideas about how things should work. In this new arena of diversity, we are, increasingly, going to be faced with a choice.

When Dorothy met the munchkins, she had a choice, too. She could have chosen to focus on the fact that these people were very different than she was—different, in fact, from anyone she had ever seen. They looked weird, they sounded weird, they wore very unusual clothes. She could have chosen to turn tail and run for the hills. Or she could have merely pretended to accept them, pretended to listen sympathetically to their problems and advice, while secretly putting them down as inferior and discounting everything they said.

Dorothy was faced with a similar choice when she encountered the scarecrow, the tin man, and the cowardly lion. But because she wasn't threatened by the obvious differences between herself and them, she could see what they had in common. She could see that they were more alike than different and that their diversity might be able to give them a real advantage, because they could compensate for each other's weaknesses and benefit from each other's strengths.

What if you choose to serve as mentor to someone who appears to be very different from you? Who comes from a different economic background? Who is a different sex, age, or nationality? Who worships in a different church and pulls different levers in the voting booth? Who wears very different clothes and has a very different lifestyle? You could both be in for a great learning experience!

Remember, the purpose of mentoring is to grow, to teach, and to learn. Of course, if you are secretly convinced of the superiority of your own perspective and values, your attitude is going to show, no matter how hard you try to hide it, and little good is likely to result. But if you both are able to openly acknowledge your ignorance about certain areas of each other's lives while expressing your willingness to learn, you'll be expanding your worldviews and stimulating your growth. You'll also be making the world a better place.

Moving On

Since the goal of an effective coach or mentor is to guide another person's growth to the point where guidance is no longer needed, sooner or later it will be time to move on. How do you know when that time has arrived? One of your first clues may be a dawning awareness that the nature of the relationship has changed. No longer clearly a mentor and protégé, teacher and student, there is now parity between you. Because you have done your job well, you have done yourself out of a job, so to speak.

Sometimes, of course, the relationship will continue in a new form. Sometimes, for a variety of reasons, it will not. As your protégé grows in expertise, he or she may need to move to a new level of coaching or mentoring, one that is frankly beyond your abilities. Either one or both of you may choose to initiate that move. Perhaps the length of your arrangement will be defined at the outset according to parameters that the two of you may or may not control. If you're a teacher or a coach, for example, you may be able to work with your protégé for only a season or two or for the duration of a high-school or college education. If you're mentoring an intern in your department, when the predetermined time scheduled for the internship has elapsed, your protégé will move on. Or perhaps your life circumstances will change (due, for example, to serious illness, family crisis, death or divorce, move to a new location, etc.), making one or both of you unwilling or unable to continue the relationship.

Whatever the reason, when it's time to move on, there are a number of ways in which the transition can be handled. There is no single right way, and the method you choose will depend on the quality and type of the relationship and the reason for its termination. Sometimes, little in a formal sense will need to be said or done, and a simple handshake or hug and best wishes for the future will feel most appropriate. Sometimes, a discussion reviewing your personal history together, including goals accomplished and any still left undone, will be called for. At other times, nothing less than a creative gesture designed to express the uniqueness and mutual value of the relationship will do—an individualized rite of passage, as it were.

A high school coach who had worked with a promising young swimmer until he was awarded a scholarship to an out-of-state school "graduated" his protégé with a mock diploma declaring him "swimma cum laude" in sportsmanship, determination, and self-discipline, predicting great things for him in the future.

A career counselor I know had a ten-year relationship as mentor and, ultimately, friend to a newly divorced young woman who was struggling to put herself through college at night while working at several menial, stressful day jobs to support two children. On the day her protégé finally earned her degree in business administration, the mentor took her out to dinner at a fine restaurant. She made arrangements ahead of time for the strolling musicians to serenade the new graduate with the song, "The Impossible Dream." Then she presented her with a sterling silver letter opener engraved with the words "Dare to dream . . . then make it real."

A similar story with a reverse twist comes from a friend of mine who was mentored through an extremely difficult adolescence by a man he calls "a surrogate father and one of the finest human beings on the planet." Shortly before he was about to be married and move to another state, he gave his mentor a handmade brass kaleidoscope with a gift card in which he wrote, "Thanks for helping me to learn that beauty is in the eye of the beholder!"

While such a keepsake or memento is wonderful to have and can symbolize many meaningful things for a mentor and protégé who are saying good-bye, it is certainly not essential. Taking the time to capture some of your reflections on what the relationship has meant to you and write them in a card or letter can be a great way to mark the point of moving on. So can a framed photograph of the two of you, autographed with affection. The point I want to make is that it doesn't matter so much what you do to mark the transition point, as long as you see it as an opportunity—perhaps a final opportunity—to reinforce your protégé's strengths and achievements and create a positive, hopeful vision for the future.

Even Good Mentors Need Mentors

Any individual or organization that has stopped learning and changing is inviting rigidity, morbidity, distress, even death. Life is motion. If you're not growing, you're not just standing still—you're shrinking. I can't conceive of ever feeling that I've completely outgrown the need for guidance and good advice. I can't imagine ever thinking that I am using 100 percent of my potential, doing all that I can do, being all that I can possibly be.

I realize that there are some folks out there who think of themselves this way—as having arrived. I've even had the misfortune to meet some of them. But the people I know who are most fully alive, most actively involved in the world around them, in helping others develop and grow, are those who are continually on the alert for someone or something that can help them do the same. That's why good mentors so often have their own coaches, mentors, teachers, and role models.

For example, do you know that some highly effective psychotherapists have their own therapists? Now some people will try to tell you that highly trained professionals who are getting paid to help others solve personal problems ought to have their lives running like well-oiled machines. At the very least, they should be able to deal with their own challenges and changes without turning to someone else for help.

But it's precisely because these professionals *are* so effective that they don't buy into the myth of godlike self-sufficiency. They don't believe in keeping themselves in a box defined by an egotistical desire to appear perfect or by other people's restrictive "should's" and "ought to's." Experience has taught them that access to wise and trusted mentors can help them live less stressful, more interesting lives, and when they're not trying to figure out and cope with everything by themselves, their personal and professional growth tends to be more rapid.

You are *never* too old, too successful, or too smart to have a coach or mentor. I know that the typical image of a protégé is one of youth and inexperience, someone who is just starting out, and the typical image of a mentor is precisely the opposite. But if you can rid yourself of these stereotypes and the scotomas they create, all you need to do is focus on some areas in which you'd like to grow and then look for someone who could serve as a mentor, teacher, role model, or guide. You'll find them everywhere. Sometimes they'll be the same sex as you are; sometimes they won't. Sometimes they'll be people whom you'll pay for their time; sometimes payment will be out of the question. Sometimes you'll ask them for help; sometimes it will simply happen. Sometimes they'll be people with whom you'll have a long, intimate relationship; sometimes your time together will be relatively brief. Sometimes they'll be considerably older than you are; sometimes they'll be much younger.

If you decided to develop your artistic talents by taking an oil painting class, you might find yourself paying for one-on-one lessons from a teacher who owns a local gallery that you've frequented for years. To become more computer literate, you could trade use of your sea kayak for lessons in how to surf the Internet from the fourteen-year-old computer wizard who lives next door. Maybe you'll study yoga with a teacher in her sixties whom you met during a free lecture at the public library. Perhaps you'll choose to focus on growth in self-understanding by making a commitment to work for an hour a week with a good psychologist. Or you could accomplish a similar objective by taking a ten-week journal writing course at a local community college. Mentors and teachers are everywhere.

Stay Open to Surprises

No matter what you choose to learn, no matter how you choose to grow, if you are willing to open your mind and heart and take the time to get to know them as individuals, you may discover that the people who are teaching you specific skills, arts, and crafts have other things to share with you, as well. You may begin to develop, and to prize, a much broader variety of mentors, teachers, coaches, and friends than you've ever had before—people who can bring a vibrant, richly textured spectrum of outlooks and perspectives to your world. And you may learn some things you never expected.

You may decide to revamp your schedule to build in more time for quiet observation and reflection as a result of the time you've spent with your art instructor. You may discover the blessing of good-natured patience with self and others from that youngster who is teaching you how to navigate in hyperspace. You may learn something important about your own mind-body connection as you gradually develop physical grace and stamina with the help of your yoga instructor.

Or maybe you'll be taught something vital concerning the positive effects of playfulness from someone who is supposed to be learning from you. That's what happened to me when I spent some time recently with the New York Jets and their head coach at the time, Pete Carroll, who is presently with the San Francisco 49ers. I was there to share some of what I know about high-performance thinking and the psychology of achievement with the Jets' coaches and players.

On the flight back to Seattle, Diane and I talked about how much we had appreciated Pete's genuine joyfulness and, sometimes, just plain silliness. Maybe it had something to do with my taking on adult responsibilities earlier than most kids, but Pete's spontaneous ability to play and make people laugh while still getting plenty of work done made a tremendous impression on me. He wasn't at all concerned about looking foolish to other people—he has far too much self-confidence for that. Diane described him perfectly when she said he was "mature enough to be able to be childlike."

Hanging out with Pete Carroll for a few days helped me to become more fully aware that it was possible, even desirable, for grown-ups to play as naturally as kids do, and it helped me to realize that I would like to have more of that kind of play in my life. When I got back home, all I needed to do was to commit to the end result, write some affirmations to support it, and add them to the others that I am currently repeating and visualizing as part of my personal program for growth and change. Every day, I visualize myself behaving, not like Pete Carroll, but like Lou Tice, having a lot of fun in the present moment, while still getting all the work done that I want to do. I see myself erasing the boundaries I learned to construct between "play" and "work."

Passing on the Baton

When I first met Sir Alec Dickson, whom I introduced you to in Chapter 9, we were at a dinner arranged by my business associates in London. Within minutes, I knew he could be a wonderful mentor. He was in his eighties at the time, and, although he was still very active, his body was frail and his health in decline. I knew that I probably wasn't going to have as much time with him as I wanted, so I had to move quickly. I invited Alec and his wife, Mora, to come to Seattle as my guests. When they arrived, they spent the better part of a day talking with my staff. Then I flew them to eastern Washington for a few days alone with Diane and me at our ranch. A year or so later, I flew them back to Seattle to be keynote speakers at our annual Global Leadership Conference and to spend a few more days with us.

Let me tell you a little more about Alec and Mora Dickson. When President Kennedy began the Peace Corps, he modeled it after an organization Alec had founded in England called Voluntary Service Overseas. Alec also founded Community Service Volunteers, a domestic organization, and his ideas have been translated into action in nearly every country in the world. He consulted with numerous governments and social/educational organizations, and he was twice honored by Queen Elizabeth. He worked hand in hand with Mora wherever he went, and for more than fifty years, they made quite a team.

Alec Dickson was one of the most creative thinkers I have ever known, and when he passed away recently, the world lost a wonderful human being. He possessed an extraordinarily high level of personal integrity and was selflessly dedicated to serving humanity. He was also very funny, with a quintessentially dry British wit. He had a formidable intellect coupled with a kind and gentle spirit that just naturally drew people to him. When he put his mind to work on a problem, he could come up with myriad ways to approach it that were so creative and yet so sensible, they would make you marvel.

One of the most important things Alec taught me was that the answer to a huge problem is not necessarily one huge solution. It is more likely to be a huge number of small, personal, individual contributions. He saw our efforts to address the problems of society as a relay race, with each of us carrying the baton for our small portion of the race, but none of us having the ability to go the entire distance by ourselves. "Each of us must do whatever we can do," he would say, "and then we pass the baton on to someone else."

When life begins, and we are infants or very young children, our focus is self-centered, revolving entirely around getting. We look to our caretakers and to the outside world to meet our needs, both physical and psychological. If these needs are well met, we progress through life in a way that causes our focus to shift. As we grow and age, we become more interested in and intent upon giving.

Later still, we learn that getting and giving are not separable. There is a continuous spiral or chain of giving and receiving, linking helper and those who are helped, linking generations, communities, nations, and, indeed, all of humanity. This is an "ongiving" perception, as well as an "ongoing" phenomenon: When I receive from you, you experience the power and pleasure of generosity, and we are both enriched. When I give to you, the same thing happens, but in reverse. Then we, in turn, pass our gifts along still further, until we come to a place in the chain where that which is given becomes the property of all. Becoming a mentor is a wonderful way of passing on the baton.

I hope this book has helped to convince you that your unique adventure of personal and professional growth never has to stop. I hope I've also helped you to realize that there is a great deal you can do to help others grow, as well. Another part of Alec and Mora Dickson's philosophy of human service, which they passed on to me, was that "you don't have to *be* good to *do* good." They believed, as I do, that *everyone* has something meaningful to give, right here and right now.

When the Dicksons set up their volunteer programs, they refused to turn away anyone who sincerely wanted to help, no matter how needy or poorly equipped a would-be volunteer might seem on the surface. They believed that one of their program's biggest challenges would lie in creatively matching donors and recipients, not in determining which volunteers to accept and which to reject. I wish you could have heard some of their stories about the results of that philosophy—the incredible transformations *on both sides* that took place when people who had very little were empowered to help those who had even less.

If you think you should postpone your efforts to help, to give, to mentor, until such time as you feel perfectly equipped, completely ready and able, it may never happen. Begin now, where you are, with what you have. Begin with the needs you see around you and the tools you have at hand to meet them. Begin with the end results you desire clearly in mind and the firm conviction that you'll be able to invent the means to achieve them as you go. But, above all, I urge you—begin.

Appendix

To order *A Message From Your Heart* (Chapter 12), to request information about The Pacific Institute's educational processes for organizations or individuals, or to share information about how the material in this book has worked for you, write:

The Pacific Institute

P. O. Box 84208

Seattle, WA 98124

phone: (206) 628-4800

fax: (206) 587-6007

email: cwatson@pac-inst.com

To order *Toward a State of Esteem: The Final Report of the California Task Force to Promote Self-Esteem and Personal and Social Responsibility*, send $4 (plus sales tax for California residents) to:

Bureau of Publications

California State Department of Education

P. O. Box 944272

Sacramento, CA 95802-0271

A separate volume, *The Appendixes to Toward a State of Esteem*, is available through the public libraries in California, or send $4 (plus sales tax for California residents) to:

Bureau of Publications

California State Department of Education

P. O. Box 271

Sacramento, CA 95802-0271

Notes

Chapter 3

1. Nathaniel Branden, *The Six Pillars of Self Esteem* (New York: Bantam, 1994), 27.
2. Charles Garfield, *Peak Performers: The New Heroes of American Business* (New York: W. Morrow, 1986), 212.

Chapter 6

1. Adam Smith, "Walking on Fire," *Esquire*, January 1984, 12.
2. Jack Nicklaus, *Golf My Way* (New York: Simon & Schuster, 1974), 119.
3. Alan Steinberg, "Positively Kirk Gibson," *Inside Sports*, September 1986, 67.
4. Ibid., 68.
5. Garfield, *Peak Performers*, 212.

Chapter 7

1. Carl Rogers, *Client Centered Therapy* (Boston: Houghton Mifflin, 1951).
2. Margo Murray, *Beyond the Myths and Magic of Mentoring: How to Facilitate an Effective Mentoring Program* (San Francisco: Jossey-Bass Publishers, 1991), 12.
3. Gerald G. Smale, *Prophecy, Behaviour and Change* (London: Routhledge, & Kegan Paul, 1979), 36.
4. Ibid., 35.
5. Ibid., 35.
6. Ibid., 17.
7. Don Kasparek, *Self-Fulfillment: Thoughts on Success, Happiness & a Meaningful Life* (Lincoln, Neb.: Timberlake Press, 1993), 13.

Chapter 8

1. Stephen R. Covey, *Seven Habits of Highly Effective People* (New York: Simon & Schuster, 1989), 137-39.
2. David Whyte, *The Heart Aroused* (New York: Currency Doubleday, 1994), 105.
3. Ibid., 106.

Chapter 9

1. Hyler J. Bracey, *Managing from the Heart* (New York: Delacorte Press, 1988), 145.
2. Daniel A. Sugarman, *Priceless Gifts* (New York: Macmillan, 1978), 202.

Chapter 10

1. Albert Bandura, *Social Foundations of Thought and Action: A Social Cognitive Theory* (Englewood Cliffs, N.J.: Prentice-Hall, 1986), 337.
2. Ibid., 281.
3. Martin E. P. Seligman, *Learned Optimism* (New York: Pocket Books, 1990), 163.
4. Ibid., 163.
5. Bandura, *Social Foundations of Thought and Action*, 322.
6. Norman Cousins, *Anatomy of an Illness* (New York: Norton, 1970), 139.
7. Ellen J. Langer, *Higher Stages of Human Development: Perspectives on Adult Growth* (New York: Oxford University Press, 1990), 303.
8. Blair Justice, *Who Gets Sick: How Beliefs, Moods and Thoughts Affect Your Health* (Los Angeles: St. Martin's Press, 1988), 102.
9. Victor Frankl, *Man's Search for Meaning* (New York: Pocket Books, 1985), 214.

Chapter 11

1. Norman Cousins, *Head First: The Biology of Hope* (New York: E.P. Dutton, 1989), 127.

Chapter 12

1. Shin'ichi Suzuki, *Nurtured by Love: A New Approach to Education* (New York: Exposition Press, 1969), 64.